D0463777

Between the Lines

A View Inside American Politics, People, and Culture

Jonathan
Alter

Foreword by Jon Meacham

STATE STREET PRESS

Published by
STATE STREET PRESS
by special arrangement with
ANN ARBOR MEDIA GROUP LLC
2500 S. STATE STREET
ANN ARBOR, MI 48104

Printed and bound in the United States of America.
ISBN 13: 978-0-681-49755-9
ISBN 10: 0-681-49755-6

10 9 8 7 6 5 4 3 2 1

Library of Congress Cataloging-in-Publication Data is on file.

For Emily, my love, who makes
it all possible.

Foreword

— Jon Meacham —

FOR ME, JONATHAN ALTER began as a byline. I remember the first time I noticed it, more than twenty years ago, in the spring of 1986. The evangelical empire created by Jim and Tammy Faye Bakker was collapsing amid news of his adultery and their financial transgressions (it got so bad that Jerry Falwell—yes, Jerry Falwell—was sent in to play Fortinbras). The story had everything, and the country was wallowing in every detail: the makeup, the garish estates, the sex. In the house I grew up in on Missionary Ridge in Chattanooga, I opened my *Newsweek* in the second week of June 1987 and read these words, the lead paragraph of a cover story about Ted Koppel, who had landed an exclusive with the fallen Bakkers: "At 11:30 PM on May 27, Johnny Carson didn't watch Johnny Carson. Having taped his program earlier, he and much of the rest of the nation tuned in to ABC News *Nightline* instead. The next day Carson called Ted Koppel to congratulate him on his luscious hour-long interview with Jim and Tammy Bakker. 'All right, enough already,' Carson said. 'If you don't stop this I'm going to have to book Charles Manson.'"

It was the most engaging opening to a story I had ever read, and I did something I had never done before: I flipped ahead to the end of the piece (where *Newsweek* author bylines used to be) to see who had written it. And there, on page 56 of the June 15, 1987, issue of the magazine, was "Jonathan Alter."

He has since become much, much more to me—he is the best of friends and the most trusted of colleagues—but my introduction to him as a reader illustrates Jon's strength as a writer and reporter:

he has the power to make words and ideas leap from the pages of the magazine (and now, of necessity, from the pixels of a screen) in ways other writers can only envy. The collection you are holding is a compilation of a great journalist's greatest work, a passionate columnist's most enduring dispatches from the present. With his eclectic interests (from politics to the Cubs), good heart, and love of country, Jon has captured virtually all of the major moments of the past quarter century, celebrating its triumphs, chronicling its shortcomings, and emerging from the hurly-burly of the crisis of the moment with an abiding sense of hope for America and its people.

Which is not to say that there is not a lot of sizzle in the pages that follow. From the Bakkers to Monica Lewinsky, Jon has been a sure and steady guide through scandals large and small, but he has also, more than most, faithfully reminded his readers that the sexy is not always the significant. He is a serious-minded man, without being self-serious.

At their best—and Jon is among the very best—columnists provoke and prod, scold and salute. His sense of optimism about democracy and about America is founded in part on his deep love of the great liberal tradition of FDR, Truman, Kennedy, and Johnson, but he is not a partisan. Part of his strength comes from his willingness "to say something bad about the good guys," an exhortation from our friend and former editor Charles Peters of the *Washington Monthly*. Nobody—no movement, no candidate, no party—is perfect, and Jon is a caring and vigilant watchman over the all the guys, good and bad.

From the first time I saw his name, I was certain that I was in the best of hands, and I am certain still, all these years distant. He is, as you will see in the following pages, the best of guides through times of tumult, tabloidism, and tragedy—and his is the most engaging of voices in the eternal struggle to make sense of a world that tends toward chaos.

Contents

Author's Note

THIS COLLECTION REPRESENTS the last 20 or so years of my work at *Newsweek*, with a special emphasis on historical context, media analysis and personal observation. Most are columns about the great stories of our time—from the Tiananmen Square Massacre in 1989 to the presidential campaign of 2008. In between came the Bushes, the Clintons, Newt Gingrich, the O.J. Simpson case and other tabloid distractions, impeachment, the disputed 2000 election, the events of 9/11, the Iraq War and the end of conservative dominance, among many other compelling stories.

I begin with my brushes with historical figures from before my time, like Martin Luther King and Richard Nixon, then move through profiles ranging from Daniel Patrick Moynihan to Warren Beatty, and end with personal essays on everything from my bout with cancer to my experience in customer service hell.

I was born at the peak of the baby boom, 1957, on the North Side of Chicago, just a few blocks from Wrigley Field, the second of four children. Our family life was steeped in civic activism. My father Jim ran a family-owned wholesale distributorship of refrigeration and air conditioning parts, and my mother Joanne entered the jungle of Chicago politics and in 1972 became the first woman Democrat elected to public office in Cook County, Illinois. I worked in political campaigns and on newspapers as a kid, graduated from Harvard in 1979 with a degree in American history and got my best training at the *Washington Monthly*, an outstanding small political magazine.

I joined *Newsweek* in 1983, at age 25, and the late Maynard Parker, then the editor of *Newsweek*, gave me my own column in 1991.

Because this was the first political column inside the pages of the magazine in more than 40 years (not including the back page), it was an experiment at first and closely tied to the news. Even now, I don't simply write on whatever catches my fancy. With space in the magazine still tight, the idea must fit with our overall coverage. The advent of *Newsweek*.com in the late 1990s eased space constraints considerably, and several of the pieces here first appeared on the web.

For my first several years at the magazine, I was a New York–based writer. That meant that I often wrote cover stories and inside "take-outs" based on dispatches from other *Newsweek* correspondents as well as on my own reporting. (I still do this occasionally.) I have not included any of those shared-byline stories, and only a few of the hundreds of straight news and feature stories I covered. They're too perishable. I've also skipped most of my columns that were closely tied to the news, like those about media ethics flaps, the horse-race of presidential politics or some long-forgotten political tussle in Washington with no larger point. My foreign trips and Q and A's with world leaders get short shrift because others cover those assignments better. I've broken several stories over the years, but there's nothing more stale than yesterday's scoop.

Almost all of the articles collected here appear as they did in *Newsweek*. I've deleted some references to "last week" and made a few other minor editing changes, especially when parts of columns were overtaken by events. But I wanted to capture events mostly as they seemed at the time. In fact, I've included a couple of examples where I appear shortsighted to show that my batting average is hardly perfect. Many columns I like could not be included because of space constraints. For most of the ones I've selected, I've added a few sentences of context to introduce them.

The idea for this book was hatched by Tim Francis and nurtured by Kathryn Popoff and Tom Dwyer at Borders Group Inc. To them, my great thanks. Lynne Johnson did terrific work preparing the manuscript for publication and Danny Nanos designed a beautiful cover.

I moonlight on television and have freelanced over the years for other publications, but *Newsweek* is my happy home. For this perfect perch, I'm grateful to the late Katharine Graham and William Broyles, who hired me straight out of the *Washington Monthly* at the recommendation of my mentor, Charlie Peters. To Maynard Parker, Rick Smith, Mark Whitaker and now Jon Meacham, all talented and dedicated editors of *Newsweek*, I also owe a debt of gratitude. They have been the best bosses I could possibly hope for. Among the other wonderful editors who have improved my copy over the years are Merrill McLoughlin, Peter McGrath, Stephen Smith, Tony Fuller, Alexis Gelber, Dorothy Wickenden, Tom Watson and Bret Begun. It's now 20 years since Mickey Kaus and I launched the "Conventional Wisdom Watch," and George Hackett and Steve Levy have been my co-conspirators on that section for more than a decade. Dan Klaidman, Evan Thomas, Howard Fineman, Michael Isikoff and so many other terrific *Newsweek* colleagues have enriched my work. Don Graham, Lally Weymouth, Ann McDaniel and Steve Fusezi have made the *Washington Post* Company feel like family. Thanks also to Ed Davis for his expert legal work.

My own family has been indispensable to everything I've done, putting up with late nights and calls from the office. To our hilarious kids, Charlotte, Tommy and Molly, I can only say: I hope this gives you some sense of political life in the United States when you were very young. To Emily, my best editor, adviser and true love, this one's for you.

Jonathan Alter
Montclair, New Jersey
May 2008

PART ONE
HISTORY

So Long, Soldier

──── 1992 ────

This was published shortly after Governor Bill Clinton defeated incumbent President George H. W. Bush in the 1992 election. It was the introduction to a special issue I edited that was dedicated to the contributions of World War II veterans, who five years later came to be known as "The Greatest Generation."

W HEN JOHN F. KENNEDY came to office in 1961, full of talk about "passing the torch," he described his generation thus: "Born in this century, tempered by war, disciplined by a hard and bitter peace." Thirty-two years later—the rough span of a generation— Kennedy would have been 75 years old. His fellow World War II veterans, symbolized by George Bush, are marching quietly offstage, making way, as they know they must, for their kids: born after the war, tempered by the 1960s, disciplined by nothing more than the knowledge of a hard future.

But before they go, before they motor off into the best-cushioned retirement in history, a pause, please, to look back at some of what the World War II generation wrought for the rest of us. Certainly the veterans themselves are already doing so; as the years pass, they tend to remember more and more about the war, its enormity like some time-release capsule in their minds. And if the immediate postwar decades were not always "The Best Years of Our Lives," they became among the most momentous in the entire life of the nation. Only the generation that founded the republic and the one that fought the Civil War can claim to have shaped the destiny of the country more than the men and women born in the first third of the 20th century. The transfer of power from Bush to Bill Clinton turns the page. The new chapter is an explosion of discombobulating color; the old was in stark black and white, with good and evil so much easier to discern. Or at least it looked that way, from under the apple tree.

Kennedy and Bush, combat veterans whose presidencies were sep-arated by 30 years, are bookends. These fellow naval veterans might have disliked one another; generational identity only takes you so far. But the farewell speech that Bush gave at Texas A&M struck a Kennedyesque tone on America's role in the world. While Bush may be viewed by history as a reactive president, it was on his watch that the great struggle of his generation—the struggle against totalitarianism—seemed to be won.

So why doesn't it feel like victory? After all, under the World War II generation, America dominated the world as perhaps no other nation ever has. Having survived the Depression, it beat fascism, built the biggest economy ever, ended America's feelings of artistic inferiority toward Europe, conquered polio, grappled with the issue of race for the first time in 100 years, put men on the moon. Most conspicuous of all, it played world policeman, arming itself to contain and eventually help undermine communism. "No other generation this century has felt (or been) so Promethean, so godlike in its collective world-bending power," write William Strauss and Neil Howe in their book *Generations*.

But ultimately the world could not be bent like some piece of 1950s plastic. The descendant of Superman, that generation's favorite cartoon character, turned out to be … Bart Simpson. Arrogance and hypocrisy bred alienation and rebellion. Orthodoxies of both the left and right calcified. Racial and economic justice stalled. Major movements for environmentalism and women's rights were deferred to the generations that followed.

As it turned out, the men and women who saved America also nearly bankrupted it. First were the entitlements: they'd won the war, right? They were entitled to the fruits, and in the case of the GI Bill, generosity paid dividends many times over. But in recent years, health and retirement benefits have grown to the point where the long-living World War II generation consumes a huge share of the economic pie, burdening their children with debt.

And then there were the trillions spent on arms—far more than necessary (especially in the 1980s), though it was hard to know that when the buildup began. The newsreel playing over and over in the minds of policymakers was the image of Chamberlain capitulating to Hitler at Munich. This was the mental baggage that eventually led to Vietnam. The ends of fighting communism were seen to justify all sorts of unsavory means. Now, with the benefit of hindsight, it's clear that the ends were nobler than the left admitted; communism was just as inhuman as it was cracked up to be. And the means were meaner than the right admitted; laws were broken and lives ruined in the name of narrow-minded patriotism.

3

To see how the balance has shifted, compare two dramas about military courts-martial. In Herman Wouk's *The Caine Mutiny*, a character named Greenwald helps convict Captain Queeg but ends up ashamed of it. "Queeg deserved better at my hands. I owe him a favor, don't you see? He stopped Hermann Goring from washing his fat behind with my mother." Greenwald's logic—that you "can't stop a Nazi with a law book"—prevails with the audience. It is exactly that of Colonel Jessep, played by Jack Nicholson in the current hit *A Few Good Men*. He's the one on the front lines at Guantánamo, facing off against the Communists. But the hero today is Tom Cruise, the Yuppie attorney. The rule of law triumphs over "national security" and military discipline.

Post-Cold War, this makes sense. Yet something connected to the success of a nation has been lost, or at least misplaced. Citizens of other countries have often respected the nobler values of the World War II veterans—shared sacrifice, hard work, old-fashioned pluck—better than have their own heirs. That's one reason our competitors have caught up. The challenge, before the World War II generation dies off, is to transmit those values within the United States, to make the odds they overcame in winning the war and preserving the peace a source of some inspiration.

Recall that wartime song: "There'll be bluebirds over / the white cliffs of Dover / tomorrow ... when the world is free." The world is, in most places, free—freer than ever, thanks in part to this historic generation. But the bluebirds are barely in sight. The soldiers can't bring them back; now it's up to their children.

Bush and FDR

The 2006 publication of my book The Defining Moment:
FDR's Hundred Days and the Triumph of Hope *got me thinking about
the similarities and differences between one of our best presidents
—and one of our worst.*

O N ONE LEVEL, it's unfair to compare a sitting president to
his predecessors, especially when he has time left before leaving
office. And it's doubly unfair to compare George Walker Bush,
currently experiencing some of the lowest approval ratings in the
history of polling, to Franklin Delano Roosevelt, who is on the list
of even conservative historians as one of our best presidents. But
juxtaposing the two men may shed some light on both Roosevelt's
unusual gifts and Bush's current troubles. FDR's presidency can offer
some useful lessons—for today's White House, and for anyone
intrigued by the mysteries of leadership.

Before reaching office, blue bloods Roosevelt and Bush had a great
deal in common, even sharing some ancestors. FDR went to Groton
and Harvard, Bush to Andover and Yale. Their academic records and
the assessment of friends suggest roughly equivalent IQs. Both grew
up with tough mothers and bearing the name of a previous American
president. Both had a clubby charm and enjoyed bestowing cutting
nicknames on aides. Both were tagged by top pundits of the day with
the exact same epithet—"lightweight." Both lost congressional races,
suffered business setbacks and experienced a personal crisis before
becoming governor of a major state.

But the crises left entirely different imprints on the political
style and character of their presidencies. FDR, stricken with polio at
age 39, spent much of the 1920s building a clinic for polio victims
at Warm Springs, Georgia. There, "Old Doc Roosevelt," as he called
himself, shed his snobbism and learned to connect with ordinary
people, as Bush does naturally. FDR restored the hope of polio

patients, though neither he nor they would ever walk again.

Two weeks after barely dodging assassination in Miami in February of 1933, Roosevelt took office and performed a similar conjuring act on a larger stage. With the banks closed and millions of Americans wiped out, FDR used his "first-class temperament" to treat the mental depression of Americans without curing their economic one. In the days following his "fear itself" Inaugural and first "Fireside Chat," the same citizens who had lined up the month before to withdraw their last savings from the bank (and stuff it under the mattress or tape it to their chests) lined up to redeposit patriotically. This astounding act of ebullient leadership marked the "defining moment" of modern American politics, when Roosevelt saved both capitalism and democracy within a few weeks and redefined the bargain—the "Deal"—the country struck with its own people.

Also at age 40, Bush conquered his own, less debilitating disease, a battle with the bottle that left his wife Laura saying, "It's me or Jack Daniels." He emerged with a single-minded focus and discipline that took him far. But when discipline hardens into dogma, a president loses the suppleness to respond to problems. Bush's adherence to routine— a frequent attribute of those who have beaten substance abuse problems—may have slowed his adjustment to new circumstances.

By contrast, Roosevelt was so flexible that many Democrats tried to stop him from gaining the 1932 presidential nomination because they saw him as a straddler and flip-flopper on issues like the League of Nations and Prohibition. (Neither "wet" nor "dry," he was a "damp.") But by calling for "bold, persistent experimentation," he turned flexibility into a principle. When man met moment in 1933, FDR cut left and right at once, putting people to work and regulating Wall Street for the first time, but also resisting pressure to nationalize the banks and slashing federal spending by 30 percent, the deepest cuts ever.

Like Bush, FDR took an expansive view of presidential power. But he didn't circumvent Congress, as Bush did on warrantless wiretapping. On March 5, 1933, his first full day in office, Roosevelt toyed with giving a speech to the American Legion in which he essentially created a Mussolini-style private army to guard banks against violence. One draft had Roosevelt telling middle-age veterans, long since returned to private life, that "I reserve to myself the right to command you in any phase of the situation that now confronts us."

When I saw this document in the Roosevelt Library, my eyes nearly popped out. This was dictator talk—a power grab. But FDR didn't give that speech. Establishment figures like the columnist Walter Lippmann urged Roosevelt to become a dictator. (Mussolini was highly popular in the United States and the word, amazingly enough, had a positive connotation at the time. Studebaker even built a popular car called "The Dictator.") But the new president decided to run everything past Congress—even the arrogant and ill-fated effort to "pack" the Supreme Court in 1937.

Roosevelt wasn't big on excuse-making. Shortly after assuming office, he said he wanted a quarter of a million unemployed young "hobos" working in the forests by summer. Every cabinet member said it couldn't be done. But because he understood the levers of power (partly from his experience in the Wilson administration, bureaucratic training that Bush lacks), he made it happen and the Civilian Conservation Corps changed the face of the country.

Had such competent leadership been present after 9/11, it's a fair bet that it would not have taken more than four years for the FBI to fix its computers and for the government to secure ports and chemical plants against terrorism. FDR would have demanded it be done in, say, four months.

After 9/11, Bush had a moment of Roosevelt-style crisis oratory. But FDR crafted his speeches to calm fears and unify the nation; Bush has sometimes used his to stoke fears and score political points. Roosevelt was also a polarizing figure; the wealthy despised him. But he knew how to pull the country together. When the challenges changed, he shifted course, declaring that "Dr. New Deal" has been replaced by "Dr. Win the War." Like Bush, he practiced deception to take the United States to war. But it was the right war at the right time. And the founder of the United Nations thought unilateralism was ruinous.

FDR's perpetual good cheer masked a cunning ability to keep everyone guessing. Often, he assigned two or more people to the same task. "He kept everyone's balls in the air except his own," Vice President Henry Wallace quipped. This could make for exasperating management, but it gave him more options and great political mobility.

Where Bush has until now placed loyalty over performance, FDR put performance over loyalty. If aides didn't do the job or keep him fully informed, he would freeze them out, even if—like Louis Howe (Roosevelt's Rove), Ray Moley and Jim Farley—they had served him for years. And where Bush has often seen the war on terror as a chance for partisan advantage, FDR viewed World War II as a time to reach across party lines. He appointed Herbert Hoover's secretary of state, Henry Stimson, his secretary of war, and the 1936 GOP candidate for vice president, Frank Knox, his navy secretary. He even brought his 1940 Republican opponent, Wendell Willkie, into the fold.

Bush is not much of a believer in accountability; FDR knew it could make him a more effective president. He held two press conferences *a week* and instead of shunning Congress's oversight of Halliburton-style profiteering during the war, he put the main critic, Senator Harry Truman, on the 1944 ticket. Roosevelt hired some toadies, but he usually wanted to know the truth. He even deployed Eleanor and her close friend Lorena Hickok, a talented journalist, as his "eyes and ears." They traveled, often coach, and reported back on what was wrong with New Deal programs, so he could fix them.

Unlike many liberals who worship him, Roosevelt wasn't wedded to any agenda. His bias was for action, and he was willing to compromise greatly. To enact Social Security in 1935, he abandoned his liberal base and endorsed the conservative version of the bill. Even so, FDR would not have approved of Bush's privatization plan, because his bedrock principle was "guaranteed return"—a much deeper concept of "security" than protection against terrorists.

The aftermath of Hurricane Katrina has kicked off a national debate over whether President Bush responded quickly enough. But almost no one argues nowadays that he should not have responded at all, that it isn't the federal government's role to address suffering. That was FDR's doing. He envisioned a nation that refused to "leave the problems of our common welfare to be solved by the winds of chance and the hurricanes of disaster." This was a new America—a country of citizens committing themselves to one another, with a set of governing values we are debating anew today.

The Kennedys' Real Legacy

—— 1999 ——

*When John F. Kennedy Jr. was killed in an airplane crash in 1998,
it offered a chance to assess the family's role in American life.*

ONE OF THE PROBLEMS with the Kennedys is that so much
of what is written and said about them quickly crystallizes into
cliché. It then becomes harder to get a clear-eyed view of what they
mean to the country politically. The whole idea of "Camelot," for
instance, grew out of a comment Jackie Kennedy made to journalist
Theodore White after the assassination, remembering that she and
the president had enjoyed listening to the album from the Broadway
musical before bed sometimes. By linking "Camelot" to the Kennedy
years, a treacly legend was launched, obscuring the unsentimental truth
about the era.

Now, with the outpouring of grief over the death of John F. Kennedy
Jr., the myths are back. The family's cultural significance may be over-
shadowing its true political legacy. The whole "triumph and tragedy"
bit, however understandable at a time like this, makes it harder to see
how the Kennedys have actually affected our real lives, not just our
fantasy lives. We know more about how they've touched us than about
how they've changed us.

They've certainly reflected us—a nearly perfect political mirror for
the 20th century. One hundred years ago, the Irish began their long
domination of urban politics—led by the Fitzgerald family of Boston.
Joe Kennedy Sr. was a Wall Street buccaneer in the Roaring Twenties
and a key FDR man in the New Deal 1930s. As the country moved
from isolationism to war in the 1940s, so did the Kennedys. In the
anti-communist 1950s, they were quintessential cold warriors, with
Bobby Kennedy even working for Joe McCarthy. The critical 1960s'
issues of civil rights and the Vietnam War were deeply enmeshed with

the Kennedys. In the 1970s, the steep consequences of family dysfunction surfaced in drug problems—in the Kennedy family and the country as a whole. The 1980s were an aberration; led by Ted Kennedy, the family "sailed against the wind" instead of championing free-market values. But by the 1990s, they were back in the swing, and willing to embrace, as John F. Kennedy Jr. did, a mix of politics and celebrity, entrepreneurship and service.

The Kennedys have this reputation as big liberals; in fact, both JFK and his son were centrist and pragmatic. Fearful of losing Southern Democrats, President Kennedy fought for little domestically—and accomplished little. In less than three years in office, his legislative record was thin, though he did help move civil rights higher on the agenda, set the adventurous Cold War goal of beating the Soviets to the moon and skillfully handled the 1962 Cuban missile crisis.

Anyone who thinks the Kennedys are overrated should study that terrifying crisis, when we came as close as ever to nuclear war. The military, the "wise men" who advised earlier presidents, and smart and experienced congressional leaders like Senators William Fulbright and Richard Russell, all favored air strikes against Cuba to remove missiles brought from the Soviet Union. Only the 45-year-old president and his 37-year-old brother Robert stood in the way, insisting on the less warlike naval blockade instead. After the Cold War, we found out that Cuba contained far more nuclear missiles than known at the time and the Soviets planned to retaliate—quite possibly commencing a nuclear war—if the United States launched air strikes.

"In his bones, John Kennedy believed in the rule of reason," says JFK aide Harris Wofford. Bobby Kennedy was different. In *his* bones, he was a rare and potent mix of moralism and toughness. His brother's assassination—and his private fear that it might have been retribution for the CIA's efforts to kill Fidel Castro—gave a tragic arc to his journey through the 1960s. But the political message of looking out for the less fortunate was serious and specific, and helped millions of Americans locate their social consciences.

In a time of plenty, when complacency might have prevailed, the Kennedys asked the country to do better. RFK's assassination in 1968 and Ted Kennedy's appalling conduct at Chappaquiddick intensified the myths but seemed to end the family's role as agents of real political change. Not so. While Ted could never be president, he directly affected countless lives with an impressive string of legislative accomplishments on health, education, deregulation and the minimum wage. He's old-fashioned and easy to ridicule, but he will be remembered in both parties as one of the giants of the postwar U.S. Senate.

The younger generation of Kennedys hasn't changed the country yet, but almost all of the cousins are trying, in smaller ways, to make a difference. Kathleen Kennedy Townsend, the moderate lieutenant governor of Maryland, made community service mandatory for high-school graduation in that state, a move that was initially criticized but is now being embraced elsewhere. The basic Kennedy message has been remarkably consistent over 100 years. "I hope that young people participate," John F. Kennedy Jr. said in one of his last television interviews, getting set to place the most overworked of Kennedy clichés in its proper context. "If they don't, then *that* really is a tragedy."

"Godspeed, John Glenn"

—— 1998 ——

In 1962, John Glenn became the first man to orbit the earth. Thirty-six years later, Glenn, at the end of a long career in the Senate, did so again in the Space Shuttle. It provided a welcome relief from scandal-ridden Washington and I went down to Cape Canaveral, Florida, to witness the launch.

SOME FIRSTHAND EXPERIENCES fail to live up to expectations; a shuttle launch is not among them. In the press grandstand where I watched Discovery rise against the cloudless sky, the media hit the abort button on cynicism. The Earth shook to the sounds of man, three miles away. The candle lit. When wide eyes narrowed again, hard questions about the future returned. But only someone stripped of awe can leave a launch untouched.

And yet the exhilaration was tinged with bittersweet yearning. This was, after all, a sequel, not vivid history itself: low orbit, not Mars. John Glenn saw his dreams made real again—would the rest of us? Or was this just the networks giving us a break from tawdry (and increasingly low-rated) Washington news, a Mark McGwire moment? A hero sandwich for a hungry nation?

No, it was more than manufactured. The nostalgia conjured a real sense of national purpose and performance. In the NBC News booth, I met Scott Carpenter, whose 1962 benediction, "Godspeed, John Glenn," still tingles every time. "I guess I said that because no one had ever gone that fast before," he explained. Repeating his send-off on the air, he had tears on his face, once the wrong stuff for stoic astronauts, now right for the occasion. Baseball legend Ted Williams, confined to a wheelchair, made the trip to the cape; he and Glenn had flown combat missions together. The day felt a bit like it must have at Fenway Park in 1960, when Williams hit a home run in the last at-bat of his career.

President Clinton and a good chunk of Congress came down; it's the new hip junket, assuring NASA funding in a recession. And they knew the press was here. Saturation City. We communicate so much more nowadays about so much less. I met an old space reporter from the *New York World-Telegram* named Richard Slawsky. When Alan Shepard became the first American in space in 1961, Slawsky said, there were 39 telephones for the press corps at Cape Canaveral. This week there were 5,000 accredited reporters, most with cell phones, plus hundreds more lines.

The classic Greek hero is young and brave—like Glenn the first time—but older, safer heroism has some practical advantages. If the odds of glory are smaller, so are those of disillusionment. We know John Glenn is not going to get arrested for date rape; the pride won't be betrayed. If the scientific justification for his trip is a little fishy, no one much seems to care. Besides, we wouldn't want someone asking what *we* bring to the party when the chance finally comes to hitch a ride.

And that was the inspirational corner turned last week—if a 77-year-old could do it, so could we. In that sense, Glenn now represents a healthy ratcheting down of the heroism required for space travel. This flight is helping to exorcise the ghosts of the Challenger disaster, which had reintroduced fear into the mental baggage Americans carry into space. After all, by the standards of 20th-century aviation, the normalization of space has been agonizingly slow. Glenn's first spaceflight, 36 years ago, was in turn nearly 36 years after Charles Lindbergh first flew solo across the Atlantic. Imagine if an elderly Lindbergh had, in 1962, offered to reprise his famous flight in a bigger, fancier plane. What a yawn. By then, passenger-jet travel across the Atlantic was already routine.

Now, with the coming commercialization of the space program, limited tourism in space may actually be less than a decade away. But first comes the space station, which will soon begin going up aboard the shuttle Endeavor in December, a far more consequential mission than this one. I toured a reproduction of it at Cape Canaveral and heard the descriptions of growing crystal proteins and converting astronaut urine into drinking water. Not surprisingly, the only question the officials wouldn't answer was the price tag, which is now estimated at close to $100 billion. Needless to say, the cheap engineering that worked so well for the Mars Pathfinder has not been applied to the space station, which is apparently being built in the priciest way possible. The most controversial portion of the project's budget is the money to prop up the Russian space program. Actually, that's the spending I find the most defensible, since out-of-work Russian scientists scare me.

In 220 years, this country has produced only two monumental generations of leadership—the Founding Fathers in the late eighteenth century and the World War II veterans in the mid-twentieth. The movies evoked at Cape Canaveral last week were not just *The Right Stuff* and *Apollo 13* but *Saving Private Ryan*. The giants of history were back for one more skirmish, fighting what Glenn calls the "couch potatoes." Their final mission is to prove there are no final missions—no age barriers to serving your country and challenging yourself. That means not just more septuagenarian space travelers but more tutors and child-care workers and counselors, perhaps tens of millions more local heroes as the baby boom retires, in a vast autumn harvest of experience.

Iraq: Echoes of Vietnam

——— 2003 ———

*Since college, where I wrote my senior thesis on the origins of
the Vietnam War, that conflict has informed my thinking. This is
one of several attempts to apply its lessons. It was written
only days after the U.S. invasion of Iraq in 2003.*

IRAQ IS NOT VIETNAM or Lebanon or anyplace else except
Iraq, and historical analogies are often land mines for the careless.
But the only thing worse than "thinking in time," as Harvard professors Richard Neustadt and Ernest May call this exercise, is thinking
outside of it—forgetting that certain lessons of history, carefully
applied, can yield useful insights for the present. The Bush administration is approaching a decision more fateful than any tactical move on
the battlefield: who should run postwar Iraq, and for how long?
History can help.

For a moment early last week, it felt like 1967. An overconfident
Secretary of Defense with slicked-back hair and a know-it-all style
was embarrassed by a ragtag, low-tech army putting up stiffer-than-
expected resistance. Instead of admitting as much, civilian and military
policymakers in Washington pretended there was nothing amiss,
opening up an LBJ-style "credibility gap." Pentagon brass, refusing to
be quoted by name, complained in the press as they did 35 years ago
about the political leadership denying them the military resources they
needed. On the ground, the outgunned underdogs adopted cruel Viet
Cong tactics, including the execution of civilians who didn't resist the
Americans.

Then in a flash the manic-depressive media mood swung back to
triumphalism. Those who scoff at the Vietnam analogy now have the
upper hand: this war looks as if it will last one month, not 10 years.
After all, Iraqis are not as good fighters as the Viet Cong were, and the
desert terrain and mind-blowing technology favor the United States in
ways they didn't in Vietnam. And while the rest of the world may be

seeing bloody pictures on TV, the United States is fighting much more humanely this time around. No sickening "body counts" or 65,000 North Vietnamese civilians killed in bombing attacks.

But if the military comparisons to Vietnam are glib, some *political* lessons remain relevant, especially those about the limits of power. The puppet regimes we installed in Saigon all lacked legitimacy, a sorry tale of failed nation-building that the United States might consider before assuming that exiles from the Iraqi National Congress, many of whom have not set foot in the country in more than 15 years, can govern for long. Offering huge economic aid won't be any more decisive. My *Newsweek* colleague Ron Moreau recalls how LBJ thought that the Vietnamese could be bought off with a big Mekong River dam.

After a period of jubilation following the fall of Saddam's regime, Iraqi nationalism will quickly assert itself. Suicide bombings (like the one carried out by two women last week) will almost certainly continue until the Americans clear out, just as attacks by the Viet Cong (clad as civilians) helped drive the United States out of Vietnam. The enemies of our enemy (Ho Chi Minh, Saddam) will not necessarily be our friends. For instance, the Al Dawa faction fighting Saddam in southern Iraq is apparently the same crowd that helped plan the 1983 bombing of the U.S. Marine barracks in Beirut. What's to stop someone from doing the same against us in Baghdad sometime soon?

Two Vietnam-era buzzwords to watch for are "pacification" and "infiltration." In the late 1960s and early 1970s, the United States believed it could "pacify" resistance by rooting out enemy agents; Pentagon planners are already talking about the same process. Iraq will require what is being called "de-Baathification" (just as Germany needed "denazification"), but if carried out by Americans alone, it will likely lead to more bloodshed. Meanwhile "infiltration" from Syria, Iran and other Arab countries has already begun. There's simply no way to prevent jihadists from slipping into Iraq to kill Americans.

This is what happened to the Israelis in Lebanon, where they were initially greeted as liberators, and to the Soviets in Afghanistan. A Soviet Army veteran on Russian TV last week offered a useful reminder: "We took the presidential palace in Kabul in three hours. We took the city in 24 hours. It was only 10 years later that we left, and there were no smiles on our faces."

I favored this war, but I'm fearful of losing the peace for reasons of history—personal history. President Bush is so angry with Gerhard Schröder and Jacques Chirac for what he considers personal betrayal that he wants to punish them by keeping Germany and France out of Iraq. Tony Blair, sensing the complexities, knows that failing to internationalize the occupation just means more dead Americans and Brits at the hands of assorted nationalists and jihadists. He wants the United Nations to run the reconstruction, which might give some contracts to greedy French doves, but would keep the occupying Americans from being sitting ducks. On this one, root for Blair. He reads more history.

King's Final Years

—— 2006 ——

I was too young for the civil rights movement,
but returned to the city of my birth, Chicago, in 2006 to see
how much the promise of the movement had been fulfilled
in the 40 years since I had I met Dr. King.

FORTY YEARS AGO this winter, I was an 8-year-old boy growing up on the North Side of Chicago. The Reverend Martin Luther King Jr. had moved into a slum in the impoverished West Side neighborhood of North Lawndale to dramatize the conditions of what were then known as "Northern Negroes." King was scheduled to visit the home of a local politician to raise money for his cash-strapped movement from white "lakefront liberals." But the politician, caught between his personal sympathies for King and his allegiance to Mayor Richard J. Daley, who was no fan of the civil rights leader, felt uncomfortable hosting the party. So he called up my parents and, to my delight, the event was moved to our house at the last minute. The fundraising was "disappointing," according to my father's diary, and King spent most of the evening on our telephone. But I got the great man's autograph and we heard him deliver an eloquent talk while standing in front of several dozen guests in our living room. At such events that year, King would sometimes scrawl a reminder to himself: "Ad lib 'We Shall Overcome.'"

This all came to mind while reading *At Canaan's Edge: America in the King Years, 1965–68*, the third and final volume of Taylor Branch's magisterial account of the most important social movement of the 20th century, which lasted only 13 years—from the Montgomery bus boycott of 1955 to King's death at age 39 in 1968. It made me think anew about how much has changed for African-Americans living in places like Chicago, and how little. In the aftermath of Hurricane Katrina, the unfinished agenda of the 1960s is under discussion again, if not in Washington then at least among the legions of local leaders still trying to better their communities.

Branch's book shows us King not as a plaster saint but an intuitive, conflicted and harried human being—running late to everything, refereeing among squabbling lieutenants, straying from his wife to the end, even slipping out to catch what one of his traveling aides said was his favorite movie, *The Sound of Music.*

But we also see that even after he became world-famous, King had reason to call his movement a civil rights *struggle.* Branch conveys in powerful detail the dramatic, chaotic, inspiring and incendiary era, from the triumphant Selma-to-Montgomery march to the passage in 1965 of the landmark Voting Rights Act and little-noticed end to discrimination against the Third World in immigration (which reshaped the face of America); from the pathos of Lyndon Johnson—caught between his breathtaking commitment to fighting injustice and the worsening Vietnam War—to the backlash against liberalism represented by Ronald Reagan's election as governor of California; and finally to King's eerie "I might not get there with you" premonition at the Mason Temple in Memphis on the night before his assassination.

For me, though, the central story of the last act of King's life takes place in Chicago. He lived there on and off for much of 1966, trying to take his movement of nonviolent civil disobedience to the next level. He failed. "It is in Chicago that the grapes of wrath are stored," King said as he launched what he called the "action phase" of his agenda. But the wrath at loose in American society derailed the civil rights movement and left a generation politically adrift. Branch's research suggests that 1966 was the year the liberal dream began to disintegrate.

King's organization, the Southern Christian Leadership Conference, came to Chicago at the suggestion of Al Raby, a teacher and community activist who had led demonstrations against the severely segregated school system. The SCLC saw Chicago as "the first significant Northern freedom movement" and the first focused on economic discrimination more than voting rights or public access: "This economic exploitation is crystallized in the SLUM ... not unlike the exploitation of the Congo by Belgium." The movement to "end slums" and create an "open city" ran straight into middle-class Chicagoans, all-white trade unions and real-estate agents as racist as anything found in the South.

On January 26, 1966, King, his wife, Coretta, and their four children moved into a third-floor walk-up at 1550 South Hamlin in North Lawndale, by then known as "Slumdale." Once a middle-class Jewish neighborhood, the area had filled up with blacks streaming north after World War II. The entryway of the building on Hamlin was used as a toilet by the neighborhood, and the apartment was tiny. "You had to go through the bedrooms to get to the kitchen," Coretta remembered. The landlord had quickly slapped a coat of paint on the apartment when he learned the identity of his new tenants (originally signed up under a false name), but it didn't help much.

The Northern campaign went into high gear with a rally at Soldier Field and a march to city hall, where King, like Martin Luther before him, nailed his 14 demands (for things like open housing and jobs in all-white industries) to the door. At first, Daley was conciliatory. He claimed that the problems all predated him and that he had already repaired more than 100,000 apartments. When a summer riot broke out in North Lawndale (Coretta told the children to back away from the windows), the mayor sought a truce with token concessions like fire-hydrant nozzles so black kids could cool off. King held all-night talks with gang leaders and Justice Department officials in the same room, but his commitment to nonviolence was belittled by newer "Black Power" leaders like Stokely Carmichael as "too Sunday school."

The point of the Chicago campaign was to show race as a national problem, and it did so with a bang when King led an integrated group of marchers into the racist enclave of Marquette Park. "I have never in my life seen such hate," said King, who was hit by a rock there. "Not in Mississippi or Alabama." But unlike the battle with Alabama state troopers the year before at Selma's Edmund Pettus Bridge, marches into Marquette Park (and later into the white suburb of Cicero) led to no national catharsis or landmark legislation. Congress defeated a new civil rights bill that would have banned housing discrimination (it finally passed in 1968). Although Northern authorities—the National Guard and Daley's police—defended the marchers rather than attack them, a backlash against the movement was setting in. "Don't you find," Mike Wallace asked King on CBS News, "that the American people are getting a little bit tired, truly, of the whole civil rights struggle?"

In 1965, King had shed a tear while watching LBJ proclaim "We shall overcome" on national television. But by mid-1966, Daley skillfully drove a wedge between King and Johnson, who would never meet again. "He [King] is not your friend," the mayor told the president. "He's against you on Vietnam. He's a goddamn faker." Even though he was privately against the war, too, Daley pledged his support for Johnson's escalation. In Chicago he outmaneuvered King by talking moderately but doing little. "Daley cut Martin Luther King's ass off," said Bayard Rustin, a more senior movement leader.

Branch does not see Chicago as a total loss. While the open-housing settlement reached there didn't end segregation, it began a process of change. Moreover, "Chicago nationalized race," Branch writes. "Without it King would be confined to posterity more as a regional figure." But it also marked the effective end to nonviolence as a potent force in the civil rights movement.

The 40 years since have been a time in the desert for the movement, bereft of strong leadership and the clarity of the fight against Jim Crow segregation. As the country saw in Katrina's wake, Washington long ago moved on from a serious engagement with the problems of poverty. "There has been a hurricane of neglect for the poor in this country for decades," says Richard Townsell, executive director of the Lawndale Christian Development Corporation. Meanwhile, the consequences of family disintegration, which King well understood, have been, if anything, more severe than Daniel Patrick Moynihan and others in the 1960s predicted.

Yet it is simply inaccurate to say that every period since King has been what he called a "valley moment." The Voting Rights Act transformed American politics, and the growth of the black middle class has changed the lives of millions of families. While New Orleans got worse, Chicago got better. Today it's a much healthier city than it was in Boss Daley's time, thanks in part to his son, Richard M. Daley, who has been mayor since 1989, and his predecessor, Harold Washington, the city's first African-American mayor.

While Chicago's public-school system remains troubled and stubbornly segregated, it now boasts several highly successful schools and realistic hope for more. Housing, too, is still largely segregated by neighborhood and is unaffordable for the poor and working class, with long waiting lists for subsidies. But notorious housing projects like the Robert Taylor Homes and Cabrini-Green have been mostly torn down and replaced by townhouse-style public housing units, a third of them owned by the residents.

Equally important have been public-private efforts spearheaded by a little-known but influential national nonprofit called the Local Initiative Support Corporation, chaired by former Treasury Secretary Robert Rubin. Since 1980, LISC's Chicago affiliate has quietly invested $120 million—and leveraged an additional $2.4 billion—in inner-city development, which has translated into 21,000 units of affordable housing and 4 million square feet of commercial space. They lack the drama of freedom marches, but stronger ties between the corporate world and dedicated community leaders are now the proven routes to urban revival. A drive down Martin Luther King Boulevard on the South Side, a thoroughfare of despair as recently as the 1980s, now yields glimpses of rehabbed million-dollar mansions and thriving retail stores. Ernest Gates, a community leader on the once burned-out near West Side, told me that "things are a lot better here now, though for the poorest of the poor, it's still pretty much the same."

North Lawndale, where King once lived, doesn't look much different than it did 40 years ago. I saw four young men in hooded parkas spread-eagled by police against a wall on Hamlin Avenue in what looked like a drug bust, directly across the street from the onetime King slum, now an empty lot. Nearly 60 percent of those over 18 have had some kind of involvement with the criminal justice system, with the number much higher among men. More than 40 percent of North Lawndale households have incomes of less than $15,000 a year (compared with 20 percent of all city residents). Fewer than a third have bank accounts. Many residents are still unable to "grow from within," in King's words, by resisting self-destructive behavior and the "gangsta" culture.

But North Lawndale is changing, too. It's still mostly poor and black, but much less densely populated, down two-thirds in size since 1960, to 41,000. The first shopping center in four decades was built in 2000, and nonprofit organizations are building a bit of new housing.

Near King's old haunts, I watched ex-convicts sitting at computer screens inside the LISC-backed North Lawndale Employment Network, printing resumes and looking for work. Many have problems with bad debt. "A job alone is not the answer—that was my big 'Aha!'" says Brenda Palms Barber, who runs the nonprofit and is teaching entrepreneurship skills to local residents (including placing beehives on empty lots that yield 4,000 pounds of profitable honey). "It's mental health, general health. The big missing piece is about financial education." A program in Chicago called First Accounts is focusing on a neglected segment of the poor now known as the "unbanked." When they do get accounts, their balances are small, but the vast majority has learned to be creditworthy.

You don't hear much about Martin Luther King in Chicago nowadays. The activists in North Lawndale hope to build a civil rights museum in his name at 1550 South Hamlin, though they don't have the money for it yet. Few Chicagoans think about the time he spent in their midst, if they remember it at all. In most parts of the country, King is now just a name like Roosevelt or Washington, a holiday on which to do some shopping. And yet books like *At Canaan's Edge* remind us that his challenge to America to "rise up and live out the true meaning of its creed" remains a powerful vision in a troubled world, as resonant today as when an 8-year-old boy watched him stand before his fireplace so many years ago.

Growing Up with Nixon

—— 1994 ——

When this was published upon Richard Nixon's death in 1994, many readers thought I was spitting on his grave. The director of the Nixon Library, the friend I tapped to bring the former president to Newsweek *in 1988, never spoke to me again.*

IN 1988, RICHARD NIXON came to *Newsweek* for coffee. After his usual tour of the political horizon, he was asked how history would view Ronald Reagan. "Well, you have to distinguish between history and the historians," he said. "Historians are liberal—like you." Now he was pointing at us, with only the slightest smile. Conservatives went into business, Nixon noted; liberals wrote the story of their times. But he argued that history was ultimately larger than the views of the historians, and history would judge Reagan on how his presidency affected the years that followed.

The same is true of Nixon himself. Critics within the press and academia who viewed him as a crook and a war criminal will increasingly give way to more balanced analysts. Even before his latest illness, old bitterness seemed to ebb, worn away by time and grit. At Nixon's death, nothing about him was "perfectly clear" anymore. Like children standing at the grave of a deeply flawed father, Americans began to construct a more complex picture of his strengths and weaknesses.

In the broad sweep, history's treatment of Nixon depends on Nixon's treatment of history. That treatment was not just his prodigious if conventional writing. It was, more significantly, his conditioning of the political culture—the way he changed public perceptions of public life and institutionalized cynicism. Is Nixon's influence on the nature of our politics still being felt? Now, more than ever.

Each generation of politically conscious Americans views Nixon differently. For those over 60, his contemporaries, it was either like (rarely love) or hate. His bundle of bromides and resentments—particularly of elites—often mirrored their own. For those under 30,

Nixon is just another figure from history, emitting a faintly noxious odor of no great consequence.

It's those in the middle—born in the 1940s and 1950s—who will render the first historical verdict. Nixon had his young supporters, but by and large we knew Nixon not as a contemporary or a dusty historical personage but as a twisted symbol of corruption and despised authority. Nixon believed deeply in that notion of authority, particularly his own. The great irony is that he did more than any modern president to undermine the very values he built his career on.

Strange as it sounds, Richard Nixon was our Franklin Roosevelt—the political leader who dominated the landscape for so long that he shaped or warped us in ways we barely understand. For someone growing up under Nixon, the invasion of Cambodia and the campus unrest that followed loomed about as large in our consciousness as, say, the Battle of the Bulge did for our parents when they were young. Nixon's resignation was our VJ Day. These events, 30-odd years apart, had opposite effects on the political sensibilities of younger people. Imagine what the heroic use of power in World War II did for a young generation's faith in their leaders. Now imagine what the criminal abuse of power in the Nixon years did to the next generation.

Analyzing Nixon without Watergate, says political scientist Nelson Polsby, is like looking at a map of Switzerland without mountains. If you doubt how severe the abuse of power was, consult J. Anthony Lukas's *Nightmare: The Underside of the Nixon Years*, a sorry catalog of lies, bald crimes and sheer contempt for democracy that extends far beyond Watergate and the cover-up. The late political scientist Hans J. Morgenthau, no longhair, wrote that the invocation of "national security" as justification for any government action was one of several practices of "a distinctly Fascist character" introduced in those years. Nixon apologists always complain that their man just did what other presidents had done. This is half true. The abuses had precedent in kind, but not degree. He was a lot worse.

Yet Watergate will not be Nixon's only legacy either. His influence is bigger than a scandal—and bigger than any foreign-policy accomplishments, such as restoring relations with China a few years earlier than expected. He dominates our political consciousness not because of what he did—for good or ill—but because of who he was. If the Kennedys personified our hopes, Nixon conjured our fears—of our parents and, in his moments of awkwardness and insecurity, of ourselves. In the mirror of television, this was uncomfortable and often funny. We

25

viewed Nixon's public humiliation almost as a joke, a memory that should bring some remorse. But the humor was influential, too. Making fun of Nixon helped shape the ironic sensibility that now so dominates popular culture.

Nixon's legacy for our politics is more serious. His character came to represent political character generally; his slashing style, imitated in a thousand attack ads, infected what we thought of every politician who followed. The anesthesia of the Reagan era never really treated the cancer that John Dean diagnosed as growing on the presidency. The real cancer was more than just the corruption of one administration; it was the corruption of politics as a whole in the mind of a generation. Nixon helped make people skeptical not just of individual politicians (a stout American tradition) but of the legitimacy of politics and government as a means of addressing their problems. Reagan exploited that. Clinton is suffering from it. He and every other politician in America are still reaping the bitter harvest of Nixon's career, in distrust of leaders, lack of respect for institutions and cynicism about public service. We don't have Dick Nixon to kick around anymore, but he'll be kicking us—and our politics—long after the historians have had their say.

If Watergate Happened Now

— 2006 —

I wrote this tongue-in-cheek column in early 2006,
when the GOP controlled all three branches of government and
it looked as if it would continue to do so. Roger Ailes,
president of the Fox News Channel, was so thin-skinned about
the column that he tried to retaliate by smearing me
as a failed job seeker at Fox, which was untrue.

FROM A DISTANCE, Watergate seems like a partisan affair. But that's because we tend to look at it nowadays through red- and blue-tinted glasses. In truth, President Nixon was forced to resign in 1974 by Republicans in Congress like Barry Goldwater, who realized from the so-called smoking-gun tape that he was a crook. This was after the Supreme Court—led by a Nixon appointee—unanimously ruled against him in the tapes case.

But imagine if Nixon were president today. After he completed his successful second term, I'd have to write a retrospective column like this:

President Nixon left office in 2005 having proved me and the other "nattering nabobs of negativism" wrong. We thought that his administration was sleazy but we were never able to nail him. Those of us who hoped it would end differently knew we were in trouble when former Nixon media adviser Roger Ailes banned the word "Watergate" from Fox News's coverage and went with the logo "Assault on the Presidency" instead. By that time, the American people figured both sides were just spinning, and a tie always goes to the incumbent.

The big reason Nixon didn't have to resign: the rise of Conservative Media, which features Fox, talk radio and a bunch of noisy partisans on the Internet and best-sellers list who almost never admit their side does anything wrong. (Liberals, by contrast, are always eating their own.) This solidarity came in handy when Bob Woodward and Carl Bernstein of the *Washington Post* began snooping around after the break-in at the headquarters of the Democratic National Committee. Once they scored a few scoops with the help of anonymous sources, Sean Hannity et al. went on a rampage. When the young reporters printed an article about grand jury testimony that turned out to be wrong, Drudge and the bloggers had a field day, even though none of them had lifted a finger to try to advance the story. After that, the Silent Majority wouldn't shut up.

Some argue the Watergate story died right there, but Nixon's attorney general wasn't taking any chances. Just as in the Valerie Plame case, the Justice Department subpoenaed Woodward and Bernstein to testify before the grand jury about their sources. When they declined, they were jailed for 18 months on contempt charges. Talkingpointsmemo.com and a few other liberal bloggers complained that it was hypocritical—top White House aides were suspected of shredding documents, suborning perjury and paying hush money to burglars—but to no avail. Public support for the media had hit rock bottom.

Whistle-blowers didn't fare much better. With Woodward and Bernstein out of business, the No. 2 man at the FBI, W. Mark Felt, held a press conference to air complaints that the White House and his own boss were impeding the FBI probe. Of course it was only a one-day story, with Ann Coulter predictably screaming that Felt was a "traitor." Rush Limbaugh dubbed Felt "Special Agent Sour Grapes" because he'd been passed over for the top FBI job. Within hours, the media had moved on to the tale of a runaway bride. And because the GOP controls both houses of Congress, there were no "Watergate" hearings to keep the probe going. John Dean and other disgruntled former aides had no place to go.

For a while, I hoped that the Nixon tapes might bring some justice. But soon the tapes just became more fodder for those legal shows on cable. The Supreme Court split 5-4, along largely partisan lines, as it did in Bush vs. Gore. That allowed Nixon to keep control of the tapes. When he burned them, the bipartisan outcry you would have heard in the old days over destruction of evidence was muffled by a ferocious counterattack from the GOP's legion of spinners. A group calling itself "Watergate Burglars for Truth" set up a 527 to argue that Bill Clinton and other Democratic presidents had ordered more burglaries than Nixon. There was nothing to prove them wrong. Reports of a tape showing that Nixon directly ordered the cover-up were just rumors, not anything that could be posted on smokinggun.com.

Nixon gave a TV interview to the British journalist David Frost in which he said, "When the president does it, that means it's not illegal." This explained why he felt comfortable approving the break-in at the office of Daniel Ellsberg's psychiatrist. Ken Duberstein and a few other principled Republicans weighed in that Nixon was bad news, but they were drowned out by former aides like Pat Buchanan and G. Gordon Liddy, who wanted to firebomb the Brookings Institution. When "Firebombing Brookings: Good Idea or Not?" became the "Question of the Day" on MSNBC, Liddy's radio show got a nice ratings boost. After Ralph Reed disclosed that Nixon and Henry Kissinger had been on their knees praying in the Oval Office, Nixon went up 15 points in the Gallup Poll, double among "people of faith." Our long national nightmare was just beginning.

PART TWO

EVENTS

Clarence Thomas Faces the Messy Truth

—— 1991 ——

*The Clarence Thomas–Anita Hill controversy of 1991 was
arguably the first big sign that hyper-partisanship had moved from
campaigning into the once-chummy confines of Congress. After word
leaked that she was charging Thomas with sexual harassment,
Hill was brought before the Senate Judiciary Committee, which was
reviewing Thomas's nomination to the Supreme Court.*

A T T H E E N D of the 20th century, our leaders sniffed each other's
underwear and put it on TV. That will be the inescapable conclusion
of history. The issue is whether they had to do so, and whether it's possible to salvage anything worthwhile from the laundry bin once the stench
abates and the senators stop knifing each other. Talk about Rashomon:
one side looks at the Senate Caucus Room spectacle and sees Joe
McCarthy. The other peers into the face of Anita Hill and finds Rosa
Parks. Maybe the peculiar nature of this sorry episode owes a little bit to
both, an American system debased and transformed at the same time.

At first glance, the whole thing looks unnecessary. Wasn't there
some way of preventing the leak of Hill's charges? Did the story have
to be publicized by the media once the leak took place? Did the Senate
have to hold a public hearing? Actually, some reasonable answers exist
for all three questions.

For starters, there's no way to plug leaks—never has been, never
will be. The proposed remedies—secrecy oaths and criminal penalties—
simply haven't ended leaks where they've been tried. Politicians and
their aides have always passed on information to the press when it is in
their interest to do so. What's different this time is a dubious inference—that the struggle over blame for the leak should somehow reflect
on the truth or falsity of Hill's charges. Why?

The attack on the media by Senator Alan Simpson and company for publicizing Hill's complaint makes no sense either. On
the one hand, these critics say that if the charges are true, Thomas
should definitely be disqualified from the Supreme Court. At
the same time, they say the media should have been responsible

enough to ignore the charge in the first place. Which is it, fellas?

Even Peter Jennings seemed convinced that the hearing could have been held in closed session. But Senator Patrick Leahy persuasively answered that it was impossible to do so. The failure of the Senate to respond promptly to Anita Hill had already cast doubt on the process. American women—not to mention the media—would have beaten down the door if the senators had tried to close it, and they would have been right. Imagine if the Senate, after meeting in closed session, rejected Thomas and didn't tell the public why.

Last week, anyway, the Republicans fought harder and dirtier than the opposition. They essentially charged that Senate Democrats were McCarthyites and racists. Both jabs were cynical and hypocritical. McCarthyism, a grossly overused word, suggests a peddler of innuendo and anonymously sourced slander. Anita Hill was hardly that. And Thomas's claim that he had been the victim of a "high-tech lynching" for being an "uppity black" avoided the inconvenient fact that Hill is black, too. Does the U.S. Senate really believe that she put herself through this ordeal at the behest of filthy-minded racists?

Thomas was on smarter tactical ground when pitting himself against the absurdity of the Senate as a whole. While the country slides into bankruptcy, senators are counting pubic hairs on the top of a Coke can. Even for people who prefer their politics raw, the lack of decorum was depressing. Strip off the bark and the core of partisanship is as putrid as any of the graphic sex: Democrats believe her; Republicans believe him. Viewers believe him or her or neither, but certainly not them. After all, these politicians actually judge character largely on the basis of party.

Now for the thin silver lining. Huge numbers of Americans express literally no interest in politics. They find it irrelevant to their lives and irredeemably boring. On TV, they will watch any program that is not politics. How to re-engage them? One answer, inadvertently arrived at, is to make politics into a dramatic TV show, especially one that relates to everyday life. Even with the Judiciary Committee members coming across as considerably more squalid and buffoonish than usual, there was finally some connection—however tawdry—between them and the inner lives of the people watching. It was as if the Senate and the public went out to see a trashy whodunit at the local cineplex. They might have been better off discussing the savings and loan crisis, but at least they were together, puzzling through the mystery.

And it wasn't as if the core issue—sexual harassment—was trivial.

Contrary to all of the hand wringing, the country will not be "ruined" by this. In fact, it will likely be made a bit more humane. Men are on notice that true sexual harassment has a price, a historic breakthrough telescoped into just a few days. Women know that if they try to destroy a man's career for some flimsy reason—a bad joke, for instance—they can expect withering cross-examination. Major social change is inevitably awkward, even excruciating. Careers are frequently destroyed in the process. But there has always been something messy about democracy. And it's always better to face the truth and feel the pain than never to have bothered at all.

Russia: The Making of a Usable Past

—— 1991 ——

The end of the Cold War was peaceful but not entirely smooth.
In 1991, Russian communists tried to stage a coup against Mikhail
Gorbachev. The president of the Russian Federation, Boris Yeltsin,
stopped them. This gave the Russians a flicker of democracy but,
as I indicate, one easily extinguished.

IN A LETTER to a friend in 1855, Abraham Lincoln suddenly made mention of a distant land. If the United States went the way of mindless inequality, he wrote tartly, "I shall prefer emigrating to some country where they make no pretense of loving liberty—to Russia, for instance, where despotism can be taken pure, and without the base alloy of hypocrisy."

A figure like Lincoln would have been wasted on the Russians then, for nothing could change that ugly verdict on their society. The masters of Russian literature were already experts at soulful evocations of the passive and fatalistic character of their nation. The genius of their art made the barrenness of the political landscape even more conspicuous. For a thousand years Russia and most of its neighboring states couldn't manage even a few crocuses, much less a full flowering of democratic ideals. In a nation obsessed with history, the rule of law and the sovereignty of the people simply had no history at all.

By the 20th century the heirs to Russia's authoritarian tradition (now dressed as Communists) wrote seemingly endless new chapters of terror, bolstered by tools of mass communications that promised "total" control. Their history became little more than a criminal enterprise. Last week alone was the 52nd anniversary of the enslavement of the Baltics, the 51st anniversary of an ice pick crashing through Leon Trotsky's skull and the 23rd anniversary of the crushing of Prague Spring.

One of the beauties of the rejection of the coup is that it contains an exquisite historical symmetry. Just as tanks in Moscow turned around to defend the institutions they were meant to attack, so the uses of history and of the mass media—once antidemocratic weapons—were liberated for the benefit of the people.

History had been especially burdensome. It was hardly surprising that during the hours when the coup seemed to be working, a round of I-told-you-sos began among those who had long believed that Russia's antidemocratic disease was incurable. Judging from the past, they argued, there could be no other outcome.

Give thanks that the past is an erratic judge, underestimating the power of change and the whims of fortune, in this case bumbling coup plotters. With a bit more luck, the events of last week will serve as an inoculation against the darkness. The task now is to create an instant democratic tradition that can be drawn on, like a booster shot. The Soviet Union is finally in a position to develop what the historian Henry Steele Commager described as essential to the success of any society: a usable past.

A usable past should not be fabricated, like that of the Bolsheviks. But it need not be entirely true, either. The young American republic, lacking any roots, quickly created a series of heroic myths about its struggle with British tyranny. Early thrilling accounts of the American Revolution invariably omitted the fact that large sections of the colonies were populated by Tories. Likewise, in Moscow last week, People Power was something of a myth; out of 291 million Soviets, at first only a few thousand courageously put themselves on the line for democracy. The vast majority stayed on the fence until the outcome was clear. But it hardly mattered. The perception of a democratic triumph quickly became the reality. People thought they had the power, and therefore they did.

This is where the role of television becomes relevant. TV is not a particularly effective conveyor of lies, as the totalitarians found over many years of failing to brainwash the masses. But it is a potent means of exaggeration, of making the dramatic symbol stand for the whole. It also has a bias for the unruly and spontaneous, much like democracy itself. In 1917, the bacillus of revolution arrived by train, with Lenin. Today, the fever of democracy moves over the air, from the Philippines to Eastern Europe and beyond. TV is not sufficient, as the Chinese proved at Tiananmen Square, but it is certainly necessary. Even the stodgy putschists knew the media is now the sea in which all politics swims. Caught between the old world of secret arrangements and the new age of tele-diplomacy, they felt obligated to televise their lies, rendering them all the more transparent. Later, it was TV that apparently helped contribute to their loss of nerve. As Boris Yeltsin reminded them, their butchery would be televised, in living color.

Democracy's triumph may be short-lived; its spirit has always been fragile, everywhere. There will surely be other assaults, if not in the form of the old totalitarianism then as part of the "gradual and silent encroachments" that James Madison warned against. But something big has changed forever. An embryonic democracy has found a way to breathe. Last week's events did more than make the world sleep easier; they created a new history—a mental videotape, to be played over and over again.

With Bush in South-Central

—— 1992 ——

In 1992, a Los Angeles motorist named Rodney King fled police in a high-speed chase. When he was caught and handcuffed, L.A. police officers kicked him and beat him, an event captured on videotape. The riots in South-Central Los Angeles after the not-guilty verdict in the police brutality trial kicked off a debate over how much the government cared about the problems of the inner city.

ALL THROUGHOUT the 1930s, '40s, '50s and into the '60s, the Democratic Party had a perfect code word: "Herbert Hoover." It summoned the Depression and Republican mismanagement of the economy. But with Democrats fouling up the economy themselves, the message finally outlived its usefulness.

The same thing just might be beginning to happen with the GOP's legendary "law and order" theme, which has worked as a way of bashing Democrats since the 1960s. After proving useful—even decisive—in five elections, the idea of exploiting fear of black crime to win white votes is looking a little tattered. It's not that there's less fear; there's more. And any national Democrat who looks squishy on crime is still politically dead. But the public seems to realize that just building more jails—the major growth area of government in the 1980s—is not going to make these problems disappear. And on whose watch did the problems get worse? Not Lyndon Johnson's. Besides, push those old buttons too often and the whole country blows up.

On his trip to L.A., George Bush appeared to understand some of this. When his cocoon was finally pierced, he responded in human terms to the carnage around him. What he failed to understand is that as president he's in a position to do something about it. Bush isn't heartless, he's clueless. And the sad part is that there are plenty of clues around for him to put together if he really wanted to solve the puzzle.

Contrary to the stage-managed TV impression, Bush didn't actually make a real walking tour of South-Central Los Angeles. His only inspection took place at one fire-damaged shopping mall sealed off from the public—at 7 in the morning. The only residents he met were a dentist and a store manager rustled up by the president's advance staff. Face to face with Belfast West, Bush appeared rather incurious; he strolled right past the bombed-out stores without really looking at them. But as the day wore on and he met eloquent black clergymen and aggrieved Korean community leaders, he seemed sincerely moved. The joke on the press bus was that the expression on his face said roughly: Marlin, somehow I don't think we're in Kennebunkport anymore.

For a man so thoroughly isolated from the lives of most Americans, the mile after mile of devastation had to be a shock. This was his country, but it looked like a foreign country—which for Bush, obsessed as he is with foreign affairs, made it perhaps a matter of more compelling interest. The Israelis last week compared the riot to their own intifada, and maybe that wasn't a completely inappropriate analogy. Despite all the rock-throwers on the West Bank, Bush views that unrest as the understandable rage of a dispossessed people. For all of the opportunistic looting, irrational arson and sheer criminality, didn't the L.A. rage reflect something real, too?

The old Republican game would have been to stigmatize those communities—and send a message to the white suburbs that they will be insulated from black crime. But even suburbanites are beginning to realize that there's no place to hide. Sensing this at last, Bush tried to talk as a president should, rejecting finger-pointing in favor of unity, compassion, the family.

Yet the hour is late for platitudes. The black residents of South-Central whom Bush didn't meet—those in the audience or outside—were remarkably consistent in their reactions. They want action, real investment in the community, not words. "I think I'd be more inclined to believe him when I see the check clear the bank," said Gale Fue, an accountant. On CNN, Claude Brown, author of *Manchild in the Promised Land*, turned to white America and said simply: "The time has come when you have to sit in on the card game and ante up."

All of this is still terribly unfashionable in Washington policy circles. While blaming Lyndon Johnson didn't go over well, Bush clings to the idea that money is no answer. Even the dumbest liberal no longer believes it's *the* answer, but how about *an* answer?

After all, it's not as if poverty pimps still roam the land, ripping off the taxpayer with their wasteful community-development programs. With 20 years of experience, it's quite clear to liberals and conservatives alike which ideas and organizations have a track record of accomplishment, and which don't. The list includes ideas like community policing, tenant ownership of public housing, early-childhood education, prenatal care and youth recreation programs like the one Bush visited in L.A. Given that agreement, how can they not be funded heavily? How can Bush say, for instance, that Head Start works, but only propose to offer it to less than one half of those children who are eligible for it? The money to pay for it is always there somewhere. Last week's bill came due for the United States' share of Desert Storm: $7.3 billion. We paid it.

The bill for our inner cities is long, long overdue. Take urban enterprise zones—no panacea, but worth a try. For 12 years, they have received bipartisan support. So why haven't they passed? Jack Kemp says it's because Democrats don't want "some Anglo-Saxon center-right Republican cutting the ribbon" on an urban renaissance. Some truth to that, no doubt. But the bigger reason is that the president never showed any real interest in the larger issue of poverty, never gave South-Central a second thought—except as a way to get votes in places like Simi Valley. Enterprise zones alone won't end poverty. Neither will any other single idea. But sustained commitment by the American leadership class can make a difference. Let's push that button for a change.

O.J. and TV: False Intimacy

—— 1994 ——

The case of O.J. Simpson, the former football star accused of murdering his wife and her friend, dominated the news for much of 1994 and 1995. This was written shortly after Simpson was apprehended and it anticipated the intimate connection Americans felt to the case. Later, I attended the trial for a day, but by then the story was hopelessly over-covered.

AFTER THE SURREALISM had lifted, after the letter, the manhunt, the cavalcade, the standoff, came the sense that we all knew more about O.J. Simpson now. Thanks to TV, we knew what his house looked like, which friends were closest, how he viewed the "downs and ups" of his marriage. But as he sat in his driveway for the last time, as Barbara Walters prattled on about how he might occupy a cell next to one of the Menendez brothers, it was somehow appropriate that he waited until it was too dark for the helicopter cameras to get the humiliating shot of his surrender. We didn't know him that well.

In fact, we didn't really know him at all. We just thought we did. The Simpson case is the best evidence yet of why all of us should learn to distrust our everyday judgments about the character of people we know only from television. "Things are seldom what they seem/Skim milk masquerades as cream," Gilbert and Sullivan wrote in *H.M.S. Pinafore.* As Americans prepare for a much-needed education about spousal abuse, this sad case might also help us learn a little modesty about our understanding of human nature. It might help us learn some necessary caution in how we view public figures—in sports, entertainment, politics, anywhere.

The false intimacy of TV is poorly understood but truly damaging to public life. Because we see familiar people moving and talking in color, "up close and personal," as ABC Sports says, we think we know them reasonably well, certainly better than we know them from a seemingly more remote medium like print. When Simpson smiled in a TV interview the week before the killings and talked about learning "to lose gracefully," this was, to all eyes, the real person talking. After all, he always seemed to be the same guy every time we got together with him to watch a football game or hear about rental cars. And we'd known him for years. Hadn't we?

So on reflection it was no real surprise that motorists cheered and blew kisses to Simpson and Al Cowlings as they made their way down the freeway. Any fugitive in similar circumstances would gain a measure of public sympathy; one man against the system is the most irresistible plot of all. But in this case it wasn't Harrison Ford playing a role, and it wasn't Lorena Bobbitt or Joey Buttafuoco or some other media confection. This was O.J.—no last name necessary. Nobody was going to let the media tell us what to think about him.

This sounds good—people judging matters for themselves. But it is a television delusion, and one connected to the more pointed ironies of American culture. Simpson's charming smile and openness were a path to some sort of success in America, even if he hadn't been a world-class running back. These good-guy qualities are a large part of this country's character, and it's how we get ahead. Friendliness—especially of a homogenized Madison Avenue sort—is the face we turn to the world. But it is a Janus face, born also of violence. In our tastes and behavior, these impulses coexist in varying degrees in all of us.

Yes, the mask extends beyond television. Simpson's friends all thought he was a good guy, too, incapable of this crime. But it is on TV that we see the mask affixed, and stripped off. This is big business now. It's the game of trying to probe beneath the mask—who's lying?—that draws millions of viewers to network news magazines, daytime talk shows and much of the rest of TV.

Americans are much savvier about media images than we once were. We think we can tell who's telling the truth and who's not. Like Oprah or Phil, we're all amateur therapists. But there are dangers in that. Last week both ABC News and CNN happened to schedule the Paula Jones interviews immediately following their O.J. Simpson coverage. This was bad news for Bill Clinton; the Simpson story no doubt boosted Jones's audience. But it should have also introduced a note of restraint to all stories that revolve around personality and character. Some viewers looked at Paula Jones and decided she was telling the truth. Others looked at her and decided she was lying.

Both are natural responses that the medium has conditioned us to formulate. But both conclusions about her are as ill-informed as anything we might have thought about O.J. The only honest answer is that the way Simpson or Jones or anyone else handles a TV appearance does not tell us much of anything about the real person. Human beings—all human beings—are much too complicated to have their entire lives reduced to how they "come across" for a few minutes on television.

Yet these fleeting assessments are how we run our public life. Forty years ago Edward R. Murrow took apart Senator Joe McCarthy on CBS. This helped end the anti-communist witch hunts, a shameful episode in modern American history. But McCarthy's televised demise helped usher in an equally disturbing era. McCarthy was fat, sweaty and uncomfortable with the medium; Murrow was thin, urbane and totally at home on TV. It was no contest. It didn't matter that Murrow made his case on the merits. The lesson, hardened after JFK looked better than Richard Nixon in the first 1960 presidential debate, was that images really count.

But even when we're sure we "See It Now," even when we watch the whole chase scene live, we really don't. So much else is going on, especially inside those hearts and minds where cameras can never really go. So instead of investing all that viewer energy in discerning the "real" O.J. Simpson or the "real" Harrison Ford or the "real" Bill Clinton, let's judge them on their actions instead of what we imagine their characters to be. That way, we're less likely to be disappointed, and more likely to be respectful of the true complexity of the human condition.

The Million Man March at Home

The "Million Man March" of 1995, led by Black Muslim leader Louis Farrakhan, gathered hundreds of thousands of African-American men in Washington, D.C. It was a separatist event, but it helped kick off some integration and fresh thinking at the local level. I've covered the rapid growth of the Boys and Girls Clubs in the years since. Today, they serve nearly a third of the 15 million at-risk youth in the United States.

L ET'S NOT BE NAIVE about the Million Man March, we're told. The message of atonement cannot ultimately be distinguished from the bigoted messenger, bent on leading blacks off the cliff of separatism. It's a valid argument. I'm still appalled at the widespread willingness to countenance attacks on Jews that would never be tolerated if they were directed toward blacks. Saying that Louis Farrakhan is right about entrepreneurship is like saying that David Duke is right about cutting taxes. Or that Hitler was nice to pets, to use a Johnnie Cochranesque formulation.

So why are so many other Americans, black and white, focusing on the positive? Why are they making the message-messenger distinction? According to a *Newsweek* poll, more than half of Americans believe the march was a necessary step toward more racial integration. An all-black event. Led by a separatist. Leading to integration? The strange thing is, they may be right.

The freshest idea to come out of the march was black America's retreat from stale victimhood. This shattered whole ice floes of political correctness, as even the conservative *Wall Street Journal* seemed to sense in an approving editorial. For all the sharp attacks on white supremacy—and even the Founders—there was little of the blame game that white America had been conditioned to expect. This shouldn't have been such a surprise; Jesse Jackson has been talking personal responsibility for years. But it was always hitched to the tired politics of grievance. By publicly conceding the central role of blacks in worsening many of their own problems, the march may let whites predisposed to neglect the inner city off the hook. But it's an axiom of our 12-step culture that if you show signs of helping yourself, others more readily pitch in, which means-down the road-more collaboration and thus integration.

My own search for common ground began on the ground. To assess the march's long-term potential, I visited the Boys and Girls Club in Paterson, New Jersey, a struggling community of 137,000, nearly 40 percent black. In every city and hundreds of housing projects, these clubs are indispensable. The evening I went to Paterson, more than 200 elementary-school-age children, finished with club-supervised sports and homework, were staying on at the club for dinner. Many of their parents are so lost to crack or other problems that they cannot even manage to provide one meal a day for their kids, much less pick them up. Scores of young children then walk a mile in the dark through the ghetto by themselves to get home, if you can call it that.

For many of these kids, "Daddy" is Don Grady, a talented 33-year-old club coordinator, coach and all-round role model. For me, Grady symbolizes the good seed of the march. He made a point of going early to Washington so as not to miss speeches by the Reverend Al Sharpton, Khalid Muhammed and other black leaders who make me see red. In Grady, however, the speakers induced not venom but vigor. The march "gives me a push to get more people involved here," Grady says. Right now, the club can count on only one coach for every 48 kids. Grady desperately needs volunteers willing to give even an hour a week. Black, white, green, anybody.

It's too early to tell how many post-march recruits he'll get, but the signs are encouraging. A black man bringing his son to the club approaches us. He missed the march but is determined to catch some of its afterglow by volunteering. Someone posts a flier at the club about a meeting to be held at the local Zion Baptist Church to capitalize on the spirit. Over in Newark, all of the march bus captains from northern New Jersey are getting together. If Grady gets black volunteers this way, they will have anything but a separatist experience. "We have a very mixed culture, with Hispanics, whites," he says. "It won't be just a black thing here."

I watch as the board of directors of the Boys and Girls Club of Paterson convenes and immediately decides to place a special ad in the Paterson paper seeking volunteers. Both blacks and whites on the board have no problem separating the march's message from the messenger. Brian Heidtke, white, the treasurer of the Colgate Palmolive Company, says "It would be a great tragedy if there's not a reaching out" in the days ahead.

When all is said and done, much more may be said than done. But Chuck Cornish, a black board member and systems engineer at Bell Atlantic who attended the march, counsels patience. First comes improving family relationships, then maybe giving time to something like their club—months, even years, from now. Cornish also attended the 1963 March on Washington, which sparked a generation of civil rights activism. "The chain was broken" in the 1970s and '80s, he says. Now, "Farrakhan is helping put the chain back together." A separatist chain? Cornish snorts derisively at what he considers the white media's lack of sophistication on this point. "Some brothers were planning to open a restaurant in Paterson and wanted to make it a black place," he said. "'You will fail,' I told them. Not enough customers. To do anything, I need money from him," he says, pointing playfully to fellow board member Tony Accavallo, a white banker. Everyone laughs.

The civil rights movement required strong national leadership and strong national pressure on Washington. Today's challenge is more daunting and depressing, but at bottom it's not about the men on top. It's about committed blacks like Don Grady and Chuck Cornish and their white colleagues pulling together to save the next generation. Last year, 126 new Boys and Girls Clubs opened across the country, and the number of disadvantaged kids participating now exceeds 2 million—nearly twice as many as a decade ago. It's a long march against long odds, but it has begun.

Clinton and Starr: In History's Bedchamber

—— 1998 ——

In early 1998, Newsweek revealed that President Clinton has carried on an affair with Monica Lewinsky, a White House intern. As it became clear over the months that Kenneth Starr, the independent counsel in the Lewinsky case, would not settle for the Senate censuring Clinton and would push for impeachment, I began to view the two men as unmatched bookends on the era. This was written when it became clear that Clinton would not be convicted by the Senate and removed from office.

IN HER MEMOIRS, the late Virginia Kelley, the president's mother, recalls how she laughed at the thought of a Baptist minister seeing her gardening on Sundays in Hot Springs, Arkansas, wearing short shorts and a tube top. According to press reports, Kenneth Starr's father, a Baptist minister in Thalia, Texas, often delivered sermons rebuking women who gardened on Sunday without being properly attired. Though he lived across the border from Arkansas, the Reverend might just as well have been talking about Clinton's mom, and she about him.

So maybe it's not so surprising that their sons have developed one of the great blood feuds of modern times. Bill Clinton's loathing of Ken Starr is said to be nearly pathological. And when Starr responded to a question last week by denying any personal animosity toward the president, he was taking a leaf from Clinton's book. He was lying.

The irony is that these two men—both politically ambitious Southern baby-boomer lawyers who came East—are stuck with each other for good. History, as Richard Nixon liked to point out, is written mostly by liberals, which means that Starr will come out worse. But more often, the two men will be viewed in tandem, as legal and cultural bookends for their times. A backlash against the 1960s led to Ken Starr's interest in the president's sex life; a backlash against that backlash allowed Clinton to escape. To make matters more complicated, the Washington media establishment has switched teams. Once liberal but always fickle, the press clearly sided with the prim, conservative Starr for much of this year, while the once conservative "Silent Majority" backed the hip, liberal Clinton, or at least the way he has handled his job.

Clinton should be down on his knees giving thanks. He goes into

1999 stronger politically than any other 20th-century president in his seventh year in office—stronger than Franklin Roosevelt in 1939, Dwight Eisenhower in 1959 and Ronald Reagan in 1987. Were he to get a deal on fixing Social Security and Medicare, he'd have a legislative record that will stand up well for a peacetime president—a solid Rockefeller Republican legacy. Feeling vindicated by Democratic gains in the midterm elections, Clinton figures the worst is over. If the economy stays strong and the accommodationist policy toward Iraq doesn't blow up in his face (two big "ifs"), the president may slide through.

But the old pendulum has a way of smacking Clinton in the head when it swings back. Without the threat of impeachment, many of those who rallied to his side will remember what they didn't like about him. As for Clinton's place in history, censure would not be the tap on the wrist that the president's critics assume. It would tarnish him permanently and send him down several notches in the polls taken among historians.

If the president hopes to improve his marks with this crowd, he has to portray himself as the victim not just of Starr personally, but of gross prosecutorial abuse. Which is why his lawyers have spent so much time raising questions about the overzealous tactics used with lesser figures and whether Starr's prosecutors asked Monica Lewinsky to wear a wire.

This all sounds sinister until you realize that Clinton has championed the same prosecutorial techniques he now assails. His response to the Oklahoma City bombing was to weaken Fourth Amendment protections against illegal searches and seizures. Prosecutors who intimidate witnesses to get convictions are promoted, not punished. Warrantless searches are up dramatically. And wiretapping—including the use of body wires—has been greatly expanded. Clinton is in no mood to change his anti–civil liberties policies, which means he can hardly play the victim for posterity.

As an "unlawful" advocate of impeachment (according to his own ex-ethics adviser, Sam Dash), Starr will naturally suffer in the eyes of history. He has lost the argument, not just politically but on its constitutional merits. Even before the election, there was no consensus in the House that perjury is a "high crime." During Watergate, the House Judiciary Committee recognized this when it rejected perjury (the underlying tax-evasion charge against Nixon) as grounds for impeachment. As for Starr's other charges, there's simply not enough evidence of obstruction of justice. And Starr's abuse-of-power claim is both flimsy and dangerous—a bid to impeach a president for delaying, litigating privileges, and otherwise acting like a lawyer.

As they drift off together to history's bedchamber, Bill Clinton and Ken Starr have weighed in on the same side of the eternal debate over ends versus means. Clinton thought the end of protecting himself from embarrassment justified the means of lying under oath; Starr thought the end of nailing Clinton justified his heedless obsession, all out of proportion to the offense. They will be forever linked, and properly so. These two guys deserve each other.

The Era of Bad Feeling

—— 1998 ——

*This was written on the afternoon of December 19, 1998,
the day that the House of Representatives voted articles of impeachment
against President Clinton. On the same day, the newly designated Speaker
of the House, Bob Livingston, was forced to resign in a sex scandal.*

*And we are here as on a darkling plain
Swept with confused alarms of struggle
and flight
Where ignorant armies clash by night*
—Matthew Arnold, "Dover Beach," 1851

THE HISTORY OF the 1990s, so peaceful and prosperous for most Americans, will be of "ignorant armies" sounding "confused alarms" over nothing much at all. Bill Clinton is a sad and compelling human specimen who will be remembered as a cross between William McKinley (popular president in relatively placid times) and Andrew Johnson (railroaded by Radical Republicans). His impeachment was history as farce without the laughs. His foreign policy looked like a game of toy soldiers. His universe, at the end of the year, feels small, surreal and a bit scary.

Where was the grandeur? Where was the majesty? While most of America shopped for Christmas, Washington, D.C., on Saturday, December 19, 1998—a day that will live in inanity—felt like the set of a bad Peter Sellers movie. In the morning, Speaker-to-be Bob Livingston quit, a de facto admission that pornographer Larry Flynt was running the country. In early afternoon, the president of the United States was impeached for denying that he touched Monica Lewinsky "with the intent to sexually arouse" and for trying to get his secretary to clean up his mess. In late afternoon, Clinton and his fellow Democrats attempted, for the first time ever, to "spin" utter political humiliation—and it may even have worked. In the evening, the commander in chief committed the United States to a long-term, open-ended policy of occasionally irritating Saddam Hussein.

This year was the culmination of an American culture war that has been nasty, brutish and long. Leonard Garment, Richard Nixon's lawyer, was once asked why so many people hated Clinton with such intensity. "Because he represents the '60s," Garment said. The golfing Southern back-slapper with the cheatin' heart is actually a figure more out of the 1950s, but Garment had a point. As the *Wall Street Journal* editorial page inadvertently confirmed, Ken Starr was prosecuting not just Bill Clinton but "the generation that produced him." What makes Republicans especially frustrated about the events of 1998 is that the cultural war is over—and the '60s sexual revolution won. The biggest surprise of the whole year is that Clinton's approval rating has stayed high—well above Ronald Reagan's in his second term—for the duration. Puritanism, once the deepest impulse in the American character, is now a minor strain. We're not quite France yet, but we're getting there.

So having lost the war, the GOP stopped at nothing to win a big battle. Any potential defectors knew they risked losing their committee chairs and other perks. Members of the House were urged to vote their consciences—as long as their consciences didn't dictate censure, which would have won easily had it been an option. Impeachment was rammed through with no chance to vote on alternatives. Representative Tom Lantos, who escaped Hungary in 1947 after working in both the anti-Nazi and the anti-communist underground, was practically shaking with rage when I saw him coming off the floor after an eloquent speech. "What distinguishes this House from the fake parliaments of police states is not voting—they all vote—but procedural fairness." To his GOP colleagues, he said: "I would defend their right to vote their conscience with my life if necessary. I find it unbelievable that they won't defend mine."

Beyond the sins of the president and Congress lie the media's many transgressions. In print, never have so many trees died to say so little. On TV, the air pollution was more toxic than ever this year. Clinton complains about "the politics of personal destruction," but he could just as easily focus on "personal distraction"—a major ailment in our celebrity-addled age. But the press, which for years has enjoyed doing stories about politicians' private lives, is not solely responsible for today's sexual Armageddon. Politics and the law have been sexualized by politicians and lawyers; they are central to any disarmament.

The consequences of this era of bad feeling will be felt for years by the president, the Congress and the press. All have been demytholo-gized in unhealthy ways. Clinton's squalid behavior helped strip his office of much of its grandeur. The Oval Office and the Lincoln Bedroom will never be viewed in quite the same light again. The House of Representatives has taken the solemn, even inspirational, bipartisan process of 1974 and turned it into just another blunt political instrument. All future attacks on future presidents will quickly descend into talk of impeachment, further debasing our currency of outrage. In fact, the I word is already losing its sting.

Meanwhile, in the real America, people are scratching their heads —and not just over why Henry Hyde and Bob Livingston seem to get all the girls. As Washington implodes, most people's lives are better reflected in the first line of Matthew Arnold's poem: "The sea is calm tonight." Even as real bombs fell on Iraq and rhetorical ones on Washington, 1998 was—by relative historical standards—tranquil. The cleavages are deeper in the Congress than in the country. Ideology is in decline. No matter what fate befalls Bill Clinton—no matter how loud our gauche *Götterdämmerung*—this will always be seen as a transitional era between the fall of the Berlin Wall and whatever overarching global drama comes next. We are cursed to live in interesting and bitter times, but not deeply consequential ones.

Bush vs. Gore

—— 2000 ——

At about 9:00 PM on Election Night, 2000, I was in a studio at NBC News when I heard that Florida had been shifted from Al Gore's column to "too close to call." After hearing rumors of irregularities in Palm Beach County, I telephoned the city desk of the Palm Beach Post *and learned that the paper planned to publish a story the next day (this was before Web sites routinely posted news) saying that thousands of voters intending to vote for Gore had accidentally voted for third party candidate Pat Buchanan because of something called a "butterfly ballot." Within minutes, I was on the air with Tom Brokaw telling the country the story. I spent a good portion of the next several weeks in Florida covering the historic recount and how it was ended by order of the Supreme Court.*

STANDING IN THE SMALL crowd outside the Florida State Supreme Court in Tallahassee last Friday, I had a flashback. Twenty-five years ago this fall, I was at Fenway Park when Boston Red Sox catcher Carlton Fisk hit a famous home run in the bottom on the 12th inning just inside the foul pole to win game six of the World Series. The Red Sox were still alive—and so was Al Gore. The next day, in game seven, Joe Morgan hit a bloop single to win the series for the Cincinnati Reds—and the U.S. Supreme Court all but handed the election to George W. Bush. Unforgettable.

As I read it, the Supremes are basically saying that the judiciary shouldn't settle elections—so we'll go ahead and settle this one. The sad thing is that in acting for the good of democracy and the legitimacy of the American presidency, the court harmed both. I was standing outside the Leon County Public Library when court officials brought out the Miami-Dade County ballots in shoe boxes, their efforts suspended halfway through a speedy and remarkably smooth hand count. The judges designated to handle the recount had none of the dire problems assessing the intent of the voters so ominously predicted by Republicans. If the process had continued, Judge Terry Lewis would have only a couple of hundred hard calls out of 9,000 votes. As vote counters all over Florida have discovered this fall, when you actually look at the undervotes, the vast majority aren't that hard to figure out.

And soon enough, under Florida's "sunshine law," anyone who wants to will get the chance.

The great irony is that a fair hand-count might well have given the election to Bush, especially with the help of still-disputed overseas military ballots. Had the count been completed, Bush would have had a lot less trouble on the legitimacy front next year. Democratic complaints would not have subsided completely; African-American voters would have continued, in any event, to believe that in some areas their votes were suppressed. But the Democrats' main argument—that all the votes had not been counted—would have been stripped away. Bush wasn't willing to take the chance, and he will pay for it in prestige.

Justice Antonin Scalia has a big intellectual rep. We're all supposed to bow down to his brilliance, even when we disagree. But his concurring opinion on the stay was one of the most logically shoddy bits of legal reasoning in recent memory. His opinion works only if the starting point of the argument is that Bush deserves to be president. If you assume uncertainty on that point, the justice's case makes no sense. Scalia had to square an impossible circle—to show that a stay of the hand-count was necessary to avoid "irreparable harm." So Scalia argued that counting controversial votes was what did the irreparable harm. Why? Because it would "cast 'a cloud' on Bush's legitimacy." To get there, he had to assume and baldly assert that any vote rejected by the machine is, by definition, of "questionable legality." This after a Bush witness who co-invented the machine testified that it wasn't reliable in close elections.

On top of that, Scalia had to find that the state and local officials he has spent his career claiming to defer to were not in a position to assess the votes cast by their neighbors. The historic stay order was historically lame. In the name of bolstering Bush's legitimacy, Scalia undermined it.

Scalia also questioned the "propriety, even the constitutionality, of letting the standards for determination of voters' intent—dimpled chads, hanging chads, etc.—vary from county to county." It may have been emotionally satisfying for the justice to make sport of chad from the bench, as his friends on the right have done. But how could those variations possibly be unconstitutional? Does Scalia believe that today's widespread differences in chad standards among *states* are unconstitutional? (Texas counts dimples, California doesn't.) Why are counties more threatening to the republic than states? The voting equipment varies from county to county in Florida. Is he suggesting that the high court should invalidate votes on those grounds, too?

In fact, the whole idea of a consistent chad standard is not nearly as appealing as it sounds. Disputed ballots are, by definition, anomalies, and anomalies can't be easily standardized. To carry the Scalia/Bush view to its logical conclusion, we must have a uniform federal chad standard. But even after this year's mess and the extra money to upgrade election equipment that will flow from Washington, elections will still be state and local matters. If one really believes the best government is closest to the people, then the vague "clear intention of the voter" standard twice articulated by the Florida State Supreme Court is the most sensible one. It relies on the common sense of individual people (often judges) looking at individual ballots. If properly supervised with a rough equivalence in party affiliation (both of which occurred over the weekend), how much more democratic can you get?

For a reporter, Tallahassee last week was a fabulous legal Disneyland, with historic court cases and legislative maneuvering played out for huge stakes, all within walking distance. But after all the stops and starts, the hits and errors in the bottom of the 12th, Judge Lewis and his faithful counters showed that Florida could figure out how it voted for president, if only it were allowed to do so.

9/11: America, Unchanged

—— 2001 ——

*I heard on the radio about an airplane flying into the
World Trade Center while waiting for a commuter bus to take me from
my home in Montclair, New Jersey, to the* Newsweek *offices in
New York. With the Lincoln Tunnel now closed, I drove to Secaucus,
New Jersey, where MSNBC then had its studios. En route,
one of the towers collapsed and I could see the smoke on the horizon
across the Hudson River—one tower up, one down. Moments later,
the second one fell. I knew I had no way to get into the city. I wrote this
first story between midnight and 3:00 AM on September 12, 2001,
at the MSNBC studios, where I spent the night.*

SUMMER IS OVER in America. Fat and happy is history, a closed
chapter in our national experience. By midday Tuesday, with the
surreal horror sinking in, the sense spread widely that life in the United
States will change as permanently as the skyline of New York City. But
change how? Despite the unspeakable carnage, maybe we shouldn't
change so much after all.

In the news business, we are in the habit of pumping up events.
INTERN MISSING! PRESIDENT CLASHES WITH CONGRESS!
Now we are trying, in the national interest, to preserve some calm. And
with good reason. For a time last Tuesday morning it felt as if some
unseen enemy might actually decapitate the nation's financial, military
and transportation systems. The Pearl Harbor analogy didn't suffice.
This was war on the American mainland for the first time since 1865,
when Grant accepted Lee's surrender at Appomattox. As the death toll
rises to stunning levels, we can't imagine going back to pedestrian
debate about Social Security and education, much less tabloid distractions. The preoccupations of the recent past look like luxuries we can
no longer afford.

But we should try to reclaim them. As my children watched the
smoke rise over lower Manhattan—a mushroom cloud for their
generation—they wondered why school wasn't canceled. I'm glad it
wasn't. For years critics like me have bemoaned our culture's short-term

memory. We get saturation coverage—of Columbine, the embassy bombings, impeachment; then, when the finger-pointing and soul-searching is over, we move on with nary a backward glance. I've often viewed this as a bad thing, a sign of national shallowness and amnesia, evidence of the Western rot that the terrorists so despise. But maybe this cultural coping strategy is not so unhealthy after all. Maybe some of our "innocence" and capacity for denial is worth clinging to. Maybe the best approach this time is to retaliate, then sublimate.

Sublimate? Impossible now. But in the weeks to come, as we sort through the material and psychological wreckage, we need to be careful about the way we process the catastrophe. If we change too much—if we give rein to anger and pessimism—we'll hand the terrorists another, bigger victory. They want America to lose forever that confident and carefree spirit they find so threatening. Why, after we mourn, should we give them that?

Obviously there are practical lessons we must learn. It's a little bit like the war in Vietnam, where an elusive adversary made our World War II military approach look obsolete. At least in Vietnam we knew the enemy forces were somewhere in the country; today, they could be anywhere in the world. Once again, we've been fighting the last war, spending less than 10 percent of our $325 billion Defense budget on what has clearly been the biggest threat of recent years. The attack should kick off a broad national debate, not just on airport security and the colossal intelligence failure, but on what national defense actually means. Missile defense, for instance, looks just a tad off the point now.

At a minimum, we should resolve never again to ignore convincing warnings of threats to our national security. In March of this year, the Rudman-Hart Commission on National Security issued its report, saying unequivocally that the biggest threat to the United States was terrorism. The report gathered dust; we didn't know real news when we saw it.

So we are paying the price of our complacency—the price of a decade-long flight from seriousness in the way we view public affairs. Since the end of the Cold War, this country has been bound together by little more than collective consumerism and a mutual thirst for distraction. Media were tabloid media. Reality was reality TV. This summer, for instance, the United States conducted 16 days of bombing against targets in Iraq. Almost no one noticed, perhaps because the story involved no sharks. Even those stories more extensively covered than we might remember—like violence in the Middle East, the No. 2 story of the summer—didn't resonate. The strife was worrisome but tiresome, and it did not seem much connected to our everyday lives.

It would be good if this week's events changed that perception, but not too much. Shattering our complacency should not mean shattering our way of life. We need to make the world safe, not just for ourselves and our children, but for at least some of our quintessentially American diversions and illusions. I'll feel much better when the next silly celebrity scandal comes along, confirming that the skies can clear eventually. That's why the collective psychological approach of the next few days is so critical. If we think of ourselves as constantly vulnerable, we will be more vulnerable. If we succumb to the modern equivalent of putting our money under the mattress, we will turn a short-term disaster into a long-term threat to who we are—and who we want to be.

It's understandable how we might be spooked in the months ahead. Except for those who fought in Vietnam or live in extremely violent neighborhoods, Americans of this generation have little experience with threats to their physical safety. Most live longer than their parents, and experience less untimely death among family and friends. That makes the loss of control—the powerlessness—all the more acute.

We felt this way after the Oklahoma City bombing, too. At first, it seemed even worse than a foreign attack. This was homegrown terrorism—a reflection of something dark in the American soul. But in retrospect, Oklahoma City was easier to take; the work of a few right-wing kooks. Maybe the Kennedy assassination is a better comparison. Some light of rationality went out, and we aren't yet sure how to adjust our vision.

Americans are a generous people, now eager to help. But there is little concrete to do. No regiments to volunteer for or bandages to wrap or victory gardens to grow. But a more subtle collective task is, in fact, at hand, one that can be fulfilled in millions of conversations and small acts across the country. That national task is to avoid depressive and sour thinking; to suggest to friends that, say, selling their stocks would be unpatriotic; to avoid scapegoating Arab-Americans and backing the indiscriminate bombing of civilians; to engage the world, instead of telling it to go to hell.

The habit of thinking that international events have no relevance at home has been exposed as just as dangerous as pre-World War II isolationism. Just as the launching of the Soviet satellite Sputnik in 1957 kicked off a boom in science and math education, maybe this will goad our schools to make international relations more central to American curriculum.

But as we learn about the Middle East we must avoid becoming like the Middle East. The challenge is to respond like the Israeli government—hitting back hard when we find the culprits—without becoming more like Israel, where soldiers patrol cafes with machine guns and life is conditioned by the daily threat of violence. If we're not careful, we will condemn ourselves and our children to endless, episodic war. They hit us. We hit them. They wait awhile, then hit us again. That cycle would destroy the America we know.

For the past decade, we've lived in a golden age. Peace and prosperity—as good as it gets. Now that feels like past tense—as good as it got. But life on a downward slope is a profoundly un-American notion. As we grieve and heal, let's not let a horrible day open a horrible era in the life of this country.

Grit, Guts and Rudy Giuliani

— 2001 —

On September 14, 2001, I was part of a small press pool that went to Ground Zero with President Bush, New York Mayor Rudy Giuliani, Senator Hillary Clinton and others and I stood fewer than five feet from Bush when he climbed on top of a collapsed fire truck, raised a bullhorn and promised he would retaliate. That week, I reconstructed Giuliani's experience on 9/11, which while accurate, to my later regret, contributed to his myth-making.

AT 9:05 PM last Wednesday Rudy Giuliani finally broke. Exactly 36 hours after he first rushed to the World Trade Center, the mayor's neo-Churchillian reputation was already secure. He had just escaped injury or death in The Attack, calmly led a terrifying retreat uptown, then inhabited the role of wartime leader with a fine mixture of brisk compassion and gritty command presence.

But now an aide caught him wolfing down half a sandwich of what she described as "oily cheese" and "meats that sweat"—a total violation of the stewed-tomato-and-fruit diet he had strictly observed as part of his treatment for prostate cancer. The mayor of New York was famished and exhausted and grieving more than the public knew. Many of the senior uniformed officers he saw every day were dead, heroes all. His staff, still barred from reoccupying a phoneless City Hall, looked like combat veterans; one executive assistant was back by the mayor's side, though her husband lay beneath the rubble. By midnight Giuliani had slipped quietly back downtown to the ruins, where his people worked all night under the floodlights, trying to find the slightest trace of their friends and coworkers, now the nation's casualties of war.

September 11 began as Primary Day to elect a new mayor of New York. It ended with the incumbent chosen by acclamation as the new mayor of America. Giuliani is restricted by term limits, and scheduled to leave office in January. But it's clear now that his country will call him back into service in some capacity. There has been talk of making him some kind of reconstruction czar, though his skills might be better served managing the infiltration of terrorist organizations the way he once busted the Mafia. The kick-ass quality that last week had him threatening price gougers, telemarketers and bogus Web sites trying to capitalize on the crisis might, with the proper checks and balances, come in quite handy after all.

In the meantime, the task before him is immense. I've been down to view the wreckage twice so far, and it's much worse than it looks on TV, a landscape out of Dante. This is something all of the politicians notice when they come through. Hillary Clinton says it dwarfs anything she has seen on her many travels to disaster sites around the world. President George W. Bush knew it was bad, but not this bad. "The scope of it surprised him, particularly from the helicopter," Giuliani told a few of us afterward. "He just looked at it, absorbed it and said: 'Oh, my.'" At the site, Bush struck exactly the right tone, connected well with the rescue crews and, for the first time all week, didn't seem overshadowed by a lame-duck mayor.

Giuliani's mobilization of the city's emergency services has been a marvel, but management alone wouldn't have created such an aura had the mayor himself not been touched by fire. Late in the week I saw both places he holed up amid the onslaught. From the looks of them now, I'm sure glad I wasn't there on Tuesday.

The first was an FDNY (Fire Department of New York) command post on West Street near the North Tower. Giuliani got a briefing on the evacuations from senior chiefs, even the most experienced of whom had no idea that the burning towers would actually collapse. But 10 minutes after the mayor left, the first tower went down. Immediately, the firefighters knew the second, closer tower would fall, too. Instead of moving backward, many, including the senior men, held their position, all but certain they would perish. They did.

From there Giuliani, needing phone lines, commandeered a Merrill Lynch back office at 75 Barclay Street. After 45 minutes someone yelled, "Get down! It's coming down!" The force of the collapse flattened the building across the street, and a huge plume of smoke blocked the exit the mayoral party needed. Giuliani, wearing a gas mask, was led running through a smoke-filled basement maze and out the other side, where the soot they're now calling "gray snow" was a foot deep. The doomed were jumping out of the remaining tower before the mayor's eyes. Except for a walkie-talkie, all connection with the outside world was cut.

Stripping off the gas mask, Giuliani and a small group set off on foot for a mile hike up Church Street, urging the ghostly, ash-caked survivors to "Go north! Go north!" A distraught African-American woman approached, and the mayor touched her face, telling her, "It's going to be OK." Farther up, a young rowdy got the mayoral "Shhhhhh!" he deserved. That set the tone. In the days since, he was sensitive and tough and totally on top of everything from DNA on toothbrushes (to help identify bodies) to structural engineering. Even his press criticism was, for once, on target. And even his harshest critics offered nothing but sincere praise.

In recent years, Rudy Giuliani has been a cranky and not terribly effective mayor, distracted by marital and health problems. But in this cataclysm, which he rightly called "the most difficult week in the history of New York," the city and the country have found that most elusive of all democratic treasures—real leadership.

The New Shape of Patriotism

—— 2001 ——

This was written a week after 9/11 as I wandered the streets of Lower Manhattan.

I WANTED TO GO to the Statue of Liberty, and figured my police press credential might get me there. Not a chance. They tell me at the ferry that it is "closed indefinitely," which depresses me as much as anything all week. I call a government official who says that the president has said privately that he wants the Statue of Liberty open as soon as possible, but he has been told that it simply is not secure. They're hoping to let tourist boats at least float past Lady Liberty soon, so the people can feel her patriotic presence.

Patriotism. Even now the word has a musty quality, like an old war-bonds poster. We spent so many years thinking of "patriots" as New England football players that the concept almost turned to kitsch. American celebrities are so out of shape, patriotically speaking, that many didn't seem to know the words to "America the Beautiful" during their "Tribute to Heroes" telethon last week. The bigger questions slide by: What does patriotism mean now? What does it require of us?

Not enlisting—at least not yet. The military has plenty of recruits. Perhaps true patriotism demands a broad national commitment to something that needs fixing. After the Soviet Union launched the first satellite in 1957, Congress used the patriotic fear over Sputnik to spend large sums on math and science education and the interstate highway system. What's the challenge now? Maybe a big push to teach students about the rest of the world, a subject that most states don't even require. (Learning Arabic would be an especially patriotic act). Or international economic development to bolster moderate Muslims. Or energy independence.

But I can't handle such extrapolations just yet, so I spend an hour or two most days just wandering the streets of lower Manhattan looking for patriotism in the flesh. I'm rarely disappointed.

I visit a firehouse on South Street. Engine 4, Ladder 15. These were the firefighters who answered the first alarm. They raced up hundreds of stairs, helped to save thousands of people, then radioed that they were in the lobby as the tower collapsed. On the blackboard is an announcement that Scott Larsen's wife had a healthy boy on September 13. I scan the list of 14 missing out of 42 from this company, and Larsen's name is among them. Patriotism is heroism—risking it all for people you don't even know.

Walking toward Ground Zero, the Stars and Stripes are especially beautiful. We have been violated, and the flag, like a brilliant dreamcoat, warms and protects us—at least for now. Inside the "red zone" of wreckage, I see one plastered on the back of a hard hat and remember what being patriotic meant a generation ago. During the Vietnam War patriotism was nationalism. If you didn't buy in, you were out. The bumper sticker read AMERICA—LOVE IT OR LEAVE IT. Now it's UNITED WE STAND. Not for long, perhaps. There will be strong political differences again soon enough. But at least the flag itself is in less danger of becoming a political weapon at home. Patriotism is meaningful symbolism—comfort and inspiration for a hurting people.

I glimpse a huge flag at the New York Health and Racquet Club on Whitehall Street. Beneath it, a handmade sign: FOOD, SHOWERS, SLEEP, BATHROOM AND MASSAGE. EMERGENCY PERSONNEL WELCOME. Twenty-four hours a day. Indefinitely. This was yuppie New York paying tribute to firefighters and other public servants who risked their lives to protect brokerage houses and restaurants and health clubs they often couldn't even afford to patronize. Now millions around the world are stepping up to help the families of the victims (including prisoners in Louisiana, making 40 cents an hour, who have raised $11,000 so far). All good. But the truest patriots will expand that commitment to others who are needy. Patriotism means community— an ethic of service beyond one-time expressions of support.

I pass Wall Street, with its chilling view of the ruins. Some institutional investors, desperate for cash, needed to sell. But how can any patriotic American below retirement age unload his portfolio at a time like this? "Anyone who has ever bet against America has lost," New York Governor George Pataki tells me as we leave Ground Zero. Patriotism rejects pessimism.

At Union Square, the lefties are out in force, organizing to stop the war before it starts. NO WAR IS A JUST WAR is typical of their handmade signs. History has proven that thinking to be disastrous. A note nearby with a wilted white rose explains why: LOVE IS NOT AN APPROPRIATE REACTION TO EVIL. APPEASING EVIL ONLY MAKES IT STRONGER. Yet the freedom we stand for includes the freedom to be offensive and naive. Pacifism is hurtful, but so is blind loyalty. As Harry Truman said during World War II, government needs to be held accountable to make it work better. Patriotism champions tolerance, or it is empty.

Entering the 14th Street subway station, I see a picture of Roshawn and Khaniladai Singh, brother and sister. He has a tattoo of a tiger on his right shoulder and served in the Army Reserves; she wears a gold chain with a key charm. They both worked on the 106th floor at the restaurant Windows on the World in guest relations, fine citizens with their whole lives ahead of them. Later I reach their aunt on the phone. I tell her that people with last names like Singh are being attacked in parts of the United States by bigots. I ask her what country her family comes from. She politely refuses to answer: "We are Americans." And patriots.

Blame America at Your Peril

—— 2001 ——

After 9/11, I grew angry at some of the dopey commentary on the left—still audible—that the United States somehow "had it coming" from the terrorists. We have done much in the Middle East since that might prompt retaliation, but at that time we had done nothing beyond stationing troops in Saudi Arabia to defend against Saddam Hussein's conquest of Kuwait. In fact, during the 1990s we intervened in the former Yugoslavia to protect Muslims.

AFTER WE ATTACK the Taliban and the terrorists strike us again, you know what's going to happen. A big old-fashioned peace movement will emerge that blames the United States for whatever further destruction is inflicted. We'll be told that we "prompted" or "provoked" the gas attack, football-stadium bombing, assassination attempt, whatever. How do I know? Because a sizable chunk of what passes for the left is already knee-deep in ignorant and dangerous appeasement of the terrorism of September 11. While moderate liberals (and even Christopher Hitchens) seem to get who the bad guys are, some of their brethren farther left—especially on college campuses—are unforgivably out to lunch.

Like President Bush and the vast majority of the country, I'm for a targeted war that tries hard to avoid civilian casualties, Islamic blowback and other unintended consequences. And I'll defend forever the right of anyone to say any stupid thing without being fired or hassled by the authorities. But some of what's being said can truly try one's patience, and I'm not just talking about Jerry Falwell and Pat Robertson's "Blame Homosexuality First" approach to explaining the attack.

The only thing worse than a silly politician analyzing art is a silly artist analyzing politics. *The New Republic's* "Idiocy Watch," which is cataloging the fatuities, is full of the musings of novelists. Best-selling writer Barbara Kingsolver, confused by the patriotism around her, asked in the *San Francisco Chronicle* whether the "flag stands for intimidation, censorship, violence, bigotry, sexism, homophobia, and shoving the Constitution through a paper shredder? Whom are we calling terrorists here?"

This mindless moral equivalency is the nub of what lefties mean when they talk about "the chickens coming home to roost," or "reaping what you sow." Talk about ironic: the same people always urging us to not blame the victim in rape cases are now saying Uncle Sam wore a short skirt and asked for it. A haughty Susan Sontag made it sound as if we were the ones being thickheaded for not seeing that September 11 was a perfectly understandable response to years of American policy.

Obviously, some policies—like the United States' stationing troops in Saudi Arabia—have contributed to Osama bin Laden's rage. But there's a big difference between understanding Islam and the history of the region, which we need much more of, and understanding evil, which is not just offensive but impossible.

Sad to say, the line between explaining terrorism and rationalizing it has been repeatedly breached by a shallow left stuck in a deep anti-American rut. For certain (fortunately powerless) tenured radicals and antiwar vets, this post-Vietnam reflex seems as comfortable as an old sandal.

While most Americans view history through a "Greatest Generation" World War II prism, this remnant remembers how wrong that analogy was for Vietnam. The left was on target then: for years the United States refused to negotiate much with the communists out of a misplaced fear of seeming to be Neville Chamberlain-style appeasers.

But history moves on, even for aging ideologues heavily invested in the past. "National security" is not a government cover story anymore, but a genuine problem. The terrorists we're looking for aren't pathetic little pamphleteers, like the American communists targeted in the Red Scare. Reactionary left-wingers are still so busy thinking the CIA is malevolent that they forget to notice that it's incompetent; they're so busy nursing stale resentments that they forget to notice someone is trying to kill them.

"The causal business is really pernicious," says Peter Awn, a professor of Islamic religion at Columbia who says it results from ignorance of the complexities of the region. "People are going back to the one area they know something about—the Israeli-Palestinian struggle—and that's a shame. It shows their ability to understand the rest of the Islamic world is minimal."

The trick is to learn some lessons from the past without implying that we had it coming. We've done that before. After World War II our leaders saw that the punitive Versailles peace treaty following World War I had helped pave the way for Hitler. So we tried the generous

Marshall Plan instead and it worked. But that came later. Only a fool would have given credence to Hitler's grievances, however legitimate a few of them were, while we were fighting him.

And none but a fool would say, as the novelist Alice Walker did in the *Village Voice*, that "the only punishment that works is love." We've tried turning the other cheek. After the 1993 World Trade Center bombing we held our fire and treated the attack as a law-enforcement matter. The terrorists struck again anyway. This time the Munich analogy is right: appeasement is doomed.

America Firsters grasped this point after Pearl Harbor and the isolationists ran off to enlist. So why can't Blame America Firsters grasp it now? Al Qaeda was planning its attack at exactly the time the United States was offering a Mideast peace deal favorable to the Palestinians. Nothing from us would have satisfied the fanatics, and nothing ever will. Peace won't be with you, brother. It's kill or be killed.

Letter from Ground Zero

—— 2001 ——

*A few weeks after 9/11, survivors of the attack
and still-grieving family members gathered for a somber
memorial service that I attended.*

I T WASN'T THE FORMAL program that got me, but the
aftermath. During the moving hour-long World Trade Center
Family Memorial Service—mercifully free of politicians at the
podium—most of the family members of the victims stayed composed,
even during beautiful renditions of "Ave Maria" and "Amazing
Grace." The tissues offered in a little packet by the Red Cross were
used sparingly. They had steeled themselves for this, as if they wanted
to hear the astonishing quiet of Ground Zero unruffled by yet more
tears. For a time, the weather, so reminiscent of September 11, seemed
to help, the brilliant autumn sunlight a balm in misery.

On the way out, the weather turned chilly, and brought more
release. While most of the audience went north on Church Street
to the buses, some moved south past 5 World Trade Center, a squat
metal outlying structure on the north side of Ground Zero, its
partially sunken middle reminded one family member of the federal
building in Oklahoma City. This building had been fully evacuated,
but behind it, the family members knew, were the towers, or what
little was left of them.

Through the wreckage, a visage in the dusk: a weary firefighter
making a slow 100-yard trek from the rubble, his hands full of tower
stones. A crowd gathered, as weeping family members took bits of the
place where their loved ones had perished. They could also receive a
city-issued urn of ashes, but this was more spontaneous and heartbreak-
ing. Soon, an impromptu ritual began. The somber firefighters carried
flowers from the survivors to a makeshift shrine in the distance, far
beyond where it was safe to go, then returned with the precious stones.

I had seen bits of such stone before; in fact I have them on my bookcase. They are from the Berlin Wall, tokens of victory and freedom. This time, in this place, they were symbols of mourning, borne forward from the Old Testament.

A woman asked a firefighter to point out the cross. It has become part of the lore of Ground Zero, a metal beam that survived, in the shape of a cross, and preserved by workers. But it's over in what they call "the pit"—and not visible to the crowd. What they can see, and remark on, is how much more vast the damage is than they imagined.

"The devastation is 100 times greater than you see on TV, where you never even see the other buildings damaged," said Nina Barnes in a remark whose truth is not diminished by its repetition. Barnes and her family are cousins of Durrell "Bronco" Pearsall, a 34-year-old firefighter from Rescue 4 with no wife, siblings or living parents. On Friday, as next of kin, they were notified that Bronco's body had been found, with seven others, in a shaft, remarkably intact.

Now, as they leave the area, a meaningful coincidence: A firefighter, wearing a blue jean jacket over his uniform, tells Nina that he is the one who found Bronco. The family, two kids in tow, wearing FDNY caps, walk over to Broadway with a closure beyond that of all but a very few. The service for Bronco, "our hero," scheduled for mid-November, can now be moved up, and called a funeral.

Deputy Chief Edward Kalletti, back on duty, is still savoring the program: "It was purely memorial, not political—that was the nice part." The site is closed for 24 hours, but plenty more work remains. "Fires are still burning down there," Kalletti says. "I knew more than 150 of the guys, and we've got a lot more to look for." The department has held 200 funerals, with 140 to go. About 80 bodies of firefighters have been recovered.

I check back in with Patricia Thompson, widow of Philip Haentzler, who worked for Kidder Peabody in the North Tower. She came to Ground Zero with three friends (each family received five tickets) and a Bible, deeply uncertain about whether she had made the right decision to return.

"This is almost a retraumatizing experience," she told me shortly before the 2 PM service began. "I think of Philip on the 101st floor, and now I'm having these questions: Did he know what was happening? Did he suffer? It's nearly two months and it feels like yesterday. My heart is broken, and being here makes me feel what I feel every day, only more intensely. I can't figure out where I am. I'm very displaced."

Afterward, it's not quite accurate to say she is glad she came, because she's not glad about much of anything these days. But she thinks she made the right choice to return. "To be here and to pray for him—being together with so many other people. It makes a difference."

Greg Hrycak feels the same way. "Just to see what evil does," he says, his voice trailing off as his eyes move across the scene. But then, a moment of certitude: "This is not where he is," he says of his father Marty, who worked for the New York State Department of Taxation in Tower Two. "He's in a better place now."

As I left the secured area, I turned back for one last look west, and saw all the way across Ground Zero a banner hanging from the World Financial Plaza: WE WILL NEVER FORGET.

On the Eve of War

——— 2 0 0 2 ———

I traveled to the Persian Gulf three months before the Iraq War
officially began, and learned that hostilities were already underway.
After reporting that, I filed this first-person piece about
my experience aboard an aircraft carrier.

I COULD GET USED to this. I mean, it isn't every day that you're saluted as an admiral on the deck of an aircraft carrier in the Persian Gulf. It happened just after I landed on the flight deck and it left red faces all around—an auspicious (for me) beginning to my two-day Christmastime visit aboard the USS *Constellation*, now the Navy's "point of the sword" in the waters off Iraq.

After an hour flight from Bahrain, we had just landed on the carrier in "The Cod"—an ancient propeller plane used to ferry visitors and mail. The 3Gs I felt when the wire on the deck "trapped" us at 130 mph had worn off and we'd unharnessed, uncrossed our arms and sat up. Now the back of the plane opened wide, and someone gestured to me and my seatmate, an AP reporter based in Indonesia with a craggy, distinguished look, to exit first.

We stepped down to find two long rows of sailors smartly saluting us. I gave them a big smile and pathetic half wave, like Bill Clinton before he learned to salute. Somehow I'd forgotten this wonderful greeting from my last trip aboard a carrier in the mid-1980s. Was it standard for visitors?

Well, no. Inside stood Captain John Miller, commanding officer of the *Constellation*, with a puzzled look on his face. When I stuck out my hand, he greeted me warily and understandably asked: "Who are you?" He was waiting for the real distinguished visitor, a Canadian admiral on our plane. I never got to ask the admiral, but I assume he was greeted with all of the pomp and circumstance normally accorded a reporter.

The *Constellation* is a 41-year-old conventionally-powered carrier on its last cruise. The ship is scheduled for decommissioning next spring, in part because it's too old to spend the money required to retrofit the berthings (sleeping cabins) and heads (bathrooms) for women. (Unlike newer carriers, this ship carries only a handful of women). Dubbed "America's Flagship" by Ronald Reagan, the *Constellation* is currently offering what the military calls "power projection" against Iraq. The pilots of the F-14s and F-18s patrol Iraq's no-fly zone around the clock. Both nights I spent aboard, bunking with a Palestinian TV crew, it felt all night as if jets were landing on our heads. They were.

The not-so-secret story out here is that the war has already started against Iraq; in fact, it has been going on for a few years. The game in southern Iraq goes like this: pilots patrolling the no-fly zone spot Iraqi anti-aircraft fire, usually somewhere on the horizon (none has come close, except to an unmanned drone downed this month). Unless they are immediately endangered, the U.S. aircraft leave the area. Later, these or other pilots return to take out one Iraqi command-and-control target for each anti-aircraft incident. The number of incidents waxes and wanes. The two days I was aboard, sandstorms meant no Iraqi sightings. But some days bring as many as 50 encounters. The result is that if and when a real war starts, the United States will have significantly degraded Iraqi communications capacity in the south. Saddam Hussein will be fighting half blind.

The nearly 5,000 sailors and airmen (including 72 pilots) onboard the *Constellation*, which only arrived in the gulf in mid-December, have been ordered not to speculate on the likelihood of war. But they know this is already the real thing, and that odds suggest they will bear the brunt of the Navy's share of it. I asked Captain Miller if this was the "exhibition season" before the war. "No, this is the regular season, and we're getting ready for the playoffs," he said.

I guess it all comes down to what the meaning of the word "war" is. Right now, we're dropping J-DAMs on southern Iraq. If "war" comes, it will likely start with cruise missiles against Baghdad. Is there that much of a difference?

But whether we have a full-scale war or just more "low-intensity conflict," it's hard not to be impressed by the readiness of the people I've met. General Richard Myers, chairman of the Joint Chiefs of Staff, came aboard for a couple of hours while I was there, accompanied by a USO contingent that included Drew Carey and Roger Clemens. Inside the huge hangar bay, I was struck by how often Myers mentioned the "joint" nature of the mission. This was the message several officers also kept pushing, and it finally convinced me that the U.S. military has changed more in recent years than most of us have noticed.

"Goldwater-Nickles was a revolution," Admiral Barry M. Costello, commander of the *Constellation* Battle Group, told me, referring to the little-known 1986 reform bill that over time swept away many of the old interservice rivalries. The Army, Navy and Air Force finally talk to each other now, often through a secure Microsoft Chat system that three years ago revolutionized military communications. Never again will a Marine officer storming the beach have to use a pay phone to call in an airstrike. (That actually happened during the invasion of Grenada in 1983.)

The better communication extends even to our adversaries. The day before we arrived, Admiral Costello recounts, a merchant ship sank in the gulf, leaving nine Iranians in the water. A Polish vessel heard the distress call, contacted an Australian ship, which radioed the *Constellation*, which sent out a chopper to rescue the Iranians, despite their government's inclusion in the American commander in chief's "Axis of Evil."

New communications systems have also changed the military experience of the average sailor. Officers and enlisted men can send e-mail home almost as often as they want (the bandwidth is occasionally prioritized for military communications, meaning interruptions for the "Hi, Mom" messages), and they can telephone from the ship much more easily than in the past. But cell phones and BlackBerries don't work onboard—too much interference. And it's hard to shoot video on the flight deck or bridge because of the radar.

With the ease of communications come new concerns about security. After September 11, new World War II-style loose-lips-sink-ships posters went up all over the carrier. My favorite features a 1940s character drinking coffee and saying: HOW ABOUT A NICE BIG CUP OF SHUT THE HELL UP. Underneath, it reads: THINK BEFORE YOU SAY SOMETHING STUPID.

On board, I go to bed at 1 AM and wake up with reveille at 6 AM, like most of the crew. The accommodating public-affairs officers cheerfully keep tabs on reporters and cheerfully keep us from getting lost amid the five and a half acres of confusing passageways, levels, ladders and hatches. It's fun just to talk to as many people as possible: The officer who confides that this deployment is tame—when women are aboard "it's Peyton Place"; the sailor just out of boot camp and the Los Angeles barrio who has found that he gets seasick; the white senior enlisted man from a famously racist American community who recounts going home for a holiday to find his father making racial epithets in front of the grandchildren. The son fumes. In more than 20 years in the Navy he has learned to trust performance, not skin color, in making judgments about people. He tells his father that he and the grandchildren won't be back again soon unless he stops talking that way.

I watch some night landings on the carrier, which are widely considered the single hardest task in the American military. I look down at the flight deck, viewed by Lloyd's of London to be among the most dangerous work sites in the world.

One afternoon, I run into an old classmate of my brother, Lieutenant Commander Matt Wright, who gives me a special tour of parts of the flight deck where public-information officers dare not tread. On this cruise, Wright's a "shooter," which means he supervises the catapult that launches the planes. Off duty, he takes me within 10 feet of the wings of the departing planes, then up to the front of the carrier. Matt keeps walking to the very bow, just inches from the edge. The wind is blowing strongly against us (carriers routinely sail into the wind to slow the planes down on landing), but I make what I consider to be the prudent decision to stop several feet short and plant my feet for balance; the gear I'm wearing—standard for anyone on the flight deck—would emit a signal if I fell 70 feet down into the drink, but I'm taking no chances. Just then an F-18 is flung out over the ocean right in front of us—a spectacular view I won't forget any time soon.

Now, it's our turn to be catapulted out over the gulf. The Cod awaits, this time with no one saluting on deck. I get one tiny foggy window, the Russian ambassador to Bahrain the other. We strap in, the "shooter" gives the thumbs up and as the flight deck disappears at super-fast-forward beneath us, the point of the sword glistens for a moment in the sun.

Saudi Arabia: The End of the Double Game

—— 2002 ——

Fifteen of the nineteen hijackers on 9/11 were Saudi nationals. The Kingdom of Saudi Arabia continues to be the largest exporter of oil. And yet the country remains largely closed from public view. In 2002, I was eventually granted a visa and traveled there for a glimpse. What I couldn't report at the time was just how much drinking I saw by high government officials. The hypocrisy was overwhelming. Average Saudis would be punished, even jailed, for consuming alcohol.

A RECENT COLUMN in a Saudi newspaper made a splash in Riyadh. The writer asked: why shouldn't women be able to play sports? (With other women, of course.) Where did the Prophet Muhammad say that women should not be able to keep in shape? Nowhere.

"Such a silly debate," my Saudi dinner partner volunteered one evening, nursing a drink in a dry country. "My wife exercises all she wants in our gym at home." And the millions of ordinary Saudis without home exercise equipment? Not mentioned that night. Nor were the women who are forced to wear the veil and barred from driving, nor the guest workers intimidated by creepy anti-vice police into praying five times a day while the princes party in London and Aspen. The topic instead was why the American media have it out for Saudi Arabia.

You can see why the Saudis are puzzled. For decades, the royal family has stayed in power by playing a complex double game. The regime nuzzles up to the United States (which buys 25 percent of its oil from Saudi Arabia and protects it militarily) while placating joyless clerics with a taste for persecution and violence. Until now, the game worked well enough. Beyond some tsk-tsking about hypocrisy, no one in the United States much noticed it.

But the fact that 15 out of 19 hijackers on September 11 were Saudis has disrupted the old balancing act. So has the Internet, where translations from Arabic on Web sites like MEMRI.org let the rest of the world know what Saudis and other Arabs are saying to each other. Inside the global village, it's hard to talk out of both sides of your mouth.

So while both the U.S. and Saudi governments insist their cooperation on fighting terrorism is strong, the overall state of relations between the two countries is tense. For every story about Saudis arresting suspected terrorists or cracking down on money laundering, five others suggest lax oversight of extremist charities and yet more involvement by Saudi nationals in the events of September 11. The regime is stung by the American press, anxious about seeking admission to the World Trade Organization, opposed to war with Iraq but nervous about being left behind by the United States. Its solution is another lavish public-relations offensive. But this time it won't work without some real, substantive changes.

I met a few thoughtful Saudis who get this. "We are re-examining ourselves," says Hassan Yassin, a former government official with long experience in the United States. "And we should listen to some of the criticism." But Yassin reflects the common view that pushing too hard will create a backlash: "He who comes between the onion and the skin gets nothing but the stink."

But sometimes making a stink is the only way to produce any change. The old, complacent American approach of winking at the regime is part of what allowed the problem to develop in the first place. Now, with the heat on, the Saudi regime is letting the press debate more reforms, urging schools to stress tolerance and telling the anti-vice police to back off a little. Change is coming, and not just because of U.S. pressure. Satellite TV is subversive. The Saudis are so upset about Al-Jazeera that the crown prince boycotted a Gulf States conference last month to protest the Emir of Qatar's refusal to rein in his network.

At bottom, the House of Saud is still haunted by what happened to the Peacock Throne in Iran in 1979, when the shah was overthrown by radical clerics. They may be fighting the last war, but the princes are still more worried about the fundamentalists than the Westernizers.

Among the worried is Prince Saud al-Faisal, the longtime foreign minister and highest-ranking Saudi who will talk to the press. When I went to see him, he said all the right things about collaring more than 3,000 suspected terrorists and even cooperating with the United States against Iraq. But the foreign minister still did not seem to grasp the essence of what so angers Americans about Saudi Arabia these days.

Why, I pressed, had Prince Nayef, the powerful Interior minister, not apologized for saying in a recent Arabic interview that September 11 was a Zionist plot? Al-Faisal first offered the Saudi government's official position—that "the hijackers were Saudis and were planted by Osama bin Laden, not by anybody else, in order to create an air of suspicion and to drive a wedge between us." But then he defended Nayef's right "to speculate on somebody [i.e., Israel] who may gain from the act."

Here, again, was a sign of the Saudis' trying to have it both ways. Nayef and his deputy (also his son) are well regarded by the United States for their help in fighting terrorism. Does he actually believe that "Zionist plot" nonsense, or was he just "playing to Peoria," as an Interior Ministry official told me? Is he truly cooperating with the United States on Al Qaeda, or just going through the motions? Welcome to Saudi Arabia.

Nayef was falcon hunting in North Africa, so I went to see the author of another notoriously noxious sentiment. Ghazi Algosaibi, former ambassador to London, now minister of water, wrote a poem last fall praising a 17-year-old female Palestinian suicide bomber. Algosaibi added that he would like to be a "martyr" too, except that "my weight does not permit this."

Who was this brutal buffoon, chewed out by the U.S. ambassador for his comments? It turns out he is a deft novelist (I read one of his books, with a racy theme) and, he would be horrified to know, a dead ringer for the late Israeli statesman Abba Eban, down to the British accent and subtle knowledge of Middle Eastern history. In a country that holds telethons for the families of suicide bombers, his views were unexceptional. But he never did answer my question: If suicide bombing works against Israel, who's the next target of that tactic? The Saudi royal family?

The best place to sense the tension between the PR script and the truth is over at the once inaccessible Ministry for Islamic Affairs, which some Western critics believe is a nest of extremist enablers and funders inside the Saudi government. Deputy Minister Tawfeeq Al-Sediry seems like he got the memo. "We need more observation and more control" of the overseas madrasas (schools), mosques and charities, he says, adding that the ministry was sending new materials stressing a tolerant interpretation of the Qur'an to Islamic teachers around the world. Ministry officials, he says, must renounce violence. "If they don't believe that, they have to leave this ministry, but we can't go inside of their heads to know what they believe."

No matter how much social change comes, these fundamentalist teachers will always be a problem. And because Saudi Arabia is the keeper of Islam's holy places, it will always live under Sharia (religious law). But that law can be made more inclusive and transparent. I met a compelling dissident named Ibrahim Al Mugaiteeb who is devoting his life to that cause. He says that talking to me could land him back in jail, but he's determined to tell the world through *Newsweek* that he has founded Saudi Arabia's first human rights organization, Human Rights First. "They'll have to kill me to stop me," he says. More likely, they will co-opt him. After promising under pressure in Geneva last year to allow a human rights organization, the royal family founded its own group, which of course defeats the purpose.

Mugaiteeb doesn't want the overthrow of the House of Saud, which would thrust the country into chaos. He is simply after the human values of free expression and association, which he argues would actually help stabilize the country. (Not to mention easing Saudi entry into the WTO.) But it's a long road. No women have signed onto Mugaiteeb's group yet out of fear of being seen as "Western puppets." They aren't quite ready to agitate yet, even for the simple right to play sports.

Abu Ghraib: The Picture the World Sees

—— 2004 ——

Believing Saddam Hussein had weapons of mass destruction, I very reluctantly supported the invasion of Iraq. But it was soon clear that the war was a fiasco. The torture scandal at Iraq's Abu Ghraib Prison instantly harmed the credibility of the United States around the world, though some conservative commentators didn't care.

A FEW YEARS AGO, I traveled to Vietnam to report on the normalization of relations. Without intending to do so, I found myself visiting the scenes of iconic photographs I remembered seeing when I was a kid: the Saigon street corner where Eddie Adams took the shot of a Viet Cong suspect being executed at point-blank range; the stretch of road the naked little girl ran down; the roof of the building near the U.S. Embassy where the last helicopter lifted off. For many of us, these images were the Vietnam War.

The same will be true of the Iraq War. Someday, when Iraq is peaceful again (and that day will come), tourists will want to see the square where the Saddam statue toppled, the spider hole he hid in and, of course, Abu Ghraib Prison. It's too early to know exactly which of the unspeakable pictures from the torture sessions will come to represent this sickening chapter in the book of superpower super-embarrassments. Will it be that prisoner wearing the hood with electrical wires attached? Those stacked naked bodies with smiling guards above? Lynndie England leading around a naked man on a leash?

The assumption in Washington is that the damage from this fiasco in the Arab world will last for 50 years, as Senator Jack Reed put it. For all the power of the humiliating images to confirm the worst assumptions about the United States and strip away its moral authority, this seems exaggerated. Pictures play powerfully on emotions, but emotions—when they don't involve immediate family—are not often enduring. They can change depending on the next pictures and the next sequence of decisions and events. The images from Vietnam—searing as they were—were ultimately a reflection of the policy failures, not the cause of them, and the hatred expressed by Vietnamese toward the Americans who bombed them lasted only a few years. The same goes for Iraq and the Middle East. Just because the damage is done doesn't mean that it cannot, over time, be undone. The problem is whether we have the right leadership to undo it.

Take one Donald Rumsfeld. First, he and President Bush and the rest of the war cabinet ignored Colin Powell's presentation of the Red Cross's evidence of abuses in Iraqi prisons. Then Rumsfeld went on the *Today* show to say he didn't have time to read the long report on Abu Ghraib (what else was so important?) but that "anyone who sees the photographs does, in fact, apologize." Anyone? Who is "anyone"? It wasn't until his job was on the line and he bothered to finally view the pictures that he delivered a proper apology before Congress. Rumsfeld said that it was the pictures that made him realize the seriousness of the reported behavior—the "words [in Pentagon reports] don't do it." But high-level government officials should be capable of responding to horrible abuses under their authority without audio-visual aids. They're paid to make decisions on words and facts and right and wrong, not just on the emotional punch of pictures—or how something might look if it came out. Character, we know, is what you do when you think no one is watching.

Of course, some people didn't even mind the pictures. Rush Limbaugh told his audience last week that the whole thing reminded him of a "Skull and Bones initiation." He argued that the torturers should be cut a little slack: "You ever heard of emotional release? You heard of need to blow some steam off?" Limbaugh's peculiar rationalization didn't get traction, but he's right about one thing: when it comes to pictures, context still counts. Sympathy for the prisoners developed in this case because few were suspected terrorists. Some were resisting Coalition forces—which is terrible but not terrorism, unless you think every civilian who ever resisted an occupying army in human history was a terrorist. Others were simply in the wrong place at the wrong time. None had anything to do with 9/11.

But imagine if these images had been of, say, Al Qaeda terrorists in captivity in Afghanistan in late 2001. There would have been no uproar at all. In fact, at that time, too many people (including me) were complacent about the use of psychological interrogation techniques that end up loosening the bonds of civilized behavior and making Americans look like hypocrites.

Is there any way forward after this excruciation? Any way to rebuild the bridges (remember that overworked Clinton metaphor?) the Bush administration is burning? For all the talk in John Kerry's campaign about America's tarnished image in the rest of the world, most U.S. voters aren't interested. In the broadest sense, they're correct. Being respected and popular again is not an end in itself; sometimes we need to do the right, unpopular thing.

But at this particular historical moment, the United States can be safer only when it is respected abroad. The only way we'll get the cooperation we need to win either the war in Iraq or the wider war on terrorism is by persuading other nations to begin looking to us again for leadership. No respect, no victory. In that sense, restoring America's prestige is a means to an end, and the 2004 presidential election, a referendum on which man can best change the picture that the whole world sees.

New Orleans Learns How to Hope

—— 2005 ——

When I traveled to New Orleans three months after Hurricane Katrina, I tried to look for some signs of hope—and found them. Since then, these schools have taken root. But the makeshift trailer parks and abandoned buildings remain.

NEW ORLEANS in December is cool and dry, and the 20 percent that wasn't flooded seems normal enough. But the pictures don't even begin to convey the scope of what 17 days of standing water will do to the delicate ecosystem of a metropolis. More than 50 million cubic yards of debris have already been picked up, including 100,000 useless refrigerators—that's 34 normal years of garbage in just three months.

Every day brings more mounds of tangled possessions and sundry junk, the stuffing of a city. I rode with a nonprofit group called Share Our Strength past the thousands of abandoned cars and handwritten WE TEAR DOWN HOUSES signs at intersections that still have no working stoplights; past the still-mysterious levee breaks and reopened Wal-Marts; past mile after eerie mile of homes and stores that for a moment look habitable enough, until you see the thick layers of dust and mold and grimy water lines four or six or eight feet up, a sure indication that the place is a total loss.

So the gutting of New Orleans has begun, but not the renovation. Why build anything yet? The place is on hold: gumbo limbo. Residents and their insurers are all waiting to see if the federal Army Corps of Engineers (responsible for the faulty levees in the first place) will fulfill its promise and at least minimally secure the city by the time the hurricane season begins again next June. The original estimate was that two-thirds of the city's 450,000 people would return and one-third would stay away. Now those numbers have been flipped, though no one actually has a clue.

The housing situation is a scandal. Of the 73,000 trailers needed, only 14,700 have arrived. And the trailer parks, while peaceful now, have the frustrated feel of future Gaza Strips. I toured "Renaissance Village"—a Baton Rouge trailer park with 1,600 people (the largest so far) which FEMA fobbed off on a subpar subcontractor. It still had no place for the residents to even pick up their mail, much less any real services. FEMA remains a disaster area, trashed in every conversation. One prominent Louisianan recalled how, just after the storm, physicians from Doctors Without Borders were told they could not give treatment to moaning victims lying on the tarmac at Louis Armstrong Airport because the doctors were not FEMA-certified.

But amid all the heartache—the still-raw feelings that can lead to tears in an instant—a few tiny rays of winter sun are slipping through. Newly created institutions like the Louisiana Family Recovery Corps and the Louisiana Recovery Authority are beginning to cut through the chaos to supervise better and plan rationally. About three months late, President Bush finally appointed a federal coordinator, Donald Powell, who doesn't have the clout that a big name would have brought but whose background in banking is appropriate to the tangled reconstruction challenge. Most encouraging, the hurricane blew away the New Orleans school district, a cesspool of corruption and neglect that made local schools among the worst in the country. With the entrenched bureaucrats and teachers-union hacks scattered to the winds, the state legislature took the opportunity to strip them of all their power.

This offers what Tony Recasner, the principal of the New Orleans Charter Middle School, calls a "magic moment" for major change. Almost all the schools that will begin reopening in 2006 (mostly in the fall) will be charter schools, where everyone works on one-year contracts (full accountability), and the principal can actually run the school. "This gives us an opportunity to fix each school as it comes back on line," says Recasner, who already has an impressive track record of academic achievement in his school. "We get to create something from our own imagination and ask: what is this going to be?"

The answer, ideally, would be a series of KIPP (Knowledge Is Power Program) schools. The nearly 50 KIPP schools around the country have an astonishing record of academic success with low-income students, not with shortcuts but with a disciplined "be nice, work hard" program. While KIPP has only one New Orleans school planned and not nearly enough leaders in its pipeline yet, Recasner and the other avatars of local school reform are eager to adapt the model. The challenge is to get the right leadership in. And because the system will go from 60,000 students to about 20,000 next fall, New Orleans will have the perfect size for a true national experiment with school reform.

Randy Ewing, the chairman of the Louisiana Family Recovery Corps, says, "Our mind-set is not to return people to normal, because normal wasn't too good. Our challenge is to take them to a better life."

That will take time, but it should not be seen as impossible.

2008: Wrong Time for an Urban Cowboy

—— 2007 ——

This tees up what I think is the central issue in the
2008 campaign—restoring American prestige in the world.
It also helps explain why Rudy Giuliani eventually went nowhere
in the GOP primaries. He was out of sync not only with
his party but with the times.

PRESIDENTIAL ELECTIONS are said to be about the future, but they also end up as verdicts on the past. Voters often reject the type of leadership they have recently experienced. In 1960, young JFK was the antidote to dowdy Ike. In 1976, Jimmy ("I'll never lie to you") Carter campaigned to wipe away the stain left by Richard Nixon. In 1980, sunny Ronald Reagan tapped into disgust with the malaise of the Carter years. In 2000, George W. Bush took on not just Al Gore, but Bill Clinton and Monica Lewinsky.

The reason the 2008 campaign favors Democrats—at least for now—is that Bush has failed so badly that the next president may be the one who resembles him least. Job One in 2009 will be reviving the prestige of the United States, which is a prerequisite for confronting nuclear threats, jihadists, climate change—you name it—none of which can be tackled by Americans acting alone.

So to be effective, Bush's successor must be a tough-minded but flexible and humble chief executive with a talent for building bridges, not burning them. For instance, preventing terrorism is less a matter of war than a subtle diplomatic challenge involving international coordination and a convincing projection of Western values. It's a group activity, which means that the next commander in chief will need a Tom Sawyer–like skill in getting other kids in the global neighborhood to paint the fence. This requires charm and leadership.

Which brings us to Rudy Giuliani, whose leadership style seems out of sync with history's pendulum. Why would voters want to replace a my-way-or-the-highway Texan with a shut-up-and-listen New Yorker? Exchange a Crawford cowboy for an urban cowboy? A woman, African-American, Hispanic, Mormon or Vietnam POW would represent a sharper break from the immediate past.

Not that Giuliani is a Bush clone. He performed in slashing crime and helping to save New York. But Rudy was often petulant and polarizing. To give just one example (minor in itself, but revealing): he broke diplomatic relations with the Manhattan Borough President Virginia Fields because she dared to criticize him. (Giuliani was feuding with Harlem politicians at the time.) When, amid a racial crisis in the city, I went to Gracie Mansion to ask him how he could refuse to speak for more than two years to the highest-ranking African-American in town, he scoffed that there was no point.

Of course, such detail about his fitness for the give-and-take of the presidency is too nuanced to be a campaign issue. So is the dictatorial way he dealt with local dissent. Unless his temper explodes on the trail, which is not as likely as his detractors predict, we probably won't squarely face the question of whether America is Ready for Petty. The mayor once described by Jimmy Breslin as "a small man in search of a balcony" has found one, and with lots of people standing in rapt attention below.

Including me. In the days after 9/11, I went with Giuliani five times to Ground Zero and to the funerals of several firefighters. Up close, his compassion and calm command were every bit as impressive as advertised. I fell hard for him and what he was doing for New York and the country. Too hard. When he said it was "cynical" to believe he should leave office at the end of his term—nearly four months after 9/11—I bought his argument for an extension. I was fearful enough to write that he had "practical reasons" for moving in an extra-constitutional direction amid the emergency. When cooler heads than mine prevailed, he eventually backed down on that idea, as well as his insistence on changing the city constitution so he could run for a third term.

Rudy was a good mayor in many ways, but his appeal now is based on fear. When terrorists attack again, we'd want him at the helm for the first few weeks. But after that? Even the most skeptical among us might bend too easily to his will, with frightening consequences. As Giuliani moves toward the big prize, voters will have to look closely at how his history and character could condition his behavior in the White House, where past is always prologue.

Clinton vs. Obama: Restoration vs. Inspiration

—— 2007 ——

I first met Hillary Clinton in 1988, when she came with her husband to a Newsweek lunch at the Democratic Convention in Atlanta. I've interviewed her several times since, most memorably in the White House in 1994 on the very day Kenneth Starr was named as the independent counsel. I first met Barack Obama in Chicago in the late 1990s and first talked to him at length in 2002 when he came to my aunt's funeral in Chicago, when he was a state legislator. In 2004, I interviewed him for his first magazine cover story. I brought along my 13-year-old son Tommy, who said the senator-elect should run for president. (I told him it was too early.) I wrote this in early 2007, but by early 2008 I continued to think it reflected the basic dynamic of the fight for the Democratic nomination.

HILLARY CLINTON has a new guru, a corporate communications consultant named John Kao, who preaches a creative process he calls "jamming" or "getting to cool." Of course if cool is her destination, this Clinton has a long journey ahead. The jazz Kao uses as his metaphor to get clients to an improvisational state of "relaxed knowingness" is more often associated with a certain easy-listening senator from Illinois.

Hillary is strong. Hillary is smart. Hillary is *not* cool. Even the effort to rebrand her as softer, more heartfelt and more in touch with working-class women may prove impossible. That's because after two decades in national life, the brand is set. We know her—and him. Or think we do. The threshold question for voters is less about putting the first woman in the White House than the second Clinton.

The obsession with polls, consultants, money—even positions on the issues—obscures the fundamental dynamic of the Democratic primary race: Restoration vs. Inspiration. A Clinton victory would offer the hope of restoring the 1990s, a fat and relatively happy time in America. The sexual politics of the Clinton years were a luxury afforded by peace and prosperity. Voters might be exhausted by the present and ready to recapture the past with more Clintonism. By this logic, the worse President Bush does, the better the Clintons look.

Conversely, for all of Bill Clinton's popularity, the public could end up tired of the whole bunch of 'em and eager for the shock of the new with Barack Obama, John Edwards (who emphasizes his freshness by all but denying he ever served in the Senate or ran for vice president) or someone else. When Obama refers seven or eight times in his stump speech to "turning the page," he's talking about moving forward to the next chapter, not re-reading the last one. It works.

Themes of dynasty and restoration have long provoked ambivalent feelings among Americans. George Washington, appalled by the idea of monarchy, made a revolutionary point by leaving office on his own accord after eight years. But soon the Adams family produced father-and-son presidents, and the Roosevelts, though only fifth cousins, dominated the presidency for two decades in the first half of the 20th century. After FDR, antiroyalists amended the Constitution to prevent presidents from serving more than two terms. But dynastic dreams endured. If he had not been assassinated in 1968, Robert F. Kennedy may well have been the first sibling president; Camelot did not die until Ted Kennedy's loss in the primaries in 1980.

In the 27 years since, each presidential election has featured a Bush or a Clinton on the ticket. Were Hillary to serve two terms and Jeb Bush to return to politics (even now, he is arguably the most popular Republican in the country) and serve eight years in the White House, a two-family dominance of American democracy would have lasted uninterrupted for more than four decades. At a minimum, Hillary's election would mean BushClintonBushClinton, a line I'm increasingly hearing from voters in a pejorative context.

But family restoration (and vindication) remains a powerful narrative in most societies. In fact, family—even a dysfunctional family—often trumps gender, as the election of wives and daughters as heads of state in highly patriarchal countries like India, Pakistan, Argentina, Indonesia and the Philippines attests.

Unsure of the applicability of that thinking in the United States, Clinton aides are leery of dynastic or restorationist appeals. While they don't want to make Al Gore's mistake and underplay the achievements of the Clinton presidency, they know that most elections here are only secondarily about the past and are primarily fights about competing visions of the future. So to make her look fresh, they are emphasizing her credentials as a caring woman. This is risky. There is little or no indication in state and local elections that women vote disproportionately for women. And men sometimes vote disproportionately against them.

A presidential primary could be different, in part because Hillary is tough, experienced and may evoke a pride among women voters that no congressional candidate could. Or maybe she won't. The impact of gender is as much of a wild card for Clinton as our dynastic ambivalence, which is why the analysts who continue to say that she is a sure winner or sure loser for the nomination may be jamming, but they're also blowing smoke.

How Does Change Happen?

———— 2007 ————

*This reflects one of my periodic efforts to speculate
on how candidates would govern. This was written before the 2008
Iowa caucuses, as "change" began to emerge as the big theme.*

WITH RESTORING PRISONERS' rights of *habeas corpus*
now a surefire applause line at Democratic events, maybe it's
time for more Latin: *modus operandi*—a way of operating (MO for
short). In a carefully prepared sound bite at last week's *Des Moines
Register* Democratic debate, Hillary Clinton thought she had found a
line to jump-start her flagging campaign: "Some believe you get
change by demanding it. Some believe you get it by hoping for it. I
believe you get it by working hard for change," she said, in thinly
veiled shots at John Edwards and Barack Obama.

But a funny thing happened on the way to the postdebate "spin
room." While Clinton's acolytes pointed to this as a key moment in a
largely dreary debate, so did Edwards's aides and Obama's. In other
words, for all the bickering, they agreed on the terrain of battle.
The contrast they offer is not about ends. Their policy goals and first-
100-days agendas are strikingly similar. It's about means—the tone
and approach required to make change happen in Washington. And
their choice of means tells us something important about who they
are and how they got into politics in the first place. For Edwards, it's
confrontation. For Obama, conciliation. For Clinton, perspiration.
The candidates who connect best to their real selves and deepest
motivations usually win. Contrary to popular belief, phonies fade fast
in politics.

Edwards sees politics as the extension of litigation by other
means. The words Hillary used to describe his MO—"demanding
change"—are fine with him. While his hard-core anticorporate
rhetoric may be a cleverly honed campaign message that's at odds

with much of his Senate record (and one likely to be softened if he survives Iowa), his adversarial approach to the world is not a pose. He first ran for office in 1998 to fill a void left in his life by the death of his 16-year-old son, Wade. The passion that works for him on the trail, as his wife, Elizabeth, explains, comes from fusing a desire to make Wade proud with a debt to those, like his millworker father, who struggled.

But this idea that power can simply be "taken" from insurance companies and drug companies does not bear scrutiny. Edwards told me last week that the special interests would see "the handwriting on the wall" after his election and capitulate to the popular will. If only it were that easy.

Obama spent much of his childhood and early adulthood figuring out who he is. He succeeded (as his book *Dreams from My Father* conveys) and became an integrated man in the fullest sense of the word. The ease with which he carries the burdens of history is what gives him his appeal. His experience as a community organizer in Chicago helps explain both his success at building a sophisticated campaign from scratch in a few months and his preference for the kind of conciliation that succeeded with skeptical community activists there—and, later, in politics. (His success in bringing together the police and the ACLU to win landmark death-penalty legislation shouldn't be discounted just because it happened in Illinois, not Washington.) But Obama's lack of experience with confrontation increases the odds that he could be swamped early in his presidency, as Bill Clinton was. Hope has a way of wilting.

Hillary would likely get off to a faster start, and her willingness to sweat the details would improve her batting average on getting those details right. But even though the "scar tissue," as she calls it, from her failed 1994 health-care plan may make her a more battle-hardened Washington operator, it could also cause her to shrink from confrontation and settle for too little. And for all of her collegiality with Republican senators and small legislative wins, no major bill yet bears her name. She is an unproven conciliator.

If Clinton fails to win the nomination—now a distinct possibility—a big reason will be that she never fully inhabited the real Hillary, who has been, as her husband accurately put it, a "change agent" at every step of her life. Instead, faced with an opponent who thoroughly embodies change, she has often come across like the cautious candidate of the Washington Democratic establishment, afraid to jeopardize her chances in the general election by sounding strident. Her best bet is to reconnect with the real Hillary, the one who spoke out passionately for children.

If only the strengths of the front runners could be melded. The strongest president would combine an instinct for a well-timed fight with an inspirational message of reconciliation and the doggedness and sophistication needed to get big things done. It's like a game of mix and match. Could a President Edwards, who settled plenty of cases before trial, mend enough fences among members of Congress to get bills through, despite what his former colleagues see as a do-nothing Senate term and an unwillingness to cooperate? Could a President Obama prove himself a natural at confronting hostile partisan fire? Could a President Clinton go over the heads of Washington insiders and rally the American people to her side?

MO matters. The candidates' histories and campaign themes don't always help us predict how they would actually operate in office (e.g., George W. Bush), but they're the only clues we've got.

Twilight of the Baby Boom

—— FEBRUARY 11, 2008 ——

I wrote this after Iowa, when I strongly sensed
the Clinton era was ending.

WHEN HE'S NOT PLAYING nice, Barack Obama likes to turn Bill Clinton's words against Hillary. He does it on the experience question by quoting Clinton's 1992 gibe against President George H.W. Bush that "real world" experience beats long years in Washington. And last week Obama began twisting the signature line of Clinton's 1996 re-election campaign by suggesting that the Clintons want to "build a bridge back to the 20th century."

The Democratic primary contest is not, as Obama claims, a battle between the future and the past. That's a gross oversimplification. But a generational struggle is nonetheless underway. It's not just that Obama has inspired young voters, who prefer him in large numbers. He also represents a new generation of leadership, even though technically he's part of the same generation as Hillary, the baby boomers. Here's where it gets a bit complicated. This tussle pits an Early Boomer vs. a Late Boomer, and the two cohorts have little in common.

Analyzing politics generationally is hazardous. Large numbers of voters and politicians defy the easy categories assigned to them. In the case of boomers—those born between 1946 and 1964—the whole frame is wrong. It's based on birthrates and birthdates, not common cultural and political affinities. Many quintessential boomer figures like Jimi Hendrix (born 1942) and Abbie Hoffman (born 1936) weren't actually in the demographic at all.

Worse, the Early Boomer sensibility gets all the attention. Five decades of newsmagazine boomer cover stories have focused on the (often narcissistic) preoccupations of the Woodstock generation as it ages. But those boomers born after 1955, now mostly in their 40s, missed Woodstock (unless a few snuck in as 14-year-olds). Our coming-of-age decade was the 1970s, not the 1960s. Our presidents were Carter and Reagan, not JFK, LBJ and Nixon. Our calling card was irony, not rebellion.

So it's no surprise that Hillary Clinton (born 1947) would have a different generational identity from Barack Obama (born 1961). Late Boomers, dubbed "Generation Jones" by activist Jonathan Pontell (because of in-between anonymity and lots of Joneses in popular '70s songs), make up the largest share of the voter pie—26 percent. Despite our size (the peak of the baby boom was 1957, the year I was born), we spent years feeling like generational stepchildren. It was as if we arrived late at the '60s party, after everything turned bitter. But if we weren't convincing flower children (or anti-hippies, like George W. Bush), we weren't part of Generation X either. The Gen-Xers were too cynical. Instead we became the perennial swing voters, with residual '60s idealism mixed with the pragmatism and materialism of the '80s. Even as demographers concluded that generations are really 10 to 15 years, not 20, no one represented us.

It's an exaggeration to say that Obama now does, but at least he understands the argument. In late 2004, I interviewed the newly elected senator for what would become the first newsmagazine cover story about him or any Late Boomer politician. What I remember most from that day was his insistence that we stop "re-litigating the 1960s." Nowadays he's dropped that lawyer talk, but not the idea. Well before he challenged the Clintons, Obama rejected what he called "the same old arguments" between left and right. His campaign is about "turning the page," not just from BushClintonBushClinton, but from the cultural contentiousness of those years.

To their credit, the Clintons have also long resisted what they call "false choices" in politics (e.g., you're either pro-labor or pro-business) in favor of a more practical "Third Way." Even the much-maligned tactic of "triangulation" was an effort to rise above the partisan clatter. But the Clintons simply cannot transcend those old fights. They cut their teeth on them on the way up and too often embodied them when they took power, even when it wasn't their fault. The reason they are still so loved and hated has little to do with what they did substantively, which was mostly moderate, and lots to do with visceral feelings touched off by the voters' own life experiences.

If Hillary loses, she can rightfully blame not just Obama, her husband, her campaign and herself, but a backlash against the entitlement and excess of her generation. For all the glowing press, it's a generation that has done a good job raising its kids, and not much else.

I've often wondered why some big-time politicians are Velcro while others, like Ronald Reagan, wear coats of Teflon. One explanation may lie in the struggles of the 1960s. Those who grew up then, from the Clintons and Al Gore to Newt Gingrich and Bush, are almost all Velcro. Everything sticks to them. Anyone who pre-dates or post-dates those polarizing cultural arguments has a decent shot at acquiring some Teflon.

Obama's Teflon comes not just from his race, which forces his critics to risk charges of racism when they attack him, but from his un-'60s (as opposed to anti-'60s) profile. His "Joshua Generation," as he calls it in a civil rights and Biblical context, is descended from the founding activists and still committed to their goals, but not trapped in the tumult of their times. That generates energy for the march forward into the twilight of the boom.

The Theater of Big Change

FEBRUARY 18, 2008

This column is another angle on the change theme
that is dominating in 2008.

THE WORD "CHANGE" is now so overused that it's in danger of sliding past platitude into meaninglessness. But it must be working, because a freshman black senator won 13 out of 22 states last week by selling it—and himself—to a surprisingly broad cross section of Americans. Will Barack Obama's appeal to independents convince those 796 pivotal Democratic superdelegates that he's got longer coattails than Hillary Clinton and thus the best chance to help expand the party? We don't know yet. But we do know that before long he's going to have to give us a more concrete sense of how this whole change business would work.

The first task is to clarify what changes we're talking about. Even the most successful presidents accomplish only two or three big things in eight years. Obama and Clinton have the same Big Three priorities: end the war in Iraq and restore America's standing in the world; fundamentally reform the health-care system so that it's cost-efficient and covers everybody, and transition to a "green economy" that cuts carbon emissions and creates jobs at the same time. Iraq is a wash: both candidates would repair the breach with our allies. It's fixing health care and leading the country to make the sacrifices necessary to address global warming that would test which one is the real changemaker.

If hope floats, change often sinks. Beating the odds of failure takes both a silver tongue and sharp elbows. So maybe the most relevant contrast is over which candidate is better at the other person's strength. Who's a double threat? To achieve real health-care reform and real energy conservation, Hillary would have to appeal over the heads of politicians with compelling speeches that rally the American people. Obama would have to match his inspirational rhetoric with the toughness needed to get stuff done in early 2009, when he'd have the most leverage.

I'm not sanguine about Hillary's ability to rally the country, when close to half of it implacably dislikes her. Obama's success is partly dependent on a victory big enough to create what he calls a "new majority," which means access to 60 votes in the Senate. We know he's not a policy wonk—that he'll never understand as much about, say, the specifics of out-of-network deductibles as Clinton does. The question is whether, as a newbie, he would know enough of the details and enough about manipulating the levers of power. I tried to use a recent interview to pursue both points. Obama drilled down into the arcane world of cap-and-trade energy auctions and insurance reimbursements for preventive care, but hastened to add that "technical" knowledge was not the problem: "Hillary and I talk to the same experts. We read the same books. There's a finite number of plans around and that's true on every issue."

As for his political chops, Obama was so intent on proving his readiness that he sideswiped the last two Democratic presidents. "One of the unfair comparisons has been to Jimmy Carter or Bill Clinton, that if you're an outsider you'll make a lot of rookie mistakes and squander the first hundred days," he said. "But one thing I've shown is that I understand Washington and I've got good bipartisan relationships there." While he denied that he'd yet prepared a short-list, I got the distinct impression that Republican Senator Richard Lugar could end up as his Secretary of State.

Of course those Washington relationships take you only so far. It's easy to forget that President Bush had a good rapport with the Democratic leadership at first. Obama's central argument for himself is simultaneously loftier and more practical. It's that his soaring rhetoric and his history of bipartisan conciliation are not gauzy, feel-good talents but crucial job skills: "The critical issue for the next president is the ability to mobilize the American public to move forward."

To that end, Obama has hatched a plan for governing in public. Instead of hammering out a health-care program behind closed doors, Obama says he would invite all the players to a conference on C-Span. (President-elect Clinton did something similar with a televised economic conference in Little Rock in late 1992. It helped lead to his breakthrough budget package.)

Dopey idea? I don't think so. All presidents who achieve big change have been first-rate communicators in the theater of the presidency. No FDR "fireside chats," no New Deal. No "Mr. Gorbachev, tear down this wall!"—and the Berlin Wall likely stays up for a while longer, whatever Ronald Reagan's other efforts. The health summit could be transformative. (One could even imagine Obama turning the floor over to John Edwards for some questioning of the drug- and insurance-company representatives, forced by public pressure to attend.) With the help of a few inspiring Obama speeches, even a boring summit would help educate the public and shape the debate. As Roosevelt used to say, an effective president must be the educator in chief.

Will we learn? The question of who can take the country to a different place is as much about us as it is about the new president. That's what Obama meant when he said on the night of Super Tuesday that "we are the ones we've been waiting for." To succeed, Barack Obama must bet not just on himself, but on the public's appetite for change. We're about to find out how hungry we really are.

The Obama Dividend

—— MARCH 31, 2008 ——

*Five weeks after this column appeared, Obama had to disavow
the Reverend Jeremiah Wright's offensive comments in much stronger terms
than he did in Philadelphia. But the race speech nonetheless reflects
Obama's potential to elevate the debate.*

"THE PRESIDENCY," Franklin D. Roosevelt told a reporter
shortly after he was elected in 1932, "is preeminently a place of
moral leadership." We don't know yet whether Barack Obama can
get himself elected president, much less prove a success in office. He
could get swamped by unanticipated problems or suffer from
crippling flaws we haven't seen yet. All presidents are blind dates. But
Obama is showing signs that he could project his voice in the theater
of the American presidency. Even if his legislative agenda founders, he
might be able to help the nation raise its sights in new ways. You
might think of it as the Obama Dividend.

As the afterglow of last week's landmark Philadelphia speech on
race fades, even many conservatives agree with liberal editorial
writers that Obama's approach was brilliant. I'm skeptical of that
adjective and reluctant to hazard a guess about the political impact of
the speech on blue-collar whites. Until the Pennsylvania primary on
April 22, we won't know if they even heard about the story of his
white grandmother, or how he gave voice to white frustration about
affirmative action and busing. But I do know that the speech was
"presidential" in the best sense of that word, and for reasons beyond
a tone of gravitas and a backdrop of American flags. To succeed in a
crisis (and the Rev. Jeremiah Wright Jr.'s inflammatory sermons were
at least a mini-crisis for Obama), presidents must do more than rally
the country enough to win backing in polls for a course of action.
That's relatively easy. The hard part is using the bully pulpit to
instruct and illuminate and rearrange our mental furniture. Every
great president has been a captivating teacher. By talking honestly and

intelligently about a subject that most Americans would rather ignore, Obama offered a preview of how he would perform as educator-in-chief.

Obama's unique assets have usually been viewed in international terms. The election of President Barack Hussein Obama would blow the minds of people in the Middle East and other regions and help restore American prestige. Of course, given unpredictable global events, the Obama Dividend abroad may last about as long as the much-hyped post–Cold War "peace dividend." It could pay returns for only weeks or months instead of years. Just look at Kenya, where one tribe involved in the recent unrest loves Obama (because his father was a member), and the other tribe has no use for him.

But in the United States, black opinion is now nearly unanimously behind Obama, with as many as 90 percent supporting him in the primaries. While Obama can do much to guide white Americans toward a better racial future and a greater appreciation that poor kids are not, as he says, "someone else's children," his most exciting potential for moral leadership could be in the African-American community.

Remember the 1998 movie *Bulworth*, where Warren Beatty plays a U.S. senator suffering a nervous breakdown? When Beatty's character tells astonished black Democrats that it's time for them to "put down the chicken and the malt liquor," it's final proof that Jay Bulworth is crazy and suicidal. But consider what happened late last month in Beaumont, Texas, when I covered Obama speaking before an African-American audience. A woman asked about health care and Obama explained how, for the first time in human history, thousands of obese children, many of them black, were being diagnosed with adult-onset diabetes—a disease that is killing millions and helping bankrupt the health-care system. He told the crowd that kids couldn't keep on "drinking eight sodas a day," then went in Bulworth's direction. "I know some of y'all got that cold Popeye's [chicken] out for breakfast. I know," Obama said with a smile. He continued: "That's why y'all laughing. You can't do that. Children have to have proper nutrition. That affects also how they study, how they learn in school ... It's not good enough for you to say to your child, 'Do good in school,' and then when that child comes home, you got the TV set on, you got the radio on, you don't check their homework, there is not a book in the house, you've got the videogame playing." Instead of being jeered, he was cheered wildly.

Obviously, not all black adults and children would suddenly start doing exactly what President Obama tells them. As he said in his Philadelphia speech, he's not naive enough to believe that one politician will transform American attitudes. But it must make at least some difference when Obama tells African-American audiences, as he did this year on Martin Luther King Jr. Day at Atlanta's Ebenezer Baptist Church, that they need to stop being homophobic and anti-Semitic. This is powerful stuff and would make him an important president even if his legislation stalled.

It's unlikely, however, that Obama would be completely stymied. The explanatory and inspirational abilities that he has already shown would help him push his program and move the nation on issues far beyond race. The reason that he has done so well so far is that he's proved levelheaded and stepped up when it counted—at the Jefferson-Jackson Day dinner in Des Moines, Iowa, last November, in his concession speech in New Hampshire and again in Philadelphia. Don't confuse his failure to close the sale with weakness under pressure. Barack Obama knows how to think big, elevate the debate, and transport the public to a new place. That's what real presidents are for.

The Tales Hillary Tells

—— April 7, 2008 ——

The particulars of Hillary Clinton's phony sniper fire story interested me less than the question of why politicians so often create their own reality.

W E K N O W W H Y P O L I T I C I A N S lie when they get in trouble: they think the consequences of telling the truth are too severe to bear. That's why Richard Nixon lied about Watergate and Bill Clinton about Monica Lewinsky. The more complicated question is why they fib—why politicians insist on stretching unimportant stories in ways that are easy to check and refute. Hillary Clinton's oft-told yarn about ducking sniper fire on the tarmac in Tuzla, Bosnia, in 1996 has gotten a lot of publicity, maybe too much. Her misrepresentation of her role in the Northern Ireland peace talks was more serious but less visual on YouTube. Even so, the Tuzla Tale tells us something about her insecurities and frustrations, which in turn helps explain why she's losing.

Everyone tells fish stories once in a while, exaggerating a tale for dramatic effect, and if they claim they never have, well, that's a fish story in itself. But there's a difference between telling your Aunt Mitzi that you caught a fish that was two feet long when it was actually 15 inches, and falsely claiming you wrote the Haitian Constitution (vice presidential candidate Franklin D. Roosevelt in 1920), or had helped liberate Nazi death camps (President Ronald Reagan to Israeli Prime Minister Yitzhak Shamir and separately to Nazi hunter Simon Wiesenthal in 1983).

Politicians by nature construct narratives about themselves, polished personal stories that make them shinier, if not larger than life. And the good ones start the self-mythologizing early. Barack Obama's memoir, *Dreams from My Father,* written before he entered politics, includes a few composite characters and disputed details (e.g., coworkers say he didn't have his own secretary when he worked at a company in New York). By some accounts he may have even exaggerated the extent of his youthful drug use to make himself seem more troubled than he really was.

Over time, the movies that politicians create in their heads become real to them. In that sense they lie, as was said of Henry Kissinger, not because it's in their interest but because it's in their nature. When certain buttons get pushed, the projector turns on and the fantasy begins.

Hillary's Bosnia whopper traces back to 1992, when she angrily told reporters who questioned her role in her husband's career that she hadn't been staying home "baking cookies and having teas" but was instead out working. This was in apparent reference to her 15 years as a corporate lawyer for the Rose Law Firm in Little Rock. On the trail she now emphasizes her "35 years of public service," which, because it presumably doesn't include corporate legal work, is a reference to her extensive nonprofit activity and to her time as First Lady of Arkansas and of the United States. While Hillary is not generally an insecure person, she is highly defensive about this record. Without it, she would have only seven years (her Senate career) of public service to cite. Hillary's "movie" of her own life, and of her presidential campaign, is dependent on those years seeming as meaningful as possible. An assault on their importance cuts deep.

Late last year, Obama began to push that button by belittling her travel to 80 countries as First Lady. He said that "having tea" with foreign leaders wasn't the big-time foreign-policy experience she claimed as a major reason to elect her. So Hillary began to tell the Tuzla story, which had first appeared in her memoirs, in a more dramatic fashion. "I don't remember anyone offering me tea on the tarmac there," she said, firing back at Obama. Michael Dobbs of the *Washington Post* fact-checked the tale in March and gave it "Four Pinocchios." It turned out to be untrue in almost every detail: no "corkscrew" landing, no sniper fire, no canceled airport reception. (She and Chelsea were greeted by an 8-year-old Bosnian girl, among others.) Sinbad and Sheryl Crow had come along to entertain the troops and saw nothing scary. Even the idea that she was the first wife of a president to go into a war zone was wrong. Both Eleanor Roosevelt and Pat Nixon had ventured closer to danger.

The media mob was slow to pick up the story—Sinbad jokes had been circulating for weeks on Hillary's press plane without anyone following up. But Clinton finally fell victim to what might be called "pattern coverage." For years, Hillary has had occasional problems with the truth when attacked. (The firing of the staffers who ran the White House Travel Office in 1993 was ridiculously overcovered, but an independent probe later proved she was lying when she claimed she hadn't ordered it.) All it takes is a few such incidents for the press to identify a dreaded pattern, into which it then fits subsequent stories. No pattern, no frenzy.

The Tuzla Tale has already had repercussions. Clinton was disappointed that the feeding frenzy over Obama's relationship with the Rev. Jeremiah Wright didn't destroy his candidacy. It's her best hope of winning the nomination, so she tried to reignite the story. But her latest approach to bashing Obama only reinforced the impression that her recent setbacks have left her desperate. She stopped by for a cozy interview with billionaire publisher Richard Mellon Scaife, the right-winger who commissioned the most hate-filled anti-Clinton stories of the 1990s. For her to seek help from Scaife in publicizing Obama's supposed tolerance of hate speech sets a new standard in campaign chutzpah. Scaife wrote (or at least paid for) the book on personal destruction. It's like the bloodied kids in the new Owen Wilson movie *Drillbit Taylor* asking the bully who has tormented them to go beat up some other kid. Classy.

The coda to the Tuzla Tale was the way Hillary tried to defuse it. Where the late New York mayor Fiorello LaGuardia said amiably, "When I make a mistake, it's a beaut!" or Obama confessed to being "boneheaded" in dealing with shady donor Tony Rezko, Hillary said sarcastically: "This proves I'm human, which for some people is a revelation." It was all there—the pain, the resentment and the sense of what it would be like to spend four or eight years listening to her respond to criticism as president.

PART THREE

BUSHES

Truman and the Man in the Mirror

—— 1992 ——

This summarized my view of George Bush as he fought unsuccessfully for re-election against Bill Clinton in 1992.

FORTY-FOUR YEARS AGO, this magazine took a poll of 50 political writers about the likely outcome of the 1948 election. When the issue appeared, Clark Clifford, then an aide to Harry Truman, tried to hide *Newsweek* under his coat. Truman discovered the magazine, saw that all 50 pundits were predicting Thomas E. Dewey to be the winner, and said, "I know every one of these 50 fellows. There isn't one of them has enough sense to pound sand in a rat hole."

I checked with some colleagues, and Harry's still right. Even today we'd try rags or Kleenex or something; not enough common sense for sand. The point is, why don't our candidates have the wit to say something this vivid when they're skewering the press? Truman wasn't an ace in the quip department, but at least he tried. Nowadays, even making a mild, nonsexual joke is seen as too risky. The press might turn it into a gaffe. The real mistake, of course, is to campaign scared of one's own shadow.

David McCullough's new best seller *Truman* is George Bush's playbook for re-election, down to drawing a Dewey mustache on the smooth face of Bill Clinton. Forget that George and Barbara were big Dewey supporters at the time. For Bush, the Truman appeal goes beyond the Congress-bashing mechanics of the great '48 comeback. It's about the man the president thinks he sees when he's shaving.

Imagine Bush's excitement when he came across this quote in McCullough's book from one 1948 voter: "I kept reading about that Dewey fellow, and the more I read the more he reminded me of one of those slick ads trying to get money out of my pocket. Now Harry

Truman, running around and yipping and falling all over his feet—I had the feeling he could understand the kind of fixes I get into."

This is a perfect facsimile of Bush's self-image. While his opponent is "slick," he's the guy who admits to an occasional case of the "yips" on the putting green. And from his childhood through the years in Texas and Washington, hadn't he always understood the "fixes" his friends and sons got into? As for regular voters down at the stock-car races, well, Bush understands 'em. Knows when to drop those g's. In fact, in his second term he's fixin' to get a fix on all the fixes they're in.

Bush's problem is that this self-image is totally at odds with his public image and his real lineage. "My father was a Missouri farmer politician. George Bush is a Connecticut elitist," Truman's daughter, Margaret, said last week, stating what's obvious to everyone but Bush himself. When Truman said during the '48 campaign that "we must fight the privileged class," he was talking about Bush and his friends. In fact, Bush is really Dewey—heir to his brand of moderate Eastern Establishment Republicanism. You can take the man out of Greenwich, but even years of swearing loyalty to country music and right-wing preachers can't take Greenwich out of the man. In that sense, Bush's Truman impersonation is almost touchingly ludicrous. It's like Bill Clinton trying to run as a war hero like Dwight D. Eisenhower.

While the sign reading THE BUCK STOPS HERE was a Truman gimmick, it says a little something about Bush's basic attitude toward presidential accountability that in 1989 he sent the old sign back into storage. Truman trashed the "Do Nothing" 80th Congress, which was controlled by Republicans. But he actually worked closely with Congress to create a bipartisan record of accomplishment that Bush can only envy. The Marshall Plan and the Truman Doctrine—now that's what you call a "New World Order." Domestically, Truman and Congress collaborated on landmark legislation to educate returning veterans. The fruits were considerable. Perhaps the biggest reason Truman won in 1948 was that the government managed to keep the economy humming right on through the election.

The other point that Bush missed was that Truman's second term was largely a failure, beset by an inconclusive Korean War and the symptoms of cronyism. In fact, the second term of every 20th-century president has been less successful than the first, from Woodrow Wilson's rigid internationalism, to Franklin Roosevelt's court-packing folly and New Deal failures, to Eisenhower's listlessness, to the scandals of Nixon and Reagan. Even if Bush won, he is hardly poised to break the streak.

In explaining Truman's historic victory, McCullough writes, "He had done it by being himself, never forgetting who he was." Just by trying to run as Harry Truman, Bush is not being himself, frequently forgetting who he is. Even a rat-hole pundit can figure that one out.

The Failed Case for War

—— 2003 ——

I've included this column because it reflects both my misjudgment in supporting the war in Iraq (because of the potential nuclear threat, which I believed was genuine) and my more acute understanding of how President Bush had mishandled the matter. At the time, on the eve of the invasion, I summarized it as: "Right war, wrong commander in chief."

H E WAS STEELY, determined, resolute—and totally unconvincing to anyone who didn't already agree with him.

At his prime-time press conference Thursday night—only his second since assuming the presidency more than two years ago—President Bush showed why he's in this diplomatic vise. He's got a good case but has made a hash out of it. His two key mistakes: a failure to build momentum and a failure to drill down to a deeper, more compelling logic for war.

Building the right momentum required a trait the late columnist Joseph Alsop found in Franklin Roosevelt: "longheadedness"—an ability to calculate how things will play out. During the past year, Bush didn't do that. For instance, at one point in the news conference, Bush said: "That happens to be my last choice—the use of force." Sounds good, but it simply wasn't believable. Everyone knows that war has been the president's *first* choice—not his last—since at least the summer of 2002. In trying to play the reluctant sheriff, Bush cast himself in a role that rang false. He has, for months, been the eager sheriff.

Imagine if instead of cowboyspeak about "regime change" and other name-calling last year, Bush had offered Saddam Hussein a timetable for disarmament. Then, after the dictator failed several tests, Bush's anger would not have seemed so "personal," as was suggested in one of last night's questions he didn't answer. That timetable could have even been independent of the United Nations—a second track alongside inspections to keep the pressure on. But if it had been offered in the spirit of a genuine desire for disarmament, Saddam's unwillingness to comply would have been more glaring. Bush's problem was that he started with a war cry and had nothing to escalate to. His anger has become a kind of monotone, which seriously depletes its effectiveness.

The same lack of long-term thinking applies to the United Nations. It's one thing for France or Russia to veto a Security Council resolution. That has happened before. But Bush seems determined to go ahead even if the United States is actually outvoted on the Council. He wants his opponents there to be on the record opposing the war. Why? To rub their faces in it after a big victory on the ground? Smart diplomacy is about preventing other countries from embarrassment, not causing it. Bush's satisfaction in being the principled loser in the Council is outweighing his long-term interest in repairing relations with our allies.

The second big problem with the Bush sales job is one of simple logic. Bush was lucky that no reporter asked him about his administration's most recent budget request for rebuilding Afghanistan—a big fat zero. (Congress added a couple of hundred million.) He seems to think we can play 52-card pickup and then simply leave the room.

The same logical inconsistency applies to North Korea, which he described as a "regional problem." Let's get this straight: Saddam's potential development of nuclear weapons five or 10 years from now constitutes an imminent threat to the United States, but North Korea's possession of them five to 10 weeks from now does not? I personally favor taking out Saddam now so that he's not Kim Jong Il in a few years. But it seems extremely unwise to ignore the threat of North Korea just because we have our heart set on hitting someone else.

The president's deeper logical problem relates to the way he uses the bully pulpit to make an argument. His habit—on display again Thursday night—is to simply assert, assert, assert until the message sinks in. It's as if war supporters believe that if they repeat the Saddam-Al Qaeda connection enough, people will eventually believe it.

Imagine if instead the president explained that terrorism—by Al Qaeda or anyone else—simply doesn't work in the long term without state sponsorship. Terrorists can deploy weapons of mass destruction but they can't make them. That requires a rogue state. Over time, no rogue states—no terrorism of mass destruction. This would have required Bush to move beyond platitudes to a more nuanced analysis of how Iraq's potential to develop nukes is at the heart of the rationale for war. The fact that he didn't offer the nuclear argument (in part out of fear of looking hypocritical on North Korea) explains in part why the larger case has been made so poorly. Instead, we get a scattershot "If it's Tuesday this must be the 9/11 connection" style of selling the war.

My biggest concern is not that Bush has already decided to go to war (You could tell that from the past tense he used: "I wish Saddam Hussein *had* listened"). It's that he made the decision not this week or last but many months ago, and he never seemed to refine it. Now the consequences of the decision are about to be out of his control. "Events are in the saddle and tend to ride mankind," Ralph Waldo Emerson wrote. Soon enough, we'll know which direction.

The "Blink" President

—— 2004 ——

I began calling George W. Bush "Incurious George"
when he first ran for president in 2000. By 2004,
the consequences of his isolation and over-reliance on
his gut were painfully obvious.

NO WONDER PRESIDENT BUSH lost the first debate in Miami: he got rusty living in the bubble. The president looked peeved in the debate cutaway shots not just because he's a competitive guy, but because John Kerry was leveling harsh criticism to his face—a new experience for him. Bush claims not to want yes men and women around him but he's had little experience in the past four years with anyone else. Not since last winter—when he handled Tim Russert poorly and botched a press conference by refusing to admit any mistakes—has Bush taken tough questions in public. Instead of responding to those failed outings with more practice, the Bush team took the most inaccessible president in 75 years and cut him off even further from reality. Anyone attending his rallies must pledge to be a Bush supporter. And now the Bush camp has told undecided voters hoping to participate in this week's Town Meeting Debate that they are not welcome. Apparently the idea of the president's having to respond to someone who hasn't made up his mind is too intimidating for the leader of the free world.

Why is he so afraid of engaging in a real argument? Because answering more than softball questions requires boning up, and this president doesn't believe in acquiring information that contradicts his assumptions. He believes in making decisions by instinct, then sticking with them without second-guessing. It's what makes him a good politician and a poor chief executive at the same time.

Instinct is an undervalued quality. In his forthcoming book *Blink*, Malcolm Gladwell, author of an influential book called *The Tipping Point*, explains the advantages of snap judgments. "Decisions made very quickly can be every bit as good as decisions made cautiously and deliberatively," he writes. Gladwell explains how the instant intuition of art experts that a Greek statue was a fake proved superior to painstaking chemical analysis. Students know from the first few seconds of class whether a teacher is good or not—and they are usually right. Bush is a "blink" president (who blinked incessantly during the debate). He sizes up people and situations from his gut, often with ample "emotional intelligence." Operating on instinct keeps everything simple and clear, without the confusion of facts. Clarity is important, as Bush keeps pointing out, and clarity works politically. The voters like it.

The problem is that while snap judgments are better than we assume, they are hardly infallible. Warren Harding looked on first impression like a real president, Gladwell notes, but he turned out to be one of the worst ever. Bush isn't in the book, but he seems to be a perfect example of the limits of intuition. The decision to go to war in Iraq was made without any formal meetings to weigh the pros and cons. It just felt right at the time. Once you enter a world where instincts and what Bush calls "core values" trump facts, you lose touch with the truth and start to fool yourself. Then things go from bad to worse.

There are ways for leaders to guard against self-delusion. Britain has a tradition called "question time," where members of Parliament pepper the prime minister with tough, sometimes vicious, questions on every issue. If something isn't working and the P.M. doesn't have a good explanation, he must fix the problem immediately. Since Franklin D. Roosevelt instituted regular press conferences in 1933, sessions with reporters have performed a similar function in the American system. In preparation for press conferences, presidents have to learn about what's going on in their own government. If, like Bush, they don't hold news conferences or venture back on Air Force One to talk with reporters, the loss isn't the media's (we can find stories elsewhere) but the president's. He becomes a prisoner of what his toadies tell him.

Kerry is also showing signs of hiding out from reporters, but at least he's not proud to be under-informed. Amid a crisis, a president who is routinely asked tough questions—one who believes that "policy analysis" is not for sissies—might be more likely to ask some tough questions himself and thus improve his odds of avoiding failure. But that's not Bush. He believes in using broad brush strokes and leaving the execution to others. When President Clinton prepared his budget—the primary instrument of governing—he would spend countless hours choosing his priorities. To govern, we know, is to choose. Bush spends only a few hours in budget meetings, if that.

We don't know much about Kerry, who has never been an executive. But he seems to be over on the other extreme, gathering huge amounts of information before making a laborious decision based on detailed knowledge of the subject.

It's not a great choice—ignorant snap judgments versus potential paralysis by analysis. The best presidents, of course, combine decisive intuition and deep knowledge of the policy implications of their actions. Maybe next time.

The Schiavo Mess

—— 2005 ——

For a few weeks in 2005, the case of Terri Schiavo, a Florida woman in a coma, dominated the headlines. President Bush even flew back to Washington from vacation just to join congressional Republicans in intervening in the case. A court order was finally carried out, allowing Schiavo to die, but the episode symbolized how rightwing radicals had seized the national agenda. I thought at the time and continue to believe that this was the high water mark of their strength.

WHEN HE WAS GOVERNOR of Texas, George W. Bush presided over 152 executions, more than took place in the rest of the country combined. In at least a few of these cases, reasonable doubts about the guilt of the condemned were raised. But Bush cut his personal review time for each case from a half hour to a mere 15 minutes (most other governors spend many hours reviewing each capital case to assure themselves that there's no doubt of guilt). His explanation was that he trusted the courts to sort through the life-and-death complexities. That's right: the courts.

I bring up that story because it's just one of several ironies that have arisen in connection with the Terri Schiavo saga, in which the president said that the government "ought to err on the side of life." Fine, but whose life? The death-row inmate who might not be guilty? The poor people across the country denied organ transplants (and thus life) because Medicaid—increasingly under the Bush budget knife—won't cover them? The poor people across the world starving to death because we won't go along with Tony Blair when it comes to addressing global poverty?

Or how about Sun Hudson? On March 14, Sun, a 6-month-old baby with a fatal form of dwarfism, was allowed to die in a Texas hospital over his mother Wanda's objections. Under a 1999 law signed by Bush, who was then governor, cost-conscious hospitals are empowered to decide when care is "futile." The Hudson case is the first time ever that a court has allowed bean counters to override the wishes of parents. "They gave up in six months," Wanda Hudson told the *Houston Chronicle.* "They made a terrible mistake." Wanda apparently was not "cable ready," as we say in the television world, and she failed to get Randall Terry and the radical anti-abortionists on her side. Tom DeLay never called.

Could there be—perish the thought—politics at work here? Knowing that they cannot deliver on a gay-rights amendment or abortion ban, Karl Rove & Company settled on bonding to the base with the Schiavo case. The beauty part, as Ross Perot used to say, was that they could be cynical and sincere at the same time, even if it meant twisting themselves into ideological pretzels. The same conservatives who have spent the last generation attacking "judicial activism" and federal intrusion in state jurisdictions were suddenly advocating what they had so long abhorred.

They argue they had a moral duty to intervene. If Terri had been on a respirator, like Sun Hudson, there would have been no issue, they claim. But a feeding tube is different. Says who? Says the pope, for one. Of course the pope also says that the war in Iraq is wrong, the death penalty is wrong and the West has been too stingy in sharing its wealth. So never mind the pope.

In a complex world, consistency is usually asking too much. (Seeing Democrats talk about "states' rights" last week was also a little rich.) But if you're going to accuse Michael Schiavo and the judiciary of murder (right-wing blogs and talk radio) or commit virtual malpractice by "examining" a patient long distance via outdated and heavily edited video (Senate Majority Leader Bill Frist) or advocate breaking the law by sending in state troopers to reattach the feeding tube (Pat Buchanan and William Bennett), you'd better be willing to look in the mirror.

As a father myself, I can sympathize with Terri's frenzied parents. There must be nothing harder in the world than watching a child die. And I still don't understand why Michael Schiavo didn't turn over custody and get a divorce. He says he's trying to carry out his wife's wishes and at the same time preserve her dignity. But the endless litigation and public spectacle have hardly achieved that goal.

The right wing should be ashamed of the way it has treated this man, who spent the first seven years after Terri's collapse doing everything imaginable to save her—even training as a nurse. For instance, Fox and CNN gave air time and credibility to one Carla Iyer, who accused Michael of shouting "When is the bitch going to die?" and claimed hospital authorities doctored her nursing charts—preposterous charges with no substantiation.

When this excruciating circus leaves town, the only sensible conclusion is a morally and constitutionally nuanced one. It should be possible to argue both that Terri Schiavo's case didn't belong in court—and that the courts are the only place to resolve such wrenching disputes when families cannot; custody laws should contain a little more flexibility where the wishes of the patient are unclear—and that the president and Congress did real damage to their own principles by sticking their noses in this mess. They replaced reason with emotion, confused law with theology and allowed politics and tabloidism to trump the privacy this agonizing family tragedy deserved.

The Price of Loyalty

—— 2005 ——

*The Valerie Plame leak case that lead eventually
to the conviction of Lewis "Scooter" Libby, a top aide to
Vice President Richard Cheney, was covered as
a Washington legal drama. I was more interested in what
it told us about how we went to war in Iraq.*

THE POSTHUMOUS PURPLE HEART rested near the folded American flag on the modest dining-room table of his parents' home in Cleveland. Edward (Augie) Schroeder, a Boy Scout turned Marine, was killed along with 13 other soldiers on their fifth trip into Al Hadithah, Iraq, to clean out insurgents. Their *fifth* trip. "When you do something over and over again expecting a different result," Augie's grieving father Paul told me, "that is the definition of insanity." As the death toll of American soldiers in Iraq reached 2,000 last week, Paul Schroeder concluded that the military had not sent enough troops to Iraq to do the job properly and that the president was incompetent: "My son's life was thrown away, his death was a waste." Then, noting that he shared a birthday with his boy, he broke down and said he would not be able to celebrate his own birthday anymore.

The Schroeders were on my mind as I watched Patrick Fitzgerald's skillful press conference. He laid out the seriousness of blowing the cover of CIA operatives. He explained clearly why Scooter Libby had been indicted. He even struck a blow against rogue prosecutors (like Kenneth Starr, though he didn't mention him) whose staffs routinely leak to the media in violation of the law. But Fitzgerald was wrong on one count, at least metaphorically. "This indictment is not about the war," he said. Oh, yes, it is.

According to Fitzgerald, Libby had conversations with at least seven other government officials about Joseph and Valerie Wilson that he did not disclose to the grand jury. Why were top White House officials and Vice President Cheney so concerned about an obscure former diplomat like Wilson? Because he had the temerity to offer

120

public dissent. By showing how evidence of Saddam's WMDs had been cooked, Wilson undermined the very reason Augie Schroeder and the rest of the U.S. military went to war. Wilson was more than "fair game," as Karl Rove called him. He was a mortal threat.

This has been the Bush pattern. Treasury Secretary Paul O'Neill presciently says a second tax cut is unaffordable if we want to fight in Iraq—he's fired. Bush's economic adviser Larry Lindsey presciently says the war will cost between $100 billion and $200 billion (an underestimate)—he's fired. Army General Eric Shinseki presciently says that winning in Iraq will require several hundred thousand troops—he's sent into early retirement. By contrast, CIA Director George Tenet, who presided over two of the greatest intelligence lapses in American history (9/11 and WMD in Iraq) and apparently helped spread "oppo ammo" to discredit the husband of a woman who had devoted her life to his agency, receives the Presidential Medal of Freedom. So does Paul Bremer, the genius behind the catastrophic decision to disband the Iraqi army.

The conventional Washington explanation is that this is just old-fashioned politics. As long as you don't lie to a grand jury, there's nothing illegal here. But the consequences of a bias for loyalty over debate—even internal debate—have been devastating. The same president who seeks democracy, transparency and dissent in Iraq is irritated by it at home. O'Neill tells his story in a book by Ron Suskind called *The Price of Loyalty*, and that title is the missing link in explaining the failure of the Bush presidency. The price of loyalty is incompetence. Issues don't get aired; downside risks remain unassessed.

Instead of reaching out and encouraging disagreement, Bush let neocons like Libby and Paul Wolfowitz hijack his foreign policy. Amazingly, the pros and cons of invading Iraq were never even debated in the National Security Council. If you had doubts, like Colin Powell, you were marginalized. (Powell's former chief of staff, Lawrence Wilkerson, said last week that a "cabal" of isolated policymakers ran a government of dangerous "ineptitude.") Consider the case of Brent Scowcroft, former President Bush's national security adviser. Bush the Elder tried to arrange a meeting between his old national security adviser (and best friend) and his son. But after Scowcroft wrote a 2002 op-ed piece titled "Don't Attack Saddam," the president has consistently refused his own father's request. Now we know that Bush's lack of curiosity has proved fatal.

Paul Schroeder says that well-meaning people offer their condolences over Augie, "then they whisper to us, 'We oppose the war, too.'

Why do they whisper?" Why? Because until now, the Bush White House has successfully peddled the idea that dissent is somehow unpatriotic. Paul and his wife Rosemary take a different view. "I think it's more patriotic to speak up," Rosemary says. "If the emperor has no clothes, or the president has no plan—then you have to speak out. Otherwise, you're putting all these lives in danger for no good cause."

The good news about the president's bad week is that even his conservative backers are no longer willing to keep quiet when they think he's wrong. And Fitzgerald was so impressive that the normal White House response—to savage the critic—was not an option this time. So Karl Rove survives, but the fear he stoked is easing. Four years after September 11, we're beginning to get our democracy back.

The Political Power of Truth

—— 2006 ——

I've covered seven presidential campaigns for Newsweek, *but thought the stakes in the 2006 midterm elections were higher than in any presidential contest. Had there been no accountability at the polls, our system would have been thoroughly broken. From the beginning of 2006, I was confident that truth could make a comeback, as reflected here. In November, Republicans lost control of Congress.*

STRANGELY ENOUGH, we may look back on Thursday, January 26, 2006, as the day America found its moral compass, long buried at the bottom of the national dirty-linen bag. To win the midterm elections in November, the Democrats, whose motto might as well be "So Lame for So Long," will need to make sure the country focuses on that compass. By "moral" I'm not talking just about the "culture of corruption" in Washington. I'm talking about restoring a reasonable respect for at least minimum standards of truth.

As usual, the iconic moment took place not in the capital but at the heart of the entertainment-industrial complex—in this case, *Oprah*. As it happens, I had just been to a screening the night before of *Thank You for Smoking*, the forthcoming movie based on the Christopher Buckley book. The story is a hilarious and gloriously politically incorrect send-up of Washington's culture of shameless spin. But the theme depressed me. The satire was all too real—more proof that "truth" and "reality" are not just pretzels to be twisted for commercial purposes but thoroughly devalued coins of the media and political realm. James Frey and Doubleday were just the latest to lie all the way to the bank.

Until Thursday. Something happened in that studio that went beyond "good TV." Such is the power of Oprah that her moment of truth seemed to shame the American public into more respect for the actual facts of a situation. As if to prove the synchronicity, there was even some truth breaking out in the White House press room at the very moment *Oprah* was airing live in the Midwest. Reporters were pressing President Bush hard. James Gerstenzang of the *Los Angeles Times* asked Bush if he subscribed to President Nixon's notion that "when the president does it, it's not illegal." This was, indeed, the essence—the truth—of the president's position on the National Security Agency's warrantless eavesdropping, which violates a 1978 law. Instead of the issue being framed in Karl Rove's phony and demagogic terms—where anyone who opposes the president's power grab doesn't want to protect us from Al Qaeda—we were edging our way toward a more accurate depiction of the controversy.

The news conference wasn't a complete truthfest. No reporter managed to ask the president about his statement of April 24, 2004, when Bush told a Buffalo audience: "Any time you hear the United States government talking about wiretap, it requires—a wiretap requires a court order. Nothing has changed, by the way. When we're talking about chasing down terrorists, we're talking about getting a court order before we do so." This statement was false, and Bush knew it when he said it. The president lied in Buffalo, just as surely as Bill Clinton lied when he said: "I did not have sexual relations with that woman, Ms. Lewinsky." Of course, Bush's Buffalo lie got a tiny fraction of the airplay of Clinton's Lewinsky lie.

The reason goes beyond Clinton's more colorful finger-wagging and sex with an intern. For four and a half years, Bush has politicized 9/11. His political motto has been "The only thing we have to use is fear itself." He was at it again last week, claiming with zero evidence that congressional scrutiny of the illegal NSA wiretapping would "give the enemy a heads-up on what we're doing." The media and the Democrats have both been intimidated by this devastatingly effective political strategy. It won the 2002 and 2004 elections for the Republicans and will continue to be their game plan for this November.

At first glance, making the Democrats seem soft on "terrorist surveillance" looks like another winner for the GOP. For Democrats to explain that they don't oppose all eavesdropping but object to the way it was done is a two-step answer that's too complicated to fly. A better approach would be to argue that Bush's NSA program has been a failure because it has threatened civil liberties and violated the law without doing anything to catch Osama bin Laden. The NSA obviously hasn't been eavesdropping on the right suspects.

This would fit with the Democrats' idea of fighting fear with failure—Bush's failure. New polls show his approval ratings in the dismal low 40s, with strong majorities believing he has failed on every score except keeping the country safe. (A majority of those polled not surprisingly support Bush on eavesdropping on terror suspects domestically. So do I. But when the constitutional questions are raised, his numbers drop.) To confront the security issue, Wesley Clark is chairing a PAC to help the nine Iraq and Afghanistan combat veterans running for Congress as Democrats (versus one as a Republican). The idea is to adopt the Rovean strategy of attacking your opponent's strength.

Will it work? In recent years, failure and incompetence have been trounced by fear at the ballot box. The former is based on reason and an examination of the facts; the latter on emotion, with 9/11 as a trump card. But now reality may be making a comeback, as Bush's authority breaks into a million little pieces.

An Alternate 9/11 History

—— 2006 ——

On the fifth anniversary of 9/11, I wrote a facetious column that tried to conjure how the world would have been different had President Bush governed differently or not been president at all. Some readers didn't understand at first that I wasn't on the level, but it generated a large response from those who agreed that with the right leadership things could have gone much better between 2001 and 2006.

F IVE YEARS AFTER 9/11, the world is surprisingly peaceful. President Bush's pragmatic and bipartisan leadership has kept the United States not just strong but unexpectedly popular across the globe. The president himself is poised to enjoy big GOP wins in the 2006 midterm elections, a validation of his subtle understanding of the challenges facing the country. A new survey of historians puts him in the first tier of American presidents.

As Bush warned, catching terrorists wasn't easy, but he kept at it. At the battle of Tora Bora, CIA operatives on the ground cabled Washington that Osama bin Laden was cornered, but they desperately needed troop support. Defense Secretary Donald Rumsfeld immediately dispatched fresh forces, and the evildoer was killed. While bin Laden was seen as a martyr in a few isolated areas, the bulk of the Arab world had been in sympathy with the United States after 9/11 and shed no tears. After their capture, Khalid Shaikh Mohammed and other 9/11 terrorists were transported to the United States, where they were given fair trials and quickly executed.

Today, Al Qaeda remains a threat but its opportunities for recruitment have been scarce, and the involvement of the entire international community has helped dramatically reduce terrorist attacks worldwide. Because Bush believes diplomacy requires talking to adversaries as well as friends, even Syria and Iraq were forced to help. By staying "humble," as he promised in 2000, he preserved much of the post-9/11 support for the United States abroad, which paid dividends when it came time to pull together a coalition to handle North Korea and Iran.

At home, some aides suggested that Bush simply tell the nation to "go shopping." But the president knew he had a precious opportunity to ask

Americans for real sacrifice. He took John McCain's suggestion and pushed through Congress an ambitious national service program that bolstered communities and helped train citizens as first responders.

Soon Bush put the country on a Manhattan Project crash course to get off oil. He bluntly told Detroit that it was embarrassing that Chinese automakers had better fuel efficiency, he classified SUVs as cars, and he imposed a stiff gas tax with a rebate for the working poor. To pay for it, he abandoned his tax cuts for the wealthy, reminding the country that no president in history had ever cut taxes in the middle of a war. This president would be damned if he was going to put more oil money into the pockets of Middle Eastern hate-mongers who had killed nearly 3,000 of our people. To dramatize the point, he drove to his 2002 State of the Union address in a hybrid car. Sales soared.

When Karl Rove said the war on terror would make a perfect wedge issue against Democrats in the 2002 midterms, Bush brought him up short. Didn't Rove know that bipartisanship is good politics? Lincoln and FDR had both gone bipartisan during wartime, he reminded Rove. So when evidence of prison camp torture surfaced and Rumsfeld was forced to resign, former Democratic senator Sam Nunn got the job. With post-9/11 unity still at least partially intact in 2004, Bush was re-elected in a landslide.

Taking a cue from Lincoln's impatience with his generals, Bush was merciless about poor performance on homeland security. When the head of the FBI couldn't fix the bureau's computers in a year's time to "connect the dots," he was out. And Bush had no patience for excuse-making about leaky port security, unsecured chemical plants and first responders whose radios didn't communicate. If someone had told him that five years after 9/11 these problems would still be unsolved, Bush would have laughed him out of the office.

In 2003, Vice President Cheney advised the president to take out Iraq's Saddam Hussein militarily. But Bush was beginning to understand that his veep, while sounding full of gravitas, was in fact reckless. When it became clear that Saddam posed no imminent threat, Bush resolved to neuter him, Kaddafi-style. When the president found, after a little asking around, that the 10-year cost of invading Iraq would be a crushing $1.2 trillion, he opted out of this war of choice.

Five years after that awful September day, even Bush's fiercest critics have learned an important lesson: leadership counts. Imagine if we'd done the opposite of these things. This country—and the world—would be in a heap of trouble.

PART FOUR
CLINTONS

The Real Character Issues

—— 1992 ——

*This was published shortly after Bill Clinton wrapped up
the Democratic nomination in March of 1992 and squared off
against President George H.W. Bush.*

FOR OBVIOUS REASONS, Bill Clinton prefers not to talk
about character. But one night in February at an Elks Lodge in
Dover, New Hampshire, he took a stab at it. For once, the smooth bark
was stripped off, and the pure sap of ambition and idealistic defiance
came pouring through. "I'll tell you what I think the character issue in
this election is," he shouted into the smoky air. "How can you have the
power of the presidency and never use it to help people improve their
lives until your life needs saving in an election?"

Clinton was overreaching. He seemed to be saying that private
behavior is irrelevant to an assessment of character—a myopic view, as
any voter (or novelist) knows. But as he spoke movingly about his commitment to public service, his commitment to "be there for you 'til the
last dog dies," the flinty New Englanders knew the good ole (college)
boy was onto something. Just bearing up so strongly under the media
onslaught—that was a form of character, wasn't it? And his concept of
political character—using power to help people—had to be at least as
important as peroxide blondes and Vietnam draft boards, right?

As the campaign gets nasty, the challenge for Clinton is to broaden
the definition of character. If the Bush campaign and lazy-minded
reporters are allowed to get away with using "character" simply as a
code word for adultery and the draft, then the meaning of the term and
Clinton himself are in trouble.

Assessing character is like eating soup with a fork. It's like Justice
Stewart's definition of pornography—you know it when you see it.
George Bush showed it in 1942 when he volunteered to risk his life
fighting in the noble cause against fascism. A young Bill Clinton

showed it in 1968 when he rushed into the Washington ghetto to pass out blankets to poor people burned out of their homes in the riots. The question is: what are their character records since?

Both are extremely loyal to old friends, honest in their financial dealings (the recent accusations against Clinton seem baseless) and run administrations that are cleaner than what came before. At the same time, each has given the voters cause to doubt his word. Bush probably knew more than he admitted about Iran-contra, and he deliberately misled the public about his attitude toward contacts with Chinese leaders after Tiananmen Square. Clinton probably knew Gennifer Flowers better than he admitted, and he could have been more candid this year about the relief he felt as a 23-year-old over being "saved" from the draft.

In the realm of political character—commitment, principle, guts—the judgments become more subjective but no less relevant. Bush has a problem here. Without blinking, he moved from pro-choice to pro-life on what is supposed to be an issue of conscience. He exploited race with Willie Horton. He was eager to amend the Bill of Rights for the first time in American history (on flag burning) for the sake of brief political advantage. On taxes, Bush must have known in 1988 that his read-my-lips pledge was hollow and cynical. Perhaps worst of all, after winning the Gulf War, he refused to expend any of his huge popularity on pushing a legislative agenda. That suggested a lack of deep belief in anything.

Actually, there are three things that George Bush seems to believe in deeply: personal loyalty (the key to his success in politics), resisting aggression abroad (his World War II enlistment, the Gulf War) and the economic value of letting the wealthy keep more of their money (cutting the capital-gains tax has been a lifelong crusade). The shortness of that list should itself be a "character issue."

Clinton's character problem is a bit more complicated than Bush's. The source of uneasiness about him is partly a result of his lack of directness—many voters ask why didn't he "fess up more on *60 Minutes*." On issues, his answers are refreshingly detailed but not always straightforward. Why fudge so much? Like many baby boomers, Bill Clinton has always thought he could have it all: an escape from the draft and the respect of the ROTC colonel; a brilliant wife, a political career and other women; the support of poor liberals and rich conservatives (and vice versa); credit for backing anti-Iraq sanctions and the president's war policy. Sometimes the calibrated position is right, sometimes it's politically effective and sometimes it's just plain slick.

To address his character issue, Clinton will have to provide direct, uncircular answers to questions. To address his, Bush will have to explain, finally, what he thinks power is for. That's what campaigns are about. And that's why the guy with the microphone in his hand should stop asking about the "character issue." If he means adultery, he should say adultery. If he means shameless political expediency, he should say it. The irony is that while the politicians and the media persist with their narrow notion of character, the public instinctively feels its way through thousands of conflicting bits of information toward the broader, truer, more democratically useful definition.

The Whitewater Farce

—— 1994 ——

*The first two years of the Clinton presidency
were marred by what seemed to be scandal after scandal.
I was skeptical of their importance.*

THE *NEW YORK TIMES* self-righteously editorialized a couple
of months ago that it was fine for Clinton political supporters
to believe Whitewater was no big deal, "but for any journalist or
news organization to be swayed by those arguments would be to
abdicate responsibility." Well, I guess I abdicate. Yes, reporters should
continue to probe various angles; they may yet find that 10 years ago
the governor of Arkansas had some friends who were crooks. But
Whitewater so far is a parody of a political scandal, full of sound and
fury, signifying next to nothing. If it walks like a duck and talks like a
duck, it must be a ... turkey.

The moment that best symbolized the absurdity of last week's
hearings may have been "Nussle Exhibit No. 1." Nussle is GOP
Representative Jim Nussle of Iowa, whose previous claim to fame was
putting a paper bag over his head to protest the House bank scandal.
This time Nussle dramatically drew former White House counsel
Bernard Nussbaum's attention to an especially significant document
that Deputy Treasury Secretary Roger Altman had sent to Nussbaum
last year. The TV audience stirred. A smoking gun? It certainly sounded
like evidence of something big. Then, the moment of truth. The document turned out to be a fax of a year-old *New York Times* clipping.
Even Nussle couldn't explain why this stale news was so meaningful.

Soon enough, someone will be made to pay for the administration's
chronic inability to get its story straight. When you lead with your chin,
as Altman has, the results are predictable. But as the Republicans
obsess over who said what to whom on which pseudo-significant date,
the giant public yawn is fully justified. Even the mystery of Vince

Foster, flogged by Senate ghouls last week, looks flat next to the O.J. Simpson story. Robert Fiske's report confirming that Foster was a suicide won't stop the grassy-knoll crowd. But Rush Limbaugh doing a bad Oliver Stone imitation isn't going to salvage these hearings for the GOP. When Representative Jim Leach demanded hearings last spring, he promised "blockbuster" revelations of "gagged" regulators. Now Leach says the Washington phase is only "1 percent" of Whitewater. Nice try.

That leaves the other 99 percent, which is presumably about what happened in Arkansas before Clinton was elected president. This should be probed by the press and special counsel, but not by Congress. Why? Because, as historian Alan Brinkley notes, the American tradition is that the political verdict on these matters should be rendered by voters in presidential campaigns, not by Capitol Hill inquisitors. For more than 200 years, partisan, even vicious, congressional committees have held scores of hearings about how presidents conduct themselves. But until now, a president's activities before taking office have never been probed. Not Chester Arthur's years as a patronage lackey. Not Harry Truman's connections to Kansas City's corrupt Pendergast machine. Not Lyndon Johnson's suspiciously profitable radio licenses.

If we're to break this precedent, let's at least consider the consequences. Imagine that Senator Bob Dole becomes President Bob Dole. Under this new Whitewater standard, his presidency might immediately be crippled by congressional hearings about the 1988 presidential campaign. That year, the Dole team consistently violated laws governing campaign spending limitations. The Federal Election Commission (FEC) imposed the largest fine in its history. What did candidate Dole know about those violations, and when did he know it? Or maybe the huge tax break Dole won for a big campaign contributor (Archer-Daniels-Midland) would be the subject. Juicy, isn't it? But turning every president's background into a congressional circus will doom the country to an even more enervating cycle of partisan score-settling.

A few years from now, nothing about Whitewater will be remembered except a few broad categories of winners and losers. The big losers will be historians. With Treasury chief of staff Joshua Steiner's diary and love letters having been turned over to authorities, only those officials with the potential for big book advances will ever again write down anything interesting. The big winners will be—surprise!— lawyers. No official of the future will dare make even an appointment in a date book without checking first with a lawyer or ethics officer.

Lisa Caputo, Hillary Clinton's press secretary, learned this lesson the hard way. She took one phone call in which a Resolution Trust Corporation spokesman told her that a couple of TV networks wanted to talk to the First Lady about Whitewater. For that—and nothing more—Caputo was hauled before a grand jury and a House committee and forced to spend thousands on legal fees.

Caputo and the rest of the White House staff were faulted all last fall and winter for not persuading Hillary Clinton and her husband to respond to questions raised in the press. That was fair criticism; the Clintons were stonewalling. But now it turns out that most of the supposedly scandalous agency "contacts" were to figure out how to handle press inquiries. Does withholding information from the press somehow constitute obstruction of justice? Even the *Times* editorial page can't honestly believe that. When one part of the government shares sensitive information with another it may look bad, but no one has yet offered any evidence that these contacts compromised any investigation. In fact, the only way in which the RTC probe has been clearly compromised is that Jay Stephens, a loudly anti-Clinton partisan, is still working for the RTC trying to gather evidence against the president who last year fired him as a federal prosecutor. Is that a conflict of interest? Paging Jim Leach.

Dr. Jekyll and Mr. Bill

—— 1998 ——

This appeared on the cover of Newsweek *just after Clinton
confessed his affair with Monica Lewinsky to the nation in August
of 1998. I was passing through London's Heathrow Airport
at the time and, sensing an angle, picked up a copy of the
Robert Louis Stevenson classic.*

I LEARNED TO RECOGNIZE *the thorough and primitive
duality of man; I saw that, of the two natures that contended in
the field of my consciousness, even if I could rightly be said to be
either, it was only because I was radically both.*
— *Dr. Jekyll and Mr. Hyde*

November 1995: The beginning of the resurrection, the beginning of
the humiliation. Historians in search of the most portentous, pivotal
moment of the Clinton presidency may end up here, amid the peculiar
calm of the famous government shutdown. Even the Washington
Monument stood silent, as irritated tourists scattered to fix blame. By
day, the politicians waged an acid-tongued budget struggle. By night,
with nonessential federal workers forced to stay home, a skeletal White
House staff plus a few interns kept the paperwork flowing, fueled by
junk food and suspense.

Into this breach, Bill Clinton. Both of him. The responsible one with
his sleeves rolled up. The heedless one with another piece of clothing
apparently zipped down. Solid and squalid. Cautious and reckless.
Supersmart and superdumb. Capable, as the world was to learn again
this week, of either exquisite escape or excruciating embarrassment.

Most of the time he was competent daytime "Dr. Clinton"—
helping to heal the American economy and tap a vein between mindless
liberalism and heartless conservatism. "Nine tenths a life of effort,
virtue and control," as Robert Louis Stevenson wrote of his infamous
19th-century London character. But sometimes, usually at night, the
president became someone else—call him "Mr. Bill"—a doughy, needy

mass of uncurbed appetites and fits of irrationality. "The Saturday Night Clinton," as Dick Morris has put it, always figuring he can seek redemption the next morning in church. This Mr. Bill was not the evil Mr. Hyde, though a throng of enemies, including Jerry Falwell, has even tried to peddle murder charges against him. But he did lead a dangerous (if hardly rare) double life. "The lower side of me, so long indulged, so recently chained down, began to growl for license," wrote Dr. Jekyll.

That November, Clinton's was growling. "I was conscious of a heady recklessness, a current of disordered sensual images running like a mill race in my fancy," Jekyll continued. The president didn't know it at the time, but the duality deep within him was reaching a fearful symmetry. One evening, 22-year-old Monica Lewinsky brought a pizza to him. There, in the dying light of 1995, Bill Clinton managed to rescue his presidency and wreck it; to ensure a second term and paralyze it; to save his legacy and soil it.

In retrospect, it was during this period that Clinton made himself the first Democrat re-elected president since Franklin D. Roosevelt. After the momentous GOP takeover of Congress in 1994, the president looked like the lamest of ducks, an almost certain loser in 1996. He brooded, he plotted and, in a series of shrewd political maneuvers, he disciplined himself to stand firm on the budget, force a showdown, then skillfully pin blame for pigheadedness on the Republicans. After riding a roller coaster in the polls for four years, Clinton started rising in popularity after the shutdowns and has stayed at high levels for the 32 months since. Most analysts see the entire 1996 election as anticlimactic, the Clinton victory a nearly foregone conclusion from late 1995 on.

Whatever the specifics of his 18-month relationship with Monica Lewinsky, it began then. Whether you call it disgraceful or irrelevant, it was certifiably stupid—a fool's gamble, as if his mother, Virginia, had wagered a year's pay on a lame pony at the Hot Springs racetrack. In contrast to most people in Clinton's orbit, Lewinsky—unmarried and gabby—had nothing to lose by talking. The psychohistorians will sort out whether the diagnosis of the president should be narcissism or masochism (or both), but the ironists will have the better of it. "I gave 'em a sword," Richard Nixon said of his enemies. "And they twisted it with relish."

The two Clintons: one uses the English language with obvious skill to comfort, as he did once again last week when the bodies of the American victims of the Africa bombings came home. The other uses it with obvious slickness to confuse, from "I have never broken the laws of my country" (his early response to the question of smoking marijuana, slipping around his drug use in England) to the latest semantic parody floated for him, where it seems you can have sex without really having sex. How romantic.

After a while, the two Clintons can give you whiplash. Dr. Clinton is a more successful president than the fevered critics can yet acknowledge. His decision to stiff liberals and play to the bond market in 1993 paid off; the economy boomed and the deficit went from $290 billion to zero. With Congress, he revolutionized welfare (rolls are plummeting nationwide), put real money in the pockets of the working poor, made community college virtually free, brought health coverage to millions of uninsured kids, passed gun control and family and medical leave. Crime is way down; the Dow has more than doubled since Ken Starr began his investigation four years ago.

For all the snickering, Clinton (or at least Clintonism) is still widely respected abroad. Britain, France, Italy, Portugal and the Netherlands have all recently elected "Clinton Democrats"—political leaders explicitly taking a leaf from the American president in finding a "third way" between the excesses of the welfare state and conservative laissez faire. Germany will likely do the same next month. Historians will give the president decent marks for saving the Democrats from failed liberalism, and easing the transition from an industrial to an information-based economy.

Then there's Mr. Bill—the one who has made it virtually impossible to talk to your kids about the American presidency or let them watch the news. This is a sorry legacy. You can blame Starr and his fellow fishing-expeditionists for losing all sense of proportion. You can blame a besotted press corps. Yet the responsibility is Clinton's first. Without Gennifer Flowers, Troopergate, Paula Jones and the rest, we could see Clinton as more of a victim. But even if some of the rumors about him were untrue, he stood warned. He had been embarrassed before, and he knew he was being watched by implacable enemies bent on destroying him. He knew that long before Lewinsky surfaced, Starr had subpoenaed plenty of Arkansans to talk about his sex life. And yet he continued to place himself in compromising positions.

With an eye on his family history, the armchair shrinks are citing sex addiction. Maybe so, but that doesn't account for what looks almost like a form of petulance. It was as if Clinton thought that the unfairness of Starr's torment and what the president calls the White

House's "gilded prison" somehow gave him license to misbehave, like a grounded adolescent who dares his parents to catch him.

Clinton supporters take the long view. In this century alone, Warren Harding conceived an illegitimate child in a White House broom closet, Franklin Roosevelt took up with his old mistress Lucy Rutherford, John F. Kennedy frolicked with naked women in the White House swimming pool. On the honesty front, Dwight Eisenhower lied about the U-2 downing, Lyndon Johnson lied about the Gulf of Tonkin incident and Ronald Reagan lied about trading arms for hostages. (It goes without saying that Richard Nixon lied repeatedly.) And those are just the bald-faced ones, each arguably worse than dishonesty about sex. Clinton might be the first to lie under oath, but he's also the first to be made a target under oath—to answer questions many Americans believe should not be asked.

Even so, there's something about Clinton that sets his behavior apart. Perhaps it's that like so many of his generation, he seems to bring a sense of entitlement to his transgressions. *I work so hard! I sacrifice so much for this lonely job! I deserve some fun!* This self-pity is especially unwelcome in someone who might have had it rough as a child, but bore none of the sacrifices of the World War II generation.

Perhaps besting Newt Gingrich was too easy, and the president had to find a worthier adversary—himself. For all his enemies, Clinton inevitably ends up contesting Clinton—fashioning his handcuffs, complaining bitterly in private as they're clapped into place, then grimly effecting his own escape. His partner in these Houdini acts is invariably his wife, who knows he needs her most then. Friends say they are never closer than when embattled in some Manichaean struggle.

It's sometimes argued that the two Bill Clintons are really one—that he practices "the politics of promiscuity," as a *Newsweek* headline put it in 1994. This analysis had some merit early on, when the profligate young president wantonly seduced and abandoned his political allies. In those days, his presidency sometimes looked like a messy midnight trip to McDonald's. But recent years have brought a striking contrast between the political and the personal. A svelte, more disciplined, more cautious Clinton has emerged. With the help of Robert Rubin, Leon Panetta, Erskine Bowles and, yes, Dick Morris (whose own experience being humiliated by philandering had no apparent effect on his boss), Clinton moved beyond the improvisation of the early period to a more structured, dependable and respectable presidency.

So when the Lewinsky story broke, the two Clintons seemed

especially at odds. The man who had triumphed in politics with the empathetic gesture seemed to show a shocking lack of empathy (call it selfishness), not just toward his family but also toward the advisers who believed his flat denials. The more mature his politics, the more immature his personal behavior looked. One Clinton grew in office; the other seemed to shrink.

In fact, Clinton's two sides are connected, but in a different way than was once assumed. The connection is the time and effort that Dr. Clinton—and his people—must devote to covering for Mr. Bill. From Betsey Wright, who patrolled "bimbo eruptions" during the 1992 campaign, to Jack Palladino, the detective she hired to dig dirt on women accusers, to Bruce Lindsey and Vernon Jordan's "counseling" women who crossed the president's path, cleaning up after Clinton became almost a way of life.

Early on, this spin-your-way-out-of-anything mentality infected the culture of the campaign and then the White House. The schemes to cover for the president on sex created an impression that he needed to be covered on everything, from the Travel Office to the Rose Law Firm. In fact, Clinton has been personally implicated in little beyond sex. Most of the much-hyped scandal "gates" have not touched him, and far fewer administration officials have been indicted than under Reagan. But you wouldn't know it by watching this White House, which consistently looks as if it's hiding something even when it's not.

Late on Election Night 1992, nursing a drink in a room in Little Rock's Capital Hotel, Lindsey explained to a couple of reporters that Clinton would insist on his own group of Arkansas folks spread throughout the administration, people he could trust. That was natural enough: every new president wants a back channel of loyalists. But this one needed something more: a human dam to hold back the tide of his past.

Almost from the first, the critics wouldn't let that past die. Until Clinton, a president's activities before he came to office were off-limits once the election took place. There are no examples in modern American history of distant pre-presidential years' being the subject of congressional, much less prosecutorial, scrutiny, and it was hardly because all other presidents were so virginal before coming to Washington. But the rules changed, and even after the Arkansas network had been all but obliterated—Vince Foster dead, Webb Hubbell convicted, most of the others burned out—Lindsey didn't grasp it. As the subpoenas mounted in mid-1996, the grim secret bearer was asked when it would all end. "After the election," he said with his usual stoicism.

Lindsey was wrong, of course. And it was the failure of Clinton's adversaries to respect his re-election that makes the First Family so bitter about them. In 1996 Bob Dole tried to frame the character question: Is this the kind of person you want as president? Where's the outrage? Nearly 50 million people answered the question by voting for Clinton. When Hillary Clinton talks about a "vast right-wing conspiracy," her friends say, what she means is that Starr and his conservative allies have managed to reopen the 1996 election. In other words, even if Clinton completes his second term, he won't truly have had one. Republicans ran again on character—this time they won.

Clinton once described character as a journey, and his began in two very different Arkansas places—Hope and Hot Springs. Hope was the birthplace of Dr. Clinton, a fine small town where he learned the importance of faith, education and racial tolerance. But Mr. Bill grew up in Hot Springs, then a gambling pleasure dome for Chicago mobsters. In that setting, Clinton essentially raised himself—a dutiful son who hid the violent outbursts of his alcoholic stepfather from even his closest friends. Early compartmentalization.

In the years that followed, Hot Springs kept bubbling back. "This is fun. Women are throwing themselves at me," Clinton reportedly told Susan McDougal after becoming governor. "All the while I was growing up I was the fat boy in the Big Boy jeans." Later he was analytic enough to see the problem: "When I was 16 I acted like I was 40, and when I was 40 I acted like I was 16."

It was at 16 that Clinton shook hands with John F. Kennedy in the Rose Garden, which his mother later said confirmed his ambition to be president. His emulation of JFK, once much noted, has been over-looked lately as Clinton evolves into his own original public caricature. But it's clearly relevant to the riddle of his recklessness. Kennedy was more cynical, ironic and cold than Clinton, but he, too, risked blackmail with his many assignations. He, too, compart-mentalized heavily—and he got away with it.

Clinton's survival skills are legendary, not just with the public but in the president's own mind. His working assumption is that his darker side will extract its pound of flesh from him politically, but not consume him. On the day the draft-dodging story broke in 1992, for example, Clinton gave one of the best speeches of his career at an Elks hall in Dover, New Hampshire, the one where he said he'd fight for the people "till the last dog dies." The grit was impressive in a potential president, and voters responded to it.

But over time, Clinton's unshakable faith in his fortitude may have actually undermined his survival. Those brushes with political death gave comfort to the more reckless angels of his nature. They made him think the political message will always be stronger than the personal baggage. He developed a perilous pattern: at his best with his back against the wall; complacent, cocky and at greatest risk when things seemed to be going well.

The ironies for a president not given to irony are endless. Consider this: the best chance for Clinton to shine in history might be for Congress to force him to pay the price for lying about sex. In the unlikely event he is pushed from office, it would take only weeks, maybe just days, before a vast national remorse set in. We destroyed our lovable rogue prince of prosperity over this? Clinton would become a martyr to a legal system run amok. His defeat would mean victory over not just sheet-sniffing prosecutors but all those who would criminalize politics with endless investigations. As legacies go, balancing the budget might look puny by comparison.

Instead, the president will probably limp to the end of his term, his accomplishments overshadowed. For Clinton, this would be a bitter fate. While other presidents have been ridiculed, he alone has become a permanent punch line, likely to be recalled by future generations mainly when the subject is sex. He and Starr will live on in history's bedroom, linked for the ages in the coarsening of public life.

Though so profound a double dealer, I was in no sense a hypocrite; both sides of me were in dead earnest; I was no more myself when I laid aside restraint and plunged into shame, than when I laboured in the eye of day, at the furtherance of knowledge or the relief of sorrow or suffering.

—Dr. Jekyll and Mr. Hyde

In a narrow sense, Bill Clinton is not a hypocrite. When he was introduced to the masses on *60 Minutes* after the 1992 Super Bowl, he admitted to "causing pain in my marriage." He never posed as a saint. At a policy level, a surprising number of his early promises have actually been fulfilled. With the passage earlier this month of worker-retraining legislation (virtually ignored by the press), another big piece of what he once called "the New Covenant" has fallen into place.

But Clinton betrayed one central if implicit clause of that covenant. The subtext of the *60 Minutes* interview and the campaign that followed was this: I'm young, I've sinned, but I won't make you ashamed if you give me a chance. This was the bond that his staff and the voters invested in, and it has been broken. "Alienation of affection," the divorce lawyers call it. All of Dr. Clinton's labors for "the furtherance of knowledge" and "the relief of sorrow" may have helped his country, but they are unlikely to save his reputation.

In his first term, Bill Clinton established that Democrats could be trusted to be more moderate and sensible. The challenge for the second term was to show that having won that trust, government could once again be a major force for good. That was a goal worthy of his ambitions and skills. Even without the scandals, Clinton was probably too cautious to try it on a large enough scale to make a dent; second terms are notoriously unproductive anyway. But until the sordid disclosures of 1998, there was always a chance. For years we've wondered whether this talented man could ever reach true greatness. Now we know.

Why Hillary Holds On

—— 1998 ——

*Shortly after a disgraced President Clinton and
First Lady Hillary Clinton walked stiffly to his helicopter with
daughter Chelsea between them, I interviewed her closest friends
for this look inside their personal lives.*

S HE WAS 21 years old then, and full of a righteous idealism that could not have fathomed a $100 necktie. It was spring 1969, the height of the student protests on American college campuses, and Hillary Rodham of Park Ridge, Illinois, was speaking at the Wellesley commencement on behalf of her generation.

"The problem with empathy is that empathy doesn't do anything," she told the audience. A quarter century later, empathy would be her husband's trademark political skill. By last week, the American public would feel plenty of it for her. But that day young Miss Rodham saw empathy as insufficient if not insincere—an emotion used mostly to cover up compromise and failure to act on social issues. In her earnest speech, so memorable that it landed her in *Life* magazine, she chose to focus on another word. "When I asked the class at our rehearsal what it was they wanted me to say for them, everyone came up to me and said, 'Talk about trust.'"

There was a lot of talk about trust in America last week, some of it undoubtedly in a guest house on Martha's Vineyard. The trust of a nation after a finger-wagging lie. The trust of a wife. Many of the questions of trust are extremely personal but suddenly relevant. What did Hillary Clinton know about the president's philandering and lies? What has kept her with him? What is the true nature of their peculiar yet compelling 27-year relationship?

No one can see behind the closed doors of someone else's marriage, especially one as perplexing as theirs. No one can know the full mysteries of love—or what it can absorb. And under normal circumstances, it's no one's business. But these aren't normal circumstances.

By committing sex acts with a 22-year-old subordinate in the White House, Bill Clinton made his marriage the nation's concern. In doing so, he victimized his wife all over again. For all her years of self-delusion, Hillary was only now bearing the full burdens of her bargain.

The Clintons had always claimed privacy to protect Chelsea. But last week, out in public, it was she who protected them. Chelsea, now 18, looked surprisingly strong and comfortable walking between her parents en route to what promised to be a hellish holiday. Her father, leading Buddy on a leash, wore an artificial smile; her mother, in sunglasses, looked straight ahead, deflated and not even pretending to be cheerful. "To say Hillary is disappointed would be a gross understatement," said one friend. She was said to believe that her husband betrayed not just her and Chelsea, but much of what they have worked together to build.

Yet they soldiered on. Hillary released a statement saying she "is committed to her marriage" and "believes in this president and loves him very much." Friends said it was more than boilerplate, and that she is certain Clinton still loves her, too. But any healing would take time. The president, by more than one account, had not yet come fully to terms with what he did. His remorse was still laced with anger at his fate and a cloying ingratiation; the bombing and other presidential business interrupted any introspection. Some friends said it was obvious the Clintons needed therapy, which the family undertook in Little Rock in the 1980s after Clinton's brother was arrested on cocaine charges. But the president was described as unlikely to submit to any counseling until he leaves office.

The Clintons' relationship had always been about more than matters of the heart. It began at Yale Law School in 1971, when Hillary spotted him bragging about Arkansas watermelons in the student lounge. On their first date, according to David Maraniss's revealing book *First in His Class*, she watched him talk their way into a closed art museum by volunteering to pick up some trash. Their intellectual partnership began during moot-court competition at the law school. They lost, but classmates remember the remarkable way that their skills complemented one another. It's hard to remember today how fiercely young people once believed they could change the world through politics. Clinton and Rodham shared the dream—and a pragmatism about needing to "win first" before they could get anything done.

As the relationship deepened, both sacrificed something to stay together. If Clinton were thinking solely of getting elected, he could have married an Arkansas beauty queen instead of a Chicago feminist. If Rodham hadn't been so madly in love, she never would have dropped a promising career as a Washington lawyer to move to Arkansas. No other man could meet her standard of likability and intellectual power, she told friends. But even when they were first dating, he sometimes saw other women on the side. When they married in 1975, Maraniss wrote, "She understood his talents and his flaws. He might not be faithful, but together they could be faithful to their larger mission in life."

Soon they became an astonishing political team—"Billary," "two for the price of one." She was not just the corporate-lawyer breadwinner, but his most trusted adviser. Clinton didn't call his wife "Mommy," as Ronald Reagan did, but through the years Hillary sometimes played that role, organizing and shaping him for advancement. Clinton's own beloved mother, Virginia, had been less of a mother than a fun-loving friend and worshiper at the shrine of Bill. Hillary, by contrast, was not subservient but equal. In intellectual terms, this worked brilliantly. But Clinton occasionally chafed at the discipline she brought to their life.

The marriage nearly ended in the late 1980s after Clinton was caught in a long-term affair (not Gennifer Flowers), but they patched it up—mostly for the sake of Chelsea, friends say—and were proud of surviving. In 1992 and 1996, they both complained that if they had simply divorced—like Reagan, Bob Kerrey and Bob Dole, among others—sex would never be an issue. In the White House, friends reported, there were plenty of loud fights—always a feature of their relationship—but no sense that the marriage was in trouble. "She was caught flat-footed this year," says one friend, who still insisted that they are bound together so deeply that they will never get divorced.

To those who didn't know the Clintons, this sounded bizarre and perhaps manufactured. With all the publicity, how could she not have known months ago about his relationship with Monica Lewinsky? Hillary Clinton, this theory goes, must have been an "enabler" who constantly covered up or even lied for her husband. According to this analysis, the White House concocted the story about her finding out for the first time just last week so that she wouldn't seem to have been lying on behalf of the president when she went on the *Today* show in January and talked about a "vast right-wing conspiracy" against them.

Hillary is described by a friend as "ticked off" by this line of analysis. Yes, she had dug her husband out of political trouble over womanizing, as she did by standing beside him in the famous 1992 *60*

Minutes interview about Gennifer Flowers. But an enabler? Hillary always relied on some strong woman staffer—Betsey Wright in Little Rock, Evelyn Lieberman in the White House—to keep the temptresses at bay. In the White House, she felt she could relax more on the perennial issue of her husband's whereabouts, which were now tightly circumscribed by the nature of the presidential cocoon. It wasn't as if Clinton was widely known within the White House to be playing around. There was no sense on her staff that she turned a blind eye to the obvious.

And for anyone who knew them, the notion that their marriage was a political "arrangement" was simply false. Eleanor Roosevelt was a heroine to Hillary, and Eleanor's fortitude amid Franklin's infidelity must have been some inspiration. But the Clintons had an entirely different sort of marriage from the Roosevelts, whose intimate physical relations apparently ended after 1918. The Clintons slept in the same bed and were constantly seen holding hands, kissing and flirting in ways that were impossible to fake.

Meanwhile, it wasn't hard for Hillary to filter out the rumors, which grew increasingly outlandish. Gary Aldrich's claim of seeing the president leave the White House with a blanket over his head? Hollywood starlets? Ridiculous, she thought. There were so many phony stories being peddled on so many topics—stories she knew to be false—that she stopped trying to sort them all out unless she was specifically preparing to testify. She rarely watched TV news, and the news summaries provided by her staff did not include stories about sex. Hillary knew a lot had happened in Arkansas—and had been angered when the Troopergate story appeared in *The American Spectator* in 1994—but she honestly believed that her husband had changed his ways once they came to Washington.

So when the Lewinsky story appeared, she told friends it was false. It seemed to come from the same sewer as so much else that she knew was untrue. This would prove to be a hoax, too, she told friends. When news broke that Lewinsky had received unusually high-level help for an intern, Hillary easily rationalized it. Lewinsky, she knew, was not just any intern, but sponsored by Walter Kaye, who has done more favors for the Clintons than almost any benefactor. (The biggest may have been figuring out how an insurance policy could be made to cover the expenses of the Paula Jones case.) She shrugged off the gifts in private just as she did to Matt Lauer on TV: everyone knew Bill was always buying trinkets for his staff; he'd done it for years.

But if Hillary was not exactly an enabler, she had become, over the years, conspicuously incurious about her husband's behavior. By the most reliable accounts, Hillary was so heavily invested in Bill that she had long since stopped asking him the hard questions. According to one version, the president did tell her in January that he had slipped briefly during the late 1995 budget shutdown—grown "too close" to Lewinsky, which was dumb and looked dumber—but that the intern was a lovesick puppy who wasn't telling the truth about a sexual relationship.

When reports of the dress first surfaced in the press, Clinton simply lied. "There is no dress," he told friends and family in January. Faced with a choice between believing her husband on the one hand, or Ken Starr and the press on the other, it was no contest for Hillary. Starr was the one she thought had lied for four years, and made her life miserable digging dry holes.

And then came mid-August. At first she learned the truth in legal terms, from the president's lawyers. And finally, on August 13, from her husband himself. As she absorbed the details—an 18-month affair with special gifts and at least a half-dozen sexual encounters—Hillary Clinton was apparently deeply angry. She still didn't doubt her husband's love for her, and she didn't blame herself. But according to friends she did turn inward, to her spiritual side.

Religion was always central to Hillary. For years, she had read widely in the theology of different faiths, including works by Gordon MacDonald, an evangelical minister defrocked for adultery, then given a second chance. She had been a regular churchgoer even in college when most of her friends were looking for other sources of insight—such as psychiatry. In recent years, Hillary came to recognize that she was not naturally disposed to the psychological perspective. Maybe now, says a friend, she will be.

Friends predicted that the First Lady would now apply her usual diligence to the task of figuring out which blend of religious traditions was best for her family. The search was potentially confusing. Hillary is a strong Methodist; over the years she had even mused about becoming a Methodist minister some day. But Methodists have a different attitude toward sin than do Baptists, the faith of her husband. One friend suggested that the redemption provided by Jesse Jackson last week might not prove enough.

Hillary's own tradition stressed the social gospel and a strong impulse to find grace in responsibility. Instead of empathy or sympathy,

Hillary wanted her friends and supporters to renew their commitment to something larger. It was that shared commitment that had bound her to Bill Clinton in the first place, a mixture of ambition and idealism she had expressed at her graduation nearly 30 years ago. The trust would have to wait.

"They Always Get It Right"

President Clinton was in New York for the opening of the General Assembly of the United Nations. It was the very day his sexually-explicit testimony in the Lewinsky case ("It depends on what the meaning of 'is' is") was played on national television—arguably the most embarrassing single day in the history of the American presidency. Because Newsweek had kicked off the scandal with the reporting of Michael Isikoff, we had been shut out from seeing the president for many months. So I snuck into a reception at New York University and, to the horror of his aides, had a few words with Clinton. The first thing he said to me was that a Latin American head of state had approached him that day at the United Nations and whispered: "You're lucky. In our country, when they stage a coup d'etat, they use real bullets."

THE SCENE WAS SURREAL—as if none of this had happened at all. On the same day his grand-jury testimony aired, I saw the president at an early-evening reception at New York University. He was up—too up—after his standing ovation earlier that day at the United Nations. His peer group—the leaders of the world—are solidly behind him, and annoyed at the U.S. Congress. Many are themselves oversexed politicians. Their fears of an arrogant United States have been replaced by fears of a crippled one. Some of the Latin American leaders apparently joked with Clinton that he's lucky: at least the coup against him is bloodless. The president of Uruguay told him: "Resist. Resist. Resist."

And he will. All the way past impeachment to a full trial in the U.S. Senate. Resignation talk is pointless. The die is almost cast: awful partisan squabbling about sex as far as the eye can see. The president, Congress and the press—locked up together in history's bedchamber. No exit. For anyone.

I asked the president if he thought the day was strange. He was preternaturally relaxed, almost nonchalant: "For 220 years, we've had a constitutional system that prevented the release of grand-jury testimony—until now." He may have had an inkling by then of the public reaction to the videotape. But even if he didn't yet know of the latest round of support, he knew that the American people were his salvation, and he talked of them the way a man would speak of the woman he loved. He trusted them "totally," "completely" and with the emphatic sincerity of the reprieved: "If they have the time to sort things out, they always get it right."

The president wasn't cocky last week, but he was getting close. And a cocky Clinton is a scary Clinton. His first encounters with both Paula Jones and Monica Lewinsky occurred during periods when he was riding high. The pattern rarely changes: when he thinks he's invincible, he thinks he's invisible. The best thing for Clinton—and the country— would be for him to act as if he's on probation: chastened, serious, not his expansive old self. With his back against the wall, he will survive— and is survivable.

The consequences of congressional cockiness are no less dire. The voters did not give Congress to the Republicans in 1994 to "get" Bill Clinton. They were sent to Washington to keep government from intruding so deeply into the lives of Americans, including their private lives. There is nothing conservative about a constitutional crisis shaking established traditions or an aggressive prosecutor spilling porn into culture. The GOP might gain ground on family values, but it will be temporary. The voters know that no party has a monopoly on them.

And then there's the media—rich, fat and greasy. Impeachment hearings would certainly make for must-see TV. ("Mr. Chairman, I yield the balance of my time for the purpose of further questioning Ms. Lewinsky about the president's contact with her breasts."). But in a larger sense, the media, as usual, are missing the story. History will eventually record that Washington's excruciating investigative culture of perjury traps and sexual witch hunts was a greater threat to the republic than Clinton's illicit sex and lying, no matter how sordid and stupid they were.

The president believes the press is driving the impeachment train. "They [the Republicans] think you're with 'em," he said with a smile. "As long as they think you all [the media] are with 'em, they'll keep on going." Actually, most Washington pundits would be satisfied to end the mess now with a plea bargain, censure and a fine. (I'd like Clinton also to undertake a couple of hours a week of community service as penance. If he can find time for illicit sex, he can find time to volunteer—with no cameras—in a school or homeless shelter.) It's the GOP leadership that wants to put the pedal all the way down. They're depressingly close to gassing the country into another six to nine months of Monica, polls be damned. First, the House Judiciary

Committee, whose GOP members come from conservative Clinton-hating congressional districts, is all but certain to vote impeachment—along party lines.

I've come to think of this as peanut-butter politics. Last week the *New York Times* ran a story about how the allergies of a few children were leading some schools around the country to ban peanut butter from their cafeterias, a blow to parents everywhere. The power of the few to thwart the will of the many is an old theme in American democracy. The founders built it into our system. But usually the committed minority has the power to stop something that the complacent majority favors, like gun control or teacher-tenure reform. In the case of banning peanut butter and impeaching the president, the minority has the power to *start* something that most people don't want.

Is there a chance this will backfire in November? The party out of the White House has picked up seats in every off-year election since 1934, often more than a dozen. That's not even including the widespread disgust with Clinton, which should drive up GOP turnout this year. But the past is not an infallible guide to the future. To use another non-Monica analogy, John W. Meriwether's hedge fund went belly-up last week after losing tens of billions. The fund had invested exclusively in what had worked in the past, but 1998 proved different. This fall is different politically, too. Unprecedented. Unpredictable. Unworthy of cockiness by anyone. House members in swing districts who vote in early October to hold impeachment hearings may go home to find a surprise—constituents who dislike Clinton, but hate what this madness is doing to the country even more.

The Lewinsky Legacy

—— 1998 ——

*This 1998 column reflected the effect
I thought the whole scandal was having on the country.*

NOT LONG AGO, my 9-year-old nephew and 9-year-old daughter prepared a skit for a family holiday. In a perfect Southern accent, my nephew said: "I did not have sexual relations with that woman, Ms. Lewinsky." As he wagged his little index finger, my daughter sashayed into view and interjected with Valley-girl weariness, "Oh, yes you did." Most of the grown-ups in attendance immediately went into cardiac arrest.

At first I thought the kids' savvy take on the news might be peculiar to my family, where the children don't know the sexual details (they think "oral sex" means *talking* about sex) but are nonetheless precocious about current events. Then I found that their level of knowledge about the scandal is not unusual. The subject is discussed by slightly older kids in many classrooms, though no longer on playgrounds. By now, kids are as bored with the whole thing as their parents. It's the consequences of that boredom that are becoming interesting. What does it mean when the behavior of politicians, like art, can't really shock anymore? How will the next generation fit this smelly case into the mental baggage they carry into adulthood? Vietnam and Watergate helped make us cynical about government. Will Zippergate change the way our children view public life?

In the short run, yes. The country will grow even more contemptuous of those who serve in what Teddy Roosevelt called "the arena." Getting good people to run for office will be hard in this meaner political culture. Future presidents will lose some of their luster, at least until the next one who succeeds. Even the good ones will be seen now as entertainment figures—and potential laughingstocks. Members of

Congress will inevitably look like Dickensian Pecksniffs, setting new standards in moral hypocrisy. (It was only last year that Newt Gingrich was reprimanded, not impeached, for "misleading" the Ethics Committee while under oath.) Prosecutors, who have long enjoyed being thought of as noble Eliot Nesses, will be recast as Ken Starrs, their motives and methods questioned as never before. The media will be seen not just as sensationalist and invasive but conservative—which is quite a switch. All will be seen as fiddling while the global economy burned.

Senator Pat Moynihan popularized the concept of "defining deviancy down," the theory being that increasing tolerance of crime made it more commonplace. Clinton has defined White House morality down. And now, impeachment is being defined down. Should the House actually vote to impeach Clinton, the story may not be so cataclysmic (assuming his chances of acquittal remain strong in the Senate). It could even be seen as a kind of super-censure. Meanwhile, children are growing up thinking that impeachment is what one party does to another when it gets really mad at the president—just another partisan weapon.

Of course, that's if they remember any of this at all. The velocity of modern life has shortened not just attention spans, but memory. Nothing makes much of a permanent impression anymore. And we pre-chew everything now, so that when the actual meal begins it is almost always anti-climactic. Impeachment? Been there (through the speculation of the talking heads), knew that.

In a larger sense, the news events themselves are just not what they used to be. Russell Baker noted last week in the *New York Times* that during the Cold War no one would have had the time for any of this nonsense. If Richard Nixon had received oral sex and lied about it, the offense would have ranked about 568th on a list of Watergate abuses, somewhere down around the millions of dollars in secret gifts from the Greek junta to the Nixon campaign. During Watergate, most Democrats decided not to vote for the article of impeachment detailing Nixon's criminal tax evasion; it was viewed as a "low" crime unworthy of so majestic a process.

Our whole era sometimes seems like a pale photocopy of real history. Today's youth missed the Kennedy assassination; they got the Princess Diana crash. They missed the Vietnam War; they got the Gulf War. They missed the civil rights movement; they got the animal rights movement. It's inspiring to see John Glenn go into the space, but it must have been more thrilling to see it the first time around. That's one reason Mark McGwire and Sammy Sosa touched a chord this year; they were making real sports history. One reason the computer revolution is so exciting is that it represents authentic history being made in our lifetimes, not another anniversary of something big that we missed.

At the same time, the reaction to Monicagate might represent an implicit rebuke to the way the computer is changing our lives. Cyberspace is dedicated to the idea that more information is better. But many of us are now experiencing info-remorse. Did we need to know all of this? In the name of "disclosure" and "openness"—bywords of the baby boomers—we got these document dumps full of gratuitous detail. Do they help us understand anything important? I'm not so sure that my kids will grow up thinking that the truth—and nothing but the truth—will truly set them free. But it might make a funny skit.

To the consternation of my children, I once spent an afternoon with Monica Lewinsky. It was at a Thanksgiving Day party in 2000, while the results of the presidential campaign were still unclear, and the subject of our conversation was, of all things, Senator Joe Lieberman. Lewinsky, who no doubt resented the senator's sanctimony in her own case, criticized him for staying on the ballot in his Senate race while running for vice president that year with Al Gore. "Why should he take the risk of losing his Senate seat?" I asked the former intern. Lewinsky batted her eyelashes and turned coy. "I thought politics was supposed to be all about taking risks," she replied, before adding with a laugh, "Oh, I guess I'm not supposed to say that."

So Long, Music Man

—— 2001 ——

This was written in early 2001, just before a
not-terribly-popular Bill Clinton left office in favor of George W. Bush.
It reflects Clinton's substantive achievements.

*H*E'S JUST A BANG BEAT, *bell-ringing, big haul, great go,*
neck-or-nothing, rip roarin', every time a bull's-eye salesman.
That's Professor Harold Hill.
— The Music Man

Los Angeles. August 2000. President Clinton, having completed his rip-roarin' speech to the Democratic convention, gives way to the Broadway cast of *The Music Man*, which marches through the aisles playing "76 Trombones." The convention planners claim the scheduling is a coincidence. Maybe. But it marks the perfect send-off for America's own Professor Harold Hill.

At first, the onetime member of his high-school band has some trouble adjusting to Washington, and loses Congress to the Republicans. *He doesn't know the territory.* All of that Beltway *pick a little, talk a little, pick a little, talk a little* is exhausting, but what drives the other political salesmen crazy is that the man never seems to suffer the consequences. *The piper pays him!* Needless to say, the womanizing is a problem. *I smile, I grin, when the gal with a touch of sin walks in. I hope, I pray, for Hester to win just one more "A"!* After being caught lying, he is nearly tarred and feathered, but then the instruments and uniforms and 22 million new jobs miraculously arrive, and everyone realizes there's less *trouble in River City* than before he showed up. Marian the Librarian goes on to the U.S. Senate, and the curtain comes down with the professor still in town and boasting 64 percent approval ratings.

Is Bill Clinton a con man? To Clinton haters, the answer seems as obvious as the bulbous nose on his ruddy face. But the surprisingly sophisticated public is more like audiences for *The Music Man*—open to the complexity of the character. For all of his squalid sexual behavior, most Americans focused on two other parts of the president's anatomy—his brain and his heart.

Clinton's *think system* actually worked; with the help of the technology revolution, he inspired huge confidence in the stock market—then thought and maneuvered his way to policy achievements. By even the most conservative estimates, he kept more than 95 percent of his 1992 campaign promises—from boosting the working poor through the earned-income tax credit to new college loans; from expanding Head Start to "ending welfare as we know it." And, despite his self-pitying temper and the widespread impression that his word was not exactly his bond, Clinton usually avoided cynicism and mean-spiritedness (managing even to get along with Newt Gingrich). It was this very ability to connect with people emotionally, to feel not just their pain but their moods, weaknesses and better instincts, that his critics so envied. As one of Harold Hill's jealous fellow salesmen says: he is *a raspberry seed in my wisdom tooth.*

The president is sometimes described as "protean," after Proteus, the powerful Greek mythological sea figure who could change into any shape, including wild beasts. The only way to get Proteus to tell the truth about the future was to hold him still, though this was almost impossible. Clinton's shapelessness and perpetual motion were not only effective politically but in tune with the borderless and high-speed times. Although he barely knows how to use a computer himself, he turned out to be the right restless steward on the trip from the Industrial Age to the Information Age.

As early as 1988, when giving his long-winded nominating speech for Michael Dukakis, Clinton spoke of "a bridge to the 21st century." (The architectural plans for his presidential library in Little Rock show a flat building that juts out over the Arkansas River like an unfinished bridge.) Exactly what lies on the other side is, in the Clinton cosmology, almost beside the point. He and Hillary were, as he repeatedly said in private, "transitional figures." Character, too, was to him "a journey and not a destination," a notion that led him to easy rationalization and trouble.

But much of the protean positioning was not easy and showed long-term thinking and guts. First, Clinton became, in his own words, an Eisenhower Republican, jettisoning traditional Democratic spending plans in favor of kissing up to the bond market with credible deficit reduction. His 1993 economic plan, passed with no GOP votes because it raised taxes on the wealthy, helped turn a $300 billion deficit into a huge surplus. By working closely with Fed chairman Alan Greenspan, Clinton made sure that fiscal and monetary policy worked in tandem for the first time in years. His unpopular decision to spend $40 billion bailing out Mexico paid off, as did the risks he took seeking peace in Northern Ireland and mobilizing NATO to fight the Serbs in Kosovo.

Politically, Clinton will be remembered for moving the Democratic Party to the center, by easing what he labeled "false choices" between economic growth and environmental protection, strong law enforcement and strong support for minorities. Whether he called it the "Third Way" or "the vital center," the approach made for creative policymaking or mushy compromise or, appropriately enough, some of both.

But every time Clinton looked to the future, his past pulled him back. The story—and the promise of his presidency—unraveled like a Shakespearean meld of tragedy and farce. It began in 1993, when the press, still too squeamish to pursue the reports of Clinton's sexual recklessness, compensated by going extra-tough on the Whitewater real estate deal, which eventually turned out to be no scandal. But at the time it forced Clinton to appoint an independent counsel, which eventually led to Kenneth Starr and impeachment.

The Clintons' tone-deaf responses—and the right-wing tabloid fantasies over the suicide of White House aide Vincent Foster—gave the scandal machine its juice. As late as the summer of 1994 Bob Dole was willing to cut a deal that would have given the Clintons most of what they wanted on health care. But the flexible president, deferring to his wife (who had him over a barrel for his earlier philandering), refused to bend at exactly the wrong time. The failure on health care led to the loss of the House and Senate to the Republicans in 1994. Everything after that was defense.

As it happened, Clinton proved extraordinarily good at that game, outwitting Gingrich on the government shutdown, finding small but popular issues like school uniforms and using the power of executive orders to impose his will without bothering with Congress, most strikingly to protect tens of millions of acres of wilderness.

This new political discipline did not apply to his private life. Soiling the White House with Monica Lewinsky was beyond stupid; it was deeply irrational. Clinton knew at the time that Paula Jones's lawyers were looking for anything to bolster their lawsuit. He was saved from forced resignation only by the excesses of Starr and the Republican Congress, proving once again that he was lucky in his enemies.

Much of that good fortune was manifest in the condition of the country as a whole, which tested him neither in depression nor war. But that does not explain his success. Somewhere along the way—through resilience, grit and a certain sunny shamelessness—Bill Clinton found the key to our deeper selves. How can there be any sin in sincere? the Music Man asks, holding his head high. *I always think there's a band, kid.*

How Tomorrow Became Yesterday

—— JANUARY 14, 2008 ——

*I wrote this a bit prematurely on the day after
Barack Obama's victory in Iowa. Because my computer broke,
I wrote it on my BlackBerry.*

IN 1992, the Clinton campaign came up with a theme song that evoked the message they hoped would turn a 46-year-old obscure Arkansas governor into the president of the United States: "Don't Stop Thinking About Tomorrow" by Fleetwood Mac. Now it's Barack Obama, also age 46, who has the claim on tomorrow, which is where presidential campaigns have almost always been won in this country. Hillary Clinton still has a chance to recover, but she's bucking this history. Although it would crimp his own foundation work, Bill Clinton desperately wants his wife to be president. But he knows "in his bones," as he likes to say in other contexts, that Obama may be his truest heir.

The 16 years since the Clintons grabbed control of the Democratic Party is the same amount of time that elapsed between the death of Franklin D. Roosevelt in 1945 and John F. Kennedy's inauguration in 1961. It's a longer period than many of us would care to admit. Kennedy operated "in the shadow of FDR," as the historian William E. Leuchtenberg put it, and he updated the New Deal to the New Frontier. But Kennedy's main argument was that "the torch has been passed to a new generation." So it is today, with the aging baby-boom generation—symbolized by the Clintons—under pressure to move aside.

But as John Edwards says (and Obama also knows, from his community-organizing days), the old order never relinquishes power without a fight. "Iowa Nice" is over. The sweet culture of the cornfields that made Hillary's weeklong attacks on Obama in late November one of the dumbest political strategies of recent years is giving way to states with a more bare-knuckle tradition. The question is how rough the

Clintons and their wide circle of political operatives will get. A frantic scramble is underway to feed reporters as much negative information about Obama as possible, but it's slim pickings. I've been leaked stories—if you can call them stories—ranging from his failure to leave more of a mark while he was in college (he made up for it in law school) to his failure to hold more hearings as chairman of the Senate Subcommittee on European Affairs. Not being Eurocentric enough for the foreign-policy establishment is hardly going to sink him.

Democrats of all stripes now have a psychic interest in Obama's success. Even if they're not for him, they're proud of him and of themselves for being in his party. They will not appreciate efforts to take him out, which puts the Clinton campaign in an excruciating bind. The harder they hit Obama, the more they reinforce the impression that all their campaign is about is a grubby struggle to keep their power in the Democratic Party. Many Obama voters I spoke with in Iowa like Hillary personally but resent this sense of entitlement. It's as if they're wearing anti-FDR Democratic campaign buttons from 1940 reading: NO THIRD TERM.

The playbook for a Clinton comeback is George W. Bush's from 2000. After being crushed by John McCain in the New Hampshire primary, he stole some of McCain's message and re-fashioned himself as a "reformer with results." Hillary is now arguing that she has "the experience to make change happen." But Obama has figured out a way to parry the no-experience rap. He simply quotes Bill Clinton from 1992, when he ran against incumbent President George H.W. Bush by arguing that real-world experience was more important than long years of government service. Then he pivots to his side of the field—change.

Hillary's electability problems couldn't be more plain: to win in November, Democrats must do better with college-educated men and with independents, the two groups where Obama is strongest and Hillary is weakest. Then there's the slight problem of hatred for the Clintons being the only thing the fractious GOP base can agree on this year. Sadly for her supporters, Hillary is indeed as much of a unifier as Obama—but of Republicans.

The strange part of all this is that Hillary has been a better-than-expected presidential candidate. She is substantive and strong and, with one notable exception, a better debater so far than Obama. But overall she is only a good candidate, not a great one. Like most women in politics, she lacks a critical asset. Male candidates can establish a magnetic and often sexual connection to women in the audience. (Just watch Bill Clinton, Obama or Edwards work a rope line.) Women candidates can't use sex appeal (except in France), which leaves them playing the sisterhood card. As Hillary learned in Iowa and other women candidates for lower office have discovered to their frustration over the years, "you go girl!" appeals are worth some votes but don't make for a winning strategy.

So that leaves grit, a quality that both Clintons have in abundance. Just as there was never any chance that President Clinton would resign after revelations that he lied about an affair with Monica Lewinsky, so there is no chance that Hillary will drop out even if she's 0-4 going into Super Tuesday on February 5, and little chance she will drop out after that date if she wins a couple of big states that day.

"Grit, resolve, displays of character under pressure are the keys to correcting course," says one senior Clinton adviser, who, like all those talking after her devastating loss in Iowa, spoke only on background. Bill Clinton set the template for that in 1992 as "The Comeback Kid" after he bounced back from womanizing and draft-dodging stories to finish second in New Hampshire and relaunch his campaign. The idea now is for Hillary to hunker down for a long struggle where she chips away at Obama's stature. With the media always looking for a new narrative, some upset somewhere is all but inevitable. But the Clintons' efforts to have the Democratic Party front-load the primaries (the idea being that Hillary could wrap it up quickly and concentrate on the fall campaign) has boomeranged badly. Hillary has only a month to get her groove fully back. If Walter Mondale had had to campaign with this schedule in 1984, Gary Hart would have been the nominee.

Another problem with the 1992 analogy is that Obama is no Paul Tsongas, the eat-your-peas winner of New Hampshire that year who was easy prey on Super Tuesday when he gave Clinton an opening on Social Security and Medicare. Hillary will continue her efforts to depict Obama as possessing an inferior health-care plan that lacks mandates and thus would not insure everyone. But Obama has successfully countered that you shouldn't be forced to buy something you cannot afford, and he has plenty of money to put this defense on the air.

Where Clinton might have a little more success is on the economy, which seems to be headed for a recession. Her husband managed to tap into anxiety about sluggish growth and the global economy without reverting to the anticorporate message of a John Edwards, which Clinton saw as part of the Democratic Party's past. We'll see if Obama can do that—and match it with concrete plans for the economy—but in the meantime his positions as a "New Democrat" are mostly indistinguishable from those of the Clintons. With Edwards now representing less than a third of Democrats (if Iowa, a strong union state, is to be believed), Clintonism has already been vindicated.

The Clintons themselves are a different matter. For all the talk of "Clinton Redux" or "Clinton Fatigue," another possibility might be "Clinton Irrelevance"—where Bill is beloved as an elder statesman and global citizen with much to contribute (his foundation has already raised hundreds of millions to fight AIDS and other global afflictions), and Hillary settles in as a widely respected senator.

In that scenario, the Clintons are part of America's past and present but not at the center of its future. Tomorrow belongs to someone else.

The Clintons' Patronizing Strategy

—— JANUARY 24, 2008 ——

After breaking the story of Ted Kennedy's split from Bill Clinton, I grew increasingly annoyed with the Clintons' campaign tactics. Their bet failed in South Carolina, which was pivotal.

T HE LAST MAJOR presidential candidate from Illinois, Adlai Stevenson, was approached by a voter in the 1950s. "Governor, you have the vote of every thinking American," she said. "That's nice," Stevenson replied. "But I need a majority."

Politics, as Bill Clinton said Tuesday in South Carolina, is "a contact sport." And while Barack Obama is trying hard to shed his professorial and all-too-Stevensonian air, he's just not a good enough eye-gouger at the line of scrimmage, especially with two people teaming up against him.

Obama's best hope is that Democratic voters aren't as dumb as Hillary and Bill Clinton think they are. The outcome of the primaries depends on whether, amid their busy lives, voters can get a general fix on who is more often telling the truth about the barrage of charges and countercharges.

This is ironic, because the way Bill Clinton survived impeachment was by betting on the intelligence of the American public. Now he's betting against it.

In South Carolina, Hillary is airing a radio ad that goes back to a theme she pushed in the debate there Monday night: that Obama liked Republican ideas. As Obama pointed out in his response ad, this is "demonstrably false," as referees from ABC News to the *Washington Post* to factcheck.org have established. (The Obama response ad ends with a new tagline that Hillary will "say anything and change nothing.")

The Republican story goes back to an interview Obama did with a Nevada newspaper in which he praised the way Ronald Reagan communicated with the public and changed "the trajectory of

American politics." He added that, unfortunately, the Republicans had some fresher ideas than the Democrats in recent decades.

These are completely ordinary comments. In fact, as Obama pointed out in the Myrtle Beach debate, Hillary is considerably more effusive about Reagan in Tom Brokaw's new book *Boom*. Bill has also made many statements over the years that were much more complimentary toward Reagan. Nobody paying attention thinks either Obama or the Clintons like Reagan's right-wing politics.

But instead of moving on to another line of attack with more grounding in what Bill Clinton called "indisputable facts," the Clinton campaign decided to bet that this Reagan horse could be flogged for more votes among less-educated voters in South Carolina who might be inclined to believe Hillary's preposterous version.

Less educated? Yes, downscale voters are their target group. Obama is stronger among well-educated Democrats, according to polls. So the Clintons figure that maybe their base among less-educated white Democrats might be receptive to an argument that assumes they're dumb. Less well-educated equals gullible in the face of bogus attack ads. That's the logic, and the Clintons are testing it in South Carolina before trying it in Super Tuesday states. They are also road-testing major distortions of Obama's positions on abortion, Social Security and the minimum wage.

I'm all for aggressive, even negative, campaigning, but I'm not so sure this patronizing approach will work for Hillary down the stretch. Let's take the battle in New Jersey, a delegate-rich state that votes on February 5. Hillary will almost certainly win there, in her backyard, but the question is by how much. New Jersey delegates are awarded proportionally, which means that if Obama can come within five or ten points, he's ahead of the game in the national delegate hunt.

As the Reagan ad aired in South Carolina, Hillary was campaigning in New Jersey. That gave the Obama campaign an excuse to assemble a rapid response team to create a little backlash in the Garden State.

Cory Booker, the inspiring mayor of Newark, is especially popular with white liberals in the suburbs. Here's what he said about the Clinton ads, beyond calling them "outrageous" and "dishonest":

"We're trying to offer an alternative to the Republicans' fear and smear campaigns, and now we're being dragged down to their level by the Clintons."

Bill Clinton rightly complained in the 1990s about the politics of personal destruction. In both 1992 and 1996 he managed to run general election campaigns against George Bush and Bob Dole that mostly stayed on the high road. Then, in 1998, he survived a withering assault by relying on the common sense of average people.

On the day his testimony about his sex life was being replayed on TV—arguably the most embarrassing day in the history of the presidency—I slipped into a reception for Clinton in New York.

He was amazingly serene. With enough time and information, the president told me, the American people figure out the truth. They aren't as dumb as [former House GOP strategist] Tom DeLay thinks, he suggested. "The people always get it right," Clinton said.

They did then, supporting Clinton against a witch hunt. But will they now?

PART FIVE
MEDIA

Mutually Assured Seduction

—— 1988 ——

*I've long been interested in the anthropology of the
reporter-source relationship in Washington and how it affects
news coverage. This article is from the Reagan Administration.
It could describe the Washington of today.*

DONALD REGAN'S* memoirs were jumping off the book store
shelf last week as if they contained stock tips or something. But
beyond disclosing that Nancy Reagan consulted an astrologer when
planning the president's schedule and more evidence of presidential
passivity, not much else was reported in news accounts. Few noticed,
for instance, Regan's attacks on the press for manipulating White
House aides, and on White House aides for manipulating the press.

Predictably enough, Regan blames leaks for leeching away his
power. But he believes "it is disingenuous to blame journalists for leaks
or call them irresponsible when they publish what has been smuggled
to them by untrustworthy government officials. The press has little
obligation to protect the government from itself." The main culprits, he
writes, were the "frivolous gossips and sycophants" in the White
House. Except the chief of staff, of course.

In settling those scores, Regan touches on one of the dirty little
secrets of life in the capital. He argues that those who fed tasty morsels
to the "wild animals" of the media received generally favorable coverage, while those who didn't leak—like himself—took a beating. He
even accuses a *Washington Post* reporter, David Hoffman, of explicitly
stating this hard reality to him in a way that amounted to blackmail, a
charge Hoffman vigorously denies.

The argument is oversimplified. Being a leaker doesn't guarantee
fawning press, just as denying access does not ensure a shellacking.

---

*Regan was Reagan's Treasury Secretary and then his White House Chief of Staff, where he tangled
with First Lady Nancy Reagan.

Besides, it's not as if Regan himself didn't try to play the leak game. He appears to have scaled back less on principle (the motive he claims in the book) than because his bullheadedness prevented him from being very good at it. But Regan's on to something when he says that reporters have developed an unhealthy form of "dependency" on high government officials who use the cloak of anonymity to stab their enemies. To keep the media attentive, officials need to come up with consistently juicy material. And to keep access open, reporters need to coddle their sources. In recent years, this cozy system of mutually assured seduction has grown corruptive.

The real danger is that good sources tend to win a measure of undeserving protection from reporters. Oliver North, a major leaker, benefited from this, as has James A. Baker III, whose failures as treasury secretary would no doubt be more fully examined if so many reporters were not indebted to him for leaks. Especially useful sources, like Robert Strauss, are rewarded with occasional "beat sweeteners." *The New York Times*, particularly on its "Washington Talk" page, has made a minor specialty of such puffy stories.

Some beat sweeteners are written partly out of hope for *future* morsels from an important source. For instance, many news organizations are scrambling to do favorable stories about Susan Estrich of the Dukakis campaign. Sure, being the first woman campaign manager is a good angle for a story. But reporters and editors are lying if they claim there is no other motive involved. Given that, Estrich should enjoy the ride while it lasts. So far she has not proven herself to be a revealing source, which means that the incentive to flatter her will dramatically diminish. The negative coverage of Hamilton Jordan, Jimmy Carter's chief of staff, corresponded roughly to his shunning of the press.

In the end, neither presidents nor the journalists who cover them get much of importance out of this way of doing business. Presidents are routinely driven to distraction by leaks that they should have expected all along. And White House reporters spend their days competing to help hoist trial balloons, uncover stories of petty backbiting and obsess over other scooplets from high-level sources that turn out to be of less than cosmic significance. The truly major stories—like Watergate and the Iran-contra scandal—were missed by the White House press corps altogether. That's partly because top aides have no incentive to reveal the biggest secrets, which are either too embarrassing or worth hoarding for one's memoirs. (Consider the astrology story, which stayed secret for years.) The valuable reporting is usually done at lower levels of government, where journalists are less likely to trade favors simply for gossip.

Notice that it is extremely rare to read hatchet jobs about people on the way up or puff pieces about people on the way down. Was Don Regan really as smart as his raves in 1985 or as foolish as his pans in 1987? In fact, like everyone else who has taken that ride, he was roughly the same guy. In the same system.

China: Unwilling Informants?

—— 1989 ——

*In the spring of 1989, pro-democracy students gathered
in Beijing's Tiananmen Square, where they were dispersed and fired on
by government troops. The Tiananmen Square Massacre
raised a series of media issues that are still relevant nearly
20 years later at the Beijing Olympics.*

T HE APPALLING AFTERMATH of the Beijing massacre is a
reminder that the media can be used to imprison as well as liberate.
The same Western TV transmissions that spread word of the democracy
movement were later scanned by Chinese authorities to help round
up suspects. But the dilemma for the press corps is not so much
technological as moral. It reaches back to the very origins of what it
means to cover the news. Like their predecessors in preliberalization
China, today's journalists are trapped between reporting the story and
avoiding complicity in the arrest of their sources. It's a tight spot.

The dangers are clearest in television. ABC News broadcast
an eight-second sound bite from Xiao Bin, an eyewitness to the
massacre. Five days later China's state television CCTV aired about 90
seconds of the same interview—suggesting that Chinese brass
perhaps lifted the shot off a satellite feed of raw footage. CCTV
followed with its own pictures of the same eyewitness under arrest,
recanting his antigovernment comments. Shocked, ABC News moved
immediately to scramble its satellite signal. The other networks
began silhouetting or otherwise disguising the faces of Chinese departing from the party line. Newspapers, too, ran more anonymous quotes.
Newsweek changed the name of one of those who might be jeopardized.

Was there any way news organizations could have anticipated
being used so cruelly? "We were totally taken by surprise," says Bob
Murphy, vice president for news coverage for ABC News. "There had
been no evidence of any repercussions." Before the crackdown, Chinese
were emboldened as never before to speak openly. Still, there is plenty
of precedent for repercussions after a crackdown is underway. Richard

Bernstein, a *Time* correspondent in Beijing from 1979 to 1982, wrote a harrowing *New York Times Magazine* story last April about discovering that he had unwittingly helped send a dissident to jail for six years. "A lot of us have found out the hard way that we can get people in trouble with what seems to be innocent reporting activity," says Fox Butterfield, a *New York Times* reporter who inadvertently caused harm to Chinese sources in the early 1980s.

The dilemma goes to the heart of how journalists view themselves. Are they reporters first, or compassionate human beings? In a situation with complexities like those in China, the question cannot be addressed so squarely. At first glance, the argument for shutting down all contact with Chinese seems compelling. Why risk helping doom them to jail or even execution? In recent days even those Chinese who support the government entirely in interviews with Western reporters have found themselves interrogated afterward by security. Some media critics went so far as to criticize NBC News anchor Tom Brokaw for merely greeting passersby in the streets of Beijing.

Of course encouraging silence is exactly the effect that the Chinese government intends. "We are intimidated, because we don't want to get more people in trouble," said Kyle Gibson, an ABC News "Nightline" producer in Beijing. The result is not only journalistic impoverishment. It also means sacrificing the larger aim of many of the people who agree to talk, which is to get details of the massacre to the world. If they go uninterviewed, they are "protected," perhaps, but not fully represented, a position that may lack compassion in its own right.

There's no pat way to resolve this journalistic tension, which exists in many other repressive nations as well. Good reporters work on a case-by-case basis. When the subject in jeopardy seems careless or naive, he is often asked if he really wants his name used—and even if he says yes, is sometimes spared identification. The problem is that ultimately this weakens the reporting of the story. Readers are less likely to believe anonymous accounts. Particularly with Chinese authorities employing a Big Lie technique, bearing witness to the world seemed, for some Chinese, worth the harsh personal price.

One of the cruel ironies of journalism is that those who need the least protection often get the most—and vice versa. The high-ranking Washington official, simply trying to exercise self-serving spin control, almost always has his request for anonymity respected. Otherwise, he won't cooperate with the reporter in the first place. By contrast, the man in the street, less wise to the implications of his actions and less valuable to the reporter in the future, is more likely to see his name in print. Perhaps the China experience can reinforce the idea that "protecting sources" should take on more resonance when one is shielding them from torture and prison than from political accountability. The most skillful and discreet reporters know how to manage that feat and cover the story at the same time.

Prime-Time Revolution

—— 1990 ——

*The role of media and technology in the fall of communism
was one of the great under-covered stories of the late 20th century.
The issues raised here predate the Internet but apply to it.*

TELEVISION IS SOMETIMES called the electronic hearth.
In Romania last week, it was more like a bonfire. Romanian viewers accustomed to pictures of happy factory workers and shiny tractors
sat down to watch the overthrow, trial and execution of their dictator
and his wife on TV. While a new regime was formed, live, extra air time
was filled with previously banned programs like *Max Headroom* and
Tom and Jerry cartoons.

The broader question—technology's role in all of 1989's mind
bending revolutions—is one of those unanswerables that will keep
symposium coordinators employed for years. In one corner are the
media triumphalists; Ronald Reagan's line that "the biggest of Big
Brothers is helpless against the technology of the Information Age" is
emblematic of this view. The opposing argument is that information
technology is value neutral; after all, the Ayatollah Khomeini
distributed thousands of cassette tapes when fomenting his despotic
revolution against the shah. By this theory, world change is produced
by economic, religious, strategic or personal forces—for example,
Soviet military restraint—that are largely independent of developments
like television. There's some truth on both sides, plus a few principles
that might fall somewhere in the middle:

TV stations are today's fortresses: Through centuries of war, battle
plans were roughly the same: secure the strategic high ground, then
attack the main garrison or palace. When the new flag went up, it was
all over. High ground is now the transmission tower; the new flag is a
different face in the anchor's chair. (Though in the case of Romania, it
was the old anchor who confessed to having lied in the past.) Last

week's new regime in Bucharest actually governed from the TV station, where some of the week's most pitched battles took place. Control of the airwaves is a pivotal sign of sovereignty, as Filipinos learned in 1986 and Czechoslovaks last year.

Controlling communications isn't new. Radio stations have been important military targets since World War II, a point that American military commanders inexplicably forgot when they failed to secure them during the invasion of Panama. But TV is even more strategically significant. Ceausescu's security forces had to see their chief's body with their own eyes on television. If they had merely heard he was dead, more might have chosen to fight on.

Totalitarians produce dull TV: With such rigid control, why didn't Ceausescu have more of a hold over the affections of the common people? One answer is that he had competition. Voice of America, Radio Free Europe. This gave Romanians hope.

It also gave them real news, which even decades of doublespeak cannot supplant. Propaganda is always a ratings loser. Night after night of paeans to "the Genius of the Carpathians" can convert even the most ardent Communist into a skeptic. In East Germany, the November purging of Karl-Eduard von Schnitzler, for 30 years the dictatorial "chief commentator" of state-run TV, was second only to the fall of the Berlin Wall as a cause for celebration. Author Peter Wyden notes that von Schnitzler's news program was so bad that only 7 percent of East German households watched it, compared with 85 percent that tuned in to Western programming.

Technology respects no borders: "The enemy of the people stands on the roof," said East German Communist boss Walter Ulbricht in 1961. But no sooner had his forces torn down the antennas than new ones popped up again. The same is true of efforts to control the use of copy equipment, computers and other technologies. By the time the real 1984 came around, George Orwell's Big Brother turned out to be thousands of unruly little cousins, sapping the government of its legitimacy.

Mikhail Gorbachev is loosening the reins in part because he knows his country can't support technology (for economic progress) and fight technology (when it's used for dissent) at the same time. The Chinese regime hasn't faced that reality yet. When Chinese exiles last year began to tie up every fax machine in China with overseas messages of freedom, the authorities issued angry but ultimately futile diplomatic protests.

Power still comes from guns: Still, the Chinese proved in Tiananmen Square that tyranny isn't always stopped by TV, and that democratization is reversible. As long as the army is loyal (a problem for Ceausescu) and the dictators bloodthirsty enough, guns can still prevail. Moreover, censorship works. Burmese authorities stifled most coverage of their massacre last year, thus forestalling international pressure. Press bans have been successful from South Africa to the Middle East (especially in the Arab world). The sad truth of the TV age is that if there's no video, it didn't really happen.

In the long run, the triumphalist argument about a "critical mass" of technology and rising democratic expectations may turn out to be valid. But there is currently no direct correlation between areas of unrest and areas that receive Western information. People choose to rebel for reasons beyond what they see on TV, as the nationalities movement within the Soviet Union suggests. By the same token, recent history shows examples of repressed peoples choosing *not* to rebel, even when the news has told them of a better, freer life. Consider how long it took the well-informed East Germans to throw off their chains. In that sense, technology may be necessary for today's revolution, but it's not sufficient. The information explosion is an explanation of why totalitarianism is doomed in the future, but not a complete answer to the riddle of the exhilarating events of 1989.

Does Bloody Footage Lose Wars?

—— 1991 ——

*This was written in 1990 during the Persian Gulf War
but it could just as easily been a piece from any time during the
last five years. In fact, I wrote in 2004 about the restrictions on
photographs at Dover Air Force Base.*

I N T V N E W S R O O M S last week, producers were asking one
another that familiar question: "Will he (or she) cry on camera?"
With a dozen Marines dead, it was time for interviews with grieving
buddies and families. Over time, such stories strike fear into the heart
of any administration trying to prosecute a war. But do weepy or bloody
pictures really sap the will to fight? Contrary to the mythology growing
out of Vietnam's "living-room war," the answer may be no.

Saddam Hussein and George Bush agree on one thing: the voracious
American media will use human-interest stories to prey on the sensibilities of the American people, who are extremely sensitive to casualties.
Saddam said as much in meetings with visiting Americans last year;
the Bush administration, determined to present as antiseptic a war as
possible, has designed its censorship program around preventing access
to such stories. Even some reporters agree that an unfettered press
would prevent the United States from sustaining a war. Steve Kroft, a
60 Minutes correspondent, admits to feeling "relieved" by the
Pentagon's decision to close Dover Air Force Base to coverage of the
arrival of body bags from the gulf. "We can't help ourselves," he says,
referring to TV's addiction to emotional pictures.

But if TV can't help itself, perhaps the public can. It doesn't take
extraordinary faith in people to believe that they will make their
decision about support for a war independent of any pornography of
grief they might see on TV. By that standard, the government should be
allowed to censor only stories affecting military security, not those that
might be inconveniently affecting.

Historically, it has censored both. In World War I, according to

177

Phillip Knightley's *The First Casualty*, censorship was so tight that even reports of a gift of wine cases to American troops by the French were deleted for fear of making the Americans look unsavory. In World War II, not only was any negative reporting censored, but no photographs of dead American soldiers were allowed to be published until 1943, more than a year after Pearl Harbor. Reporters covering the Korean War, still very much on the team, actually requested censorship to help them stay on the right side of the authorities. Only the undeclared Vietnam War lacked censorship, though the networks voluntarily avoided airing the goriest shots.

Does that help explain why Vietnam was also the only war the United States lost? Not really. Traditionally, Americans' initial reaction to damage inflicted by the other side is anger, not defeatism. A 1967 *Newsweek* survey, for instance, found that the vast majority of viewers said the televised images of death actually made them more hawkish on Vietnam. A similar dynamic was at work this year when the Iraqis displayed mistreated American pilots.

Over time, large-scale casualties can diminish public appetite for war. In the gulf conflict, the deaths may generate reminders of Vietnam that are unhelpful to the war effort. But low tolerance for casualties in fact predates both Vietnam and bloody TV pictures. The popularity of the Korean War dropped in half in just one week after heavy casualties—in an era before TV. Clearly it is the results of war, not the esthetics, that in the long run sway public opinion.

Whatever TV's true power, the perception of that power carries great weight. That's why the Gulf War restrictions on access to combat (as distinct from censorship as such) are greater than in any previous major war. The military says it cannot accommodate a horde of reporters, but it did during World War II. On D-Day, 558 journalists were accredited to travel with the invasion forces. In all major wars until this one, reporters like Richard Harding Davis and Ernie Pyle mingled freely with troops, who mostly liked the attention.

It may be, as author David Halberstam says, that this country is "extraordinarily ill-prepared emotionally for this war." But if it is— if doubts about the war's purpose, length and human cost come bubbling forth—the explanation will lie a lot deeper than the airing of maudlin, exploitive footage on television.

Why the Old Media Is Losing Control

—— 1992 ——

In 1992, well before the advent of online news and blogging, the mainstream media already seemed to me to be losing its grip.

"**N**ATTERING NABOBS of negativism" has a permanent place in the museum of memorable political rhetoric. It was among the more colorful attacks on the press launched in 1970 by Vice President Spiro Agnew (or, more accurately, William Safire). These gibes were as strong or stronger than anything offered this year by Ross Perot. But there's one big difference. When Agnew was in office and the three big networks sat astride the TV medium, the "nabobs" were the only game in town. Richard Nixon's Silent Majority was stuck with the elite Eastern media as practically its sole source of national news. Now these folks can vote with their channel clickers.

This may be remembered as the year that the mainstream political press lost control. The reporters who troop from New Hampshire to the conventions to November, playing "expectations" games all the way, are looking a tad irrelevant. Perot suggests that it "doesn't matter" what's on the front page of the *New York Times*. "Hit me again," he says to the press, because his polls just keep going up. If he's right, what will the shape of the new American news system be?

The system is splitting in two. There's Old Media: the nets, big newspapers and news magazines, Washington-based op-ed chin-pullers, public TV and influential journals of political opinion. Then there's New Media: CNN, C-Span, infotainment talk shows like *Larry King Live* and *Donahue*, computer bulletin boards and satellite hookups. Old Media is far from dead, especially in agenda-setting. The Perot phenomenon wouldn't have been taken seriously if the mandarins of the business hadn't paid attention to it. But it's now possible to go over the heads of the old players as never before.

New Media is less elitist and more democratic, which is good. But it's less analytical, which isn't good. Turn-of-the-century humorist Finley Peter Dunne (alias " Mr. Dooley") used to say that the Supreme Court "followed th' iliction [sic] returns." The same is now true of much of the media. They tend, often unconsciously, to pump someone when he's up and kick him when he's down. Local news anchors don't often ask tough questions to popular candidates.

Some Old Media outlets have made efforts to bring Perot back to earth. Not long ago, National Public Radio ran a story that convincingly suggested that Perot was not being candid when he said that he "openly" sought a huge personal tax break in the 1970s from the federal government; it was actually sought at first in secret. On the air, Perot said that he had never heard of NPR's "All Things Considered." Charming, especially for disaffected voters. But then Perot angrily called anchor Linda Wertheimer's questions "a classic setup. Whoever you're trying to do a favor for, you've done it, and I'm sure you had a smirk on your mouth as you got me into this." This suggests some of the odd, conspiracy-minded petulance that is an important if almost completely unexplored dimension of his character. If the New Media can't manage to air that less-attractive part of the Perot phenomenon, all the fresh choices on the channel changer won't mean much.

The Beast Is Always Hungry

—— 1992 ——

*When Bill Clinton ran into trouble during the 1992 presidential
primaries over philandering and his Vietnam-era draft record, it gave
me a chance to explain the strange folkways of the political press.*

GROUND ZERO of American politics this time of year is the
bar of the Sheraton Wayfarer in Bedford, New Hampshire. Sure
it's stupid that a bunch of reporters hanging out together in a pleasant
but totally unrepresentative white-bread state should be helping select
the leader of the new world order. But that's the way it is. And, hey,
it's fun. Anyway, one night last week, a group of us groused that there
wasn't any news. By news we didn't mean candidates confronting issues
that people care about. Amazingly, they were already doing that—not
with complete candor, of course, but with a lot more substance than it
seems on TV. No, by news we meant a shocking new poll or a devastating new ad or a convincing new bimbo—something, anything, to
spin the campaign off in a different direction and give dozens of
reporters the same fake-fresh angle. You could almost hear the chant in
the icy wind outside: Feed the beast! Feed the beast!

Not to worry. That powerful news vacuum - the force that both
energizes and trivializes our politics - was filled the next morning
by an article in the *Wall Street Journal* about Bill Clinton and his experience with the draft. Suddenly we had a "story of the day" to get us
through the night. The way it played out makes for a handy example
of the peculiar media psychodynamics of politics. Would it be a classic
blood-in-the-water feeding frenzy, or just a normal snack for the horde?
The outcome depended on many variables, some subconscious, others
serendipitous.

For starters, there's what could be called the Fertile Soil
Syndrome. On one level, that represented a kind of lazy slavery to
sequence (first Gennifer Flowers, now this ...) as if the rapid succession

of revelations was itself a Clinton character flaw. But the search for a pattern had a certain logic: Clinton was developing a reputation for being a bit slick, and this youthful episode seemed to confirm it. It's the same reason that George Bush got bashed for his abortion flip-flop in 1980, and Gary Hart for his name and age changes in 1984. The specific becomes a shorthand way of communicating an abstract insight. The problem is that in the real world, where most people are only barely paying attention, the shorthand becomes "Bill Clinton, draft dodger," which he wasn't. Draft finesser is closer.

Then there's the Dan Quayle pattern—if we decked him for what he did to avoid going to Vietnam, we have to deck Clinton. Quayle was unluckier; the pack at the 1988 GOP convention was larger and even hungrier for something new. And the details differed. Quayle, unlike Clinton, never exposed himself to the lottery, though he did serve for six years in the National Guard. As a war supporter who implausibly suggested that Guard duty might take him to Vietnam he was more vulnerable than Clinton (who opposed the war) on the hypocrisy front.

Still, the plausibility of Clinton's response ran up against the personal experiences of those covering him. The measured, largely accurate reporting of the story didn't reflect the intensity of their feelings. Many reporters are roughly Clinton's age, whether they served or not (several did); they assume Clinton was just as anxious to avoid the military as they were. So why couldn't he just admit that like everyone else? It was left to reporters younger (like me) or older—less tormented by those times—to point out the unreasonableness of asking the man to commit political suicide.

As usual, just when the Wayfarer regulars thought Clinton was surely doomed, the story ebbed. Because the details were complicated—not "Clinton Fled to Canada"—it didn't lend itself to TV. When only one of four networks played it on the evening news, that sent a powerful signal to the rest of the media to back off. Nothing about the next day's coverage in major newspapers (mostly off the front page) demanded a rethinking of that judgment. WMUR-TV, New Hampshire's omnipresent and influential local station, used the story as an example of unfair piling-on-the-front-runner. People began pointing out that Pat Buchanan avoided service with a bad knee and Defense Secretary Dick Cheney had numerous deferments. Ronald Reagan spent World War II in Hollywood.

Polls that assess the damage of the draft and infidelity stories are imprecise at best. All that's clear is that the reports of Clinton's political death have been greatly exaggerated. Say he loses New Hampshire after being tagged an adulterous smoothie, and Mario Cuomo enters. That's steak tartare for the press—the "New York nightmare" alone is worth a few thousand stories. Sick of Slick Willie? Try Mean Mario! Everyone is a caricature-in-waiting. Paul Tsongas's trickle-down sanctimony, Bob Kerrey's erratic existentialism, Tom Harkin's nasty New Deal nostalgia—it all looks bad if you're ahead. To update the old saw: politics ain't bean curd. In the reporters' bars beyond New Hampshire, the beast will never go hungry for long.

Go Ahead, Blame the Media

—— 1992 ——

Press-bashing is a hardy perennial for politicians,
but it was made central by President George H.W. Bush
as he faced a tough re-election fight in 1992.

IN OCTOBER, the vineyards of American polities traditionally yield a wide selection of fine whines. At the end of any campaign, when all of the other bogeymen have been flayed to the point of futility, there's always the media. Almost any trailing candidates of any party at any level of politics eventually indulge in at least private press-bashing; it's a way of venting a bit of understandable, even justifiable, bitterness. After all, losers have usually caught fewer breaks from the press. Their failure to handle the media is one of the reasons that they're failing in the first place.

But politicians don't seem to understand that the press is not a useful scapegoat. While railing against pundits may stir up anger and intensify support (especially among Republicans), it doesn't drive voting behavior. Can anyone name a contest in which blaming the media has provided the winning margin? Everywhere he goes, Bush mentions his favorite bumper sticker: ANNOY THE MEDIA: RE-ELECT BUSH. This red meat may be tasty for the faithful, but it's largely irrelevant to the issues of trust and change that are shaping the outcome. If Bush wins, it won't be by tapping distrust of the media. Americans take the presidency too seriously to base their decision on whether they like Sam Donaldson.

Still, Bush's complaint falls into fertile soil. Let's face it: reporters do tend to lean against the president. So do commentators, even though the majority of them—contrary to popular impression—are conservative. (William Safire and George Will are both deeply skeptical of Bush.) Yes, it's preposterous for Bush supporters to claim that Bill Clinton is getting off easy; just look at how much more he has been hounded on the draft this fall than Bush has been over the Irangate story. And reporters will almost always choose a juicy story over some vague political preference. But the tilt in the tone of the coverage is undeniable. A Bush victory, however terrific as a one-night upset story, would indeed annoy—even depress—many journalists, who overwhelmingly believe that he has not been a good president.

The explanation for this is less ideological than institutional: change makes a much better narrative than the status quo. Think back to 1980, when the press gave Ronald Reagan better treatment than Jimmy Carter. Then, too, the prospect of a second term seemed dull and enervating, devoid of much new (i.e., "news"). The only exception to this institutional impulse is when the challenger's chances look hopeless, in which case reporters don't want to appear naive and out of step with public opinion. If Clinton were behind by 15 points this year, he would be pilloried in the press.

That's because the highest value of all is placed on staying "in step." This is the media's greatest blessing—keeping current—and its greatest curse. The real fault of the press is not that it leads too much—tells the whom to vote for—but that it follows too much; it wires itself to polls, then reverberates with an amplified impression of what it thinks the public already believes. For all of the improvements this year in the coverage of issues, an institution designed to be an independent voice has too often become a huge echo chamber.

The irony is that in trying to be closer to the voters, the American news media have moved farther away from them. This year has seen two angry rebellions: one against politics-as-usual, the other against media-as-usual. The rise of "talk-show democracy," where voters dispense with the journalistic middleman, has encouraged the public to believe that the press is more of a hindrance than a help in learning about the candidates. While these angry voters are right to feel afflicted by too many polls and horse-race stories, they're mistaken to believe that they can draw all of the necessary conclusions just from watching the candidates directly. Candidates—all candidates—distort the record in speeches and debates. The job of the press is to fill in the gaps with inconvenient facts and impertinent questions. To be fully informed without the help of journalists requires watching C-Span five or six hours a day. Of course if you do that, you'll see plenty of interviews with ... journalists. In other words, you can't escape us. We'll be around long after Bush, Perot and Clinton have slunk offstage. No term limits, either.

Let's Stop Crying Wolf on Censorship

—— 1993 ——

This column was seen by some as an attack
on rap music when my real aim was to protect critics
of it from heated charges.

IMAGINE THAT a big record-company executive signed a new skinhead band called Aryan Nation and distributed 2 million copies of a song with the lyrics: "Rat-a-tat and a tat like that/Never hesitate to put a nigga on his back." This frank call for whites to kill blacks might run into a few problems around Hollywood. It's not likely, for instance, that President Clinton's advisers would recommend that their man appear at a gala fund-raiser at the executive's house. If radio stations declined to air Aryan Nation's songs advocating lynching, no one would scream "censorship."

Those lyrics in fact come from a rap song by Dr. Dre, whose label is Death Row/Interscope, which is partly owned by Time Warner. Interscope is headed by Ted Field, a movie-and-record mogul who hosted Bill Clinton's big Hollywood fund-raiser last year. "A lot of this [criticism of rap] is just plain old racism," Field told the *Los Angeles Times* last month. "You can tell the people who want to stop us from releasing controversial rap music one thing: Kiss my ass."

Since Hollywood already has enough people who spend their days eagerly taking Ted Field up on that offer, I thought I'd try a different tack. It is Field and other phony liberals of his ilk, wrapping themselves in constitutional pieties, who are applying the racial double standards and devaluing legitimate civil liberties concerns. It is they, more than the rappers themselves, who are responsible for spreading irresponsibility. And it is those who oppose them—private citizens rebuking or boycotting sociopathic entertainment—who are engaged in free expression in its best, most democratic sense.

That word—censorship—has been thrown around much too casually

186

in recent years. If a record company executive or an art gallery owner or a book publisher declines to disseminate something, that's not censorship, it's judgment. It might be cowardly judgment or responsible judgment, but it is what they are paid to do. Garry Trudeau makes this point whenever some wimpy newspaper decides not to run a controversial *Doonesbury* strip: his fans say he was censored; he rightly calls it bad editing.

How did we get to a point where "art" became a code word for money? As record executive David Geffen said last year about Time Warner Chief Gerald Levin's lame rationalizations for Ice-T's "Cop Killer," "To say that this whole issue is not about profit is silly. It certainly is not about artistic freedom." In other words, the Constitution guarantees all Americans the right to rap, but it says nothing about Dr. Dre's right to a record contract.

In fact, if censorship means companies like Sony and Time Warner and Capitol Records begin to think harder about the messages they're sending young African-Americans, then maybe we need more of it. If censorship means executives bear greater personal accountability for what their companies produce—if it means that when Ted Field walks into a Beverly Hills restaurant, the patrons turn around and say with disgust, "Hey, that's the guy who tells blacks to shoot each other"— then it could help. But that's not what the word means.

Real censorship is when the government—*the government*—bans books in school libraries, prosecutes artists and writers for their work, seizes pornography, and exercises prior restraint. And there's the whiff of censorship when the government hints at future action, as Attorney General Janet Reno did last month with the TV networks. The line here gets tricky. Tipper Gore was way ahead of her time, and she never advocated censorship, only voluntary labeling of albums. But as the wife of the vice president, she's probably wise to go light on the issue now. Otherwise it might begin to feel censorious. A few private institutions—like schools that try to punish offensive student speech—could also be categorized as engaging in real censorship.

Beyond that, let's give the word a rest. If an editor wants to change the text of an article about ghetto life, that's editing. But if a rap producer wants to change sociopathic lyrics, that's seen as censorship. Why? Even if you assume that rap is superior esthetically to journalism, is it really more worthy of protection? Is rap an inherently more valid form of expression than prose with no beat behind it? After all, they are both "voices of the community" waiting to be heard.

This is not an argument for applying a harsh moral standard to art, for easy listening everywhere on the dial, for record company executives to sponsor nothing that they don't personally embrace. But even at its grimmest, music is meant to enhance life. Like tobacco executives, artists and record moguls who market death bear at least some responsibility for the consequences of their work. Let's confront that—and stop crying wolf on censorship.

Journalism as a Blood Sport

—— 1993 ——

This appeared after the 1993 suicide of Vince Foster,
a White House aide and close friend of Hillary Clinton.

ACKCLOTH AND ASHES don't fit comfortably on the
Washington pundit class. After the release of Vincent Foster's note
last week blaming the press for some of his unhappiness, there was a
moment of self-examination. But only a moment. Then came the
rationalizations. After all, Lani Guinier, Clarence Thomas and lots of
others got it much worse than Foster, who was untouched outside the
pages of the *Wall Street Journal*. And Foster was obviously a deeply
troubled man whose suicide raises many still-unanswered questions.
And of course Washington isn't any more vicious than New York or
Los Angeles or corporate America. And hey, if we pull our punches out
of fear that someone might kill himself, then we couldn't engage in
good, aggressive journalism. Message: we didn't kill the guy.

This is all true as far as it goes. The problem is that the *Journal*
editorial page attack that helped make Foster so despondent was not
good, aggressive journalism. It was bad, hypocritical journalism, as the
columnist Michael Kinsley has shown. The same executive branch
prerogatives that were praised by the *Journal* when George Bush's
counsel asserted them were viewed as near crimes when Clinton's legal
team came in. More broadly, the rationalizers don't understand how
lame they sound to the public. Foster's note—especially the line "Here
ruining people is considered sport"—captured what so many people
despise about the Washington media culture.

That line deserves some deconstruction. On one level, politics has
always been viewed as akin to sports, and properly so. When public
figures stop being a source of amusement, democracy is in trouble.
Despots close the peanut gallery first. What has changed is that a

contact sport has become a blood sport. This savagery is actually a throwback to an earlier era. The *Journal* editorial page, for instance, resembles nothing so much as the rabidly partisan 19th-century newspapers that routinely—often brilliantly—slandered anyone on the other side of their barricades. In the modern era the *New York Times* and other papers reacted against this by developing a cult of objectivity and respectable editorializing that is only now beginning to break apart.

The new tone has meant sharper writing (including on the *Times* editorial page), but also shouting on television and a general coarsening of public dialogue. Lied to repeatedly over the years by public officials, reporters can no longer be deflected when they pick up a scent. In 1964, when an aide to Lyndon Johnson was arrested for disorderly conduct in a YMCA men's room, Clark Clifford persuaded the *Washington Post* to downplay the story. If that happened today, mini-series rights would be sold by noon.

Once a bit of poison is dropped into the media bloodstream, it's hard to retrieve. Foster saw the White House Counsel's Office blamed for everything that went wrong. It became a press litany: Zoë Baird, Kimba Wood, Lani Guinier ... In truth, Foster's office had nothing to do with the Baird fiasco. Did anyone change the litany? Of course not. Or consider the famous Clinton-haircut story. According to the *Post* ombudsman, the haircut was mentioned 50 times in the paper, including nine times on the front page. But when *Newsday* reported that a review of FAA records showed that the haircut had in fact not held up traffic at the Los Angeles airport, the *Post* ran one measly paragraph on it. Same with other big papers. *Newsweek* printed no correction at all until now.

After Foster's death, the media pathology he loathed continued apace. His note was found in little pieces. Good story. Fine. But when the White House delayed turning it over to the U.S. Park Police for a day so that his widow could see it first, the press reacted as if it were Oliver North's shredding party. Perhaps there's more of the suicide story to tell. It's certainly the media's job to probe. But not to hype.

Foster, emotionally over-wrought, sadly failed to recognize that Washington's cruelty is tempered by its amnesia. For instance, one of his predecessors as deputy counsel, Fred Fielding, was deeply involved in Watergate. A few years later he was back as Ronald Reagan's counsel as if nothing had happened. No one expected the tiny *Washington Monthly* even cared. Yes, major figures—Bert Lance, Donald Began—are sent packing under media assault. But short of indictment, which stigmatizes people for life (even if they're innocent), a brief run of bad publicity doesn't usually destroy careers.

For those on the receiving end, that's little comfort. When you're in the crosshairs, you twitch, no matter how famous or obscure you are. You imagine that everyone you meet is privately thinking about your embarrassment. You get a little paranoid. But the media beast's very insatiability eventually provides a measure of safety for its prey. A charge must be reprinted 100 times and turned into a Jay Leno joke to have much real impact. Even then it's soon forgotten. The Japanese have a maxim: after 75 days, no one remembers.

Insiders understand this. Some even shamelessly trade on short memory to behave badly ("Hell, it's only a one-day story at most," the unspoken logic goes). The rest of the country wonders how something as precious as one's reputation can be considered so casually in Washington by both press and public officials. If the tragedy of Vince Foster can help other people regain the sense of perspective he lost, some small good might yet come of it.

The Manic-Depressive Media

—— 1993 ——

*I noticed this phenomenon in the relationship
between the press and Bill Clinton in 1993 but had no idea it would
continue for eight years and eventually apply to Hillary, too.*

IN HIS BOOK *Chaos*, an account of recent scientific advances,
James Gleick writes that "a physicist could not truly understand
turbulence or complexity unless he understood pendulums." The same
can be said of politics. Bill Clinton's debut certainly looks like chaos.
Before his first week was over, official Washington, bolstered by the
radio static it interprets as the voice of the people, was already writing
him off as a klutz and a naif, a Jimmy Carter II Gets Taken to the
Cleaners. But beneath the turbulence, as scientists are finding in all
complex systems, lies a deeper, stranger sense of order. The news cycle
is now so short—the oscillation of opinion so intense—that Clinton's
stumble may actually have set him up for future surges. What goes
down must come up. And down and up and down and up until we're
all dizzy.

With a manic-depressive media, honeymoons are history. The same
need for an ever-new narrative that led the press to favor change (and
thus Clinton) during the campaign now demands that he be savaged—
at least for a few days. He was a hero on Election Day, a goat during
his early disorganized transition, a hero at the Little Rock economic
conference, a goat during the week before taking office, a hero at the
Inauguration, a goat during the fights over Zoë Baird and gays in the
military. In each case, there may have been sound reasons to reach
those judgments but little acknowledgment of their evanescence.

"Clinton faces a policy defeat from which his presidency might
never recover," editorialized the *Daily Oklahoman* last week. Paging
the pundit police. At last count it was one week down and 208 to go.
Yes, showy Senate hearings have been scheduled, which guarantees the

gays in the military drama a long TV run; Republicans who didn't exploit the issue during the campaign will make hay with it now in their direct-mail solicitations. But the ever-hungry media beast will soon need a comeback story to sate its appetite. Clinton will be on top again before long, because the nature of journalism requires it.

On the other hand, if the pummeling continues, American politics might witness something truly new: a liberal backlash against the media. Annoyance with the press for piling on the president has been a staple of Republican politics for at least a quarter century. When they were out of power, Democrats traditionally took the opposite tack: if they criticized the media at all, it was for being too docile, not too aggressive. No more. The new attitude within the Clinton camp seems to be that much of the press is stupid and obnoxious. At the Inaugural gala, a tape was shown of well-known pundits pronouncing Clinton politically dead last year.

Under chaos theory, "air resistance" affects pendulum swings in unpredictable and irregular ways. In other words, talk radio has become what scientists call "friction." The most familiar sound in Washington last week was a busy signal, as more calls poured in than at any time since the shooting of Ronald Reagan. The news cycle has become a powerful loop: voters see an easy-to-grasp story like Nannygate* or gays in the military on the news, then they call in to Washington and their local talk shows, then they see all the TV stories about them calling in—and the process begins again.

But the harder they call, the harder they fall. The more intense the reaction, the more quickly it passes. Remember the huge level of interest during the Gulf War? Poof. All of those war opponents who were supposed to have been trapped on the wrong side of overwhelming popular opinion got off without a scratch. Already, the TV image of the receptionist answering a busy phone in a congressional office has become a visual cliché. Vox pop means people are caring again, and they have to care in order to bring change. But when radio earthquakes become commonplace, the Richter scale reading required to shake Congress will grow higher.

The same is true of the press. When Clinton makes a more serious blunder than on gays and the military, the media will have trouble moving to an even higher threshold of attention and outrage.

*When Clinton's first two nominees for Attorney General, Zoë Baird and Kimba Wood, were withdrawn after revelations that they hadn't paid employment taxes on their domestic help's wages.

This is potentially good news for the president. It means that when he starts making tough budget decisions that anger voters and light up the switchboards, it may be easier to ride out the storm. (A million calls on the gas tax? The press corps ate George Stephanopoulos for lunch? Oh, yeah, that happened last week, and the week before, too. Not such a big deal.)

James Gleick writes: "For a pendulum steadily losing energy to friction, all trajectories spiral inward toward a point that represents a steady state—in this case, the steady state of no motion at all." That suggests a media culture so exhausted by its nervous exertions that it's soon ready for a big hand to start the pendulum again.

America Goes Tabloid

—— 1994 ——

*Here I'm trying to put the tabloid mania that began
in the early 1990s in some historical context. That many of the
once-famous names below are only dimly recognizable today
helps prove the point. (Hints: Bobbitt had his penis cut off by his
wife. Harding put out a hit on her figure skating rival Kerrigan.
Shapiro was one of O.J. Simpson's attorneys.)*

FIFTY YEARS from now, long after Kato Kaelin has given up
his lounge act, the mid-1990s will be remembered as a golden age
of tabloid news. Only some perverse celestial alignment (maybe the tab
horoscopes can explain it) could have brought us Lorena and John
Wayne Bobbitt, Tonya Harding and Nancy Kerrigan, Heidi Fleiss,
Paula Jones, O.J., Susan Smith killing her kids, and fabulous Chuck-
and-Di adultery tales all in one year. Or, more precisely, only some
black hole in our cultural universe can explain the level of interest and
coverage these stories generated. But before we get all huffy about it,
let's try to understand that our own tabloid epoch is just the latest in a
long, swampy tradition.

From at least the time of the ancient Greeks, sex, disfigurement and
murder have sold. ("Oprah, my name is Oedipus Anderson and I'm
in a support group for men who have slept with their mothers and
blinded themselves.") The 1890s are better remembered for Lizzie
Borden whacking her parents than for, say, the Free Silver Movement.
In a fine 1994 biography of Walter Winchell, the original gossip columnist, Neal Gabler explains that even the glory days of midcentury
tabloids saw plenty of hand-wringing. The poet e. e. cummings, for
instance, fretted over how the tabloids encouraged "an infantilism in
American life." Sound familiar?

Winchell's paper in the early years was the notorious *New York Graphic*,
which ran "composographs"—outrageously doctored pictures. In 1924, the
Graphic ran a composograph of a "witness" in the famous Peaches Browning
divorce trial standing buck naked (viewed from the back) before the jury.
Even Maury Povich or Sally Jesse Raphael might draw the line at that today.

The latest round of sensationalism grows out of an anomaly in recent journalistic history. Strangely enough, daily tabloid newspapers have failed in this country since World War II. Even Rupert Murdoch's print invasion in the late 1970s could not resuscitate them, except in New York. The big success story in print has been profitable, quality urban dailies in the major cities. For years, the weekly supermarket tabloids were seen as a popular but low-credibility and not particularly influential form of entertainment.

Then, in the early 1980s, Rupert Murdoch and others discovered tabloid TV, and the loosening of the old network system led to syndicated talk shows, *A Current Affair, Hard Copy* and the rest. These programs invaded the turf of the supermarket tabloids and made their fare more vivid and central to mass culture. The shows became so pervasive that mainstream news organizations like ABC News, the *New York Times* and *Newsweek* began to play catch-up, though with higher standards. (The mainstream press doesn't pay its sources, which means the sources have less incentive to exaggerate.)

Until the 1980s, network news divisions were largely insulated from moneymaking pressures. They were ornaments of respectability useful for status and license renewal. But now the ratings pressure is unrelenting, and the emphasis is on the hot story or interview. Add to that the proliferation of TV news-magazine shows, each trying to outsizzle the other. Even here the standards varied in 1994. Diane Sawyer's interview with the family of Nicole Brown Simpson was OK; Connie Chung's softball interview with Faye Resnick, a woman who claimed to be a friend of Nicole's but had written a book with a *National Enquirer* reporter detailing the sex life of her "friend," should have been beneath the dignity of CBS.

All of these stories tapped a deep ambivalence—even hypocrisy—within viewers. You know that you're addicted—that you're losing irretrievable July days outdoors in order to hear some minor pretrial motion by a hot dog like Robert Shapiro. But you can't help yourself. That Paula Barbieri interview is coming up. At the same time, when everyone else complains about too much coverage, you join in: Isn't it awful? This should touch off a little self-examination on all sides. The people who run the news business should ponder whether they are selling out their principles for ratings and circulation. And the people who are consuming the stuff should acknowledge their contradictory feelings. If they don't like it, all they have to do is turn it off. But that doesn't mean they have to make everyone else turn it off, too.

The most pointless journalism of the year was the effort to lend analytical weight to the froth. Yes, Lorena Bobbitt's act had repercussions for feminism and the now quaint notion of personal responsibility; yes, Tonya Harding's behavior raised questions about the pressures of big-time sports, and yes, the trial of O.J. Simpson involved some intriguing issues of race and celebrity in American culture. But that's like saying we eat popcorn for the roughage. We eat popcorn because it tastes good with our entertainment. These stories were horrendous (Susan Smith) or humorous (Heidi Fleiss) but always irresistible. Only the most pompous news executive could ignore them altogether.

The long-term consequences of the tabloidization of news are unmistakable. While viewers know rationally that *A Current Affair* is not, say, NBC News, it all blurs together, especially when everyone is doing the same stories. When readers and viewers can't recall or don't trust the source of something—especially something sensational—they are right to believe less of it. And when they believe less of it, the credibility of the entire news industry declines. That, ultimately, leads to fewer customers. Beyond ethics and taste, tabloid excesses are simply bad for the news as a business.

If it is amusing or gripping enough, any quirky news brief can now seize the nation. Lorena Bobbitt is far from the first woman ever to cut off a man's penis; she wasn't even the first in 1993. Her story started off tiny and made its way into the headlines only because the watercooler conversation grew impossible to ignore. As 1994 progressed, the time lag shortened, so sharply that when teenage Michael Fay was sentenced to a "caning" for minor vandalism in Singapore he became the celebrity *du jour* within hours.

The Simpson story would have been big in any era; with the possible exception of comedian Fatty Arbuckle in the 1920s, he is the most famous person ever tried for murder in this country. (Almost every other famous defendant became a celebrity as a result of the crime, not before it.) His fame, the televised chase and the broader appetite for sensation created the mother of all tabloid stories. To paraphrase Garrett Morris in the old *Saturday Night Live* baseball sketch, "O.J. been bery, bery good to media."

This may sound cynical, but Tabloid America is also democracy in action. Readers and viewers who have overdosed on these stories may be irritated at the coverage, but the plain fact is that they are outnumbered. Once a significant portion of the public tires of the story, the media—via overnight Nielsens, newsstand sales and so forth—will immediately sense it and pull back. In other words, the public as a whole is getting almost exactly what it wants. The channel changer is a kind of ballot box.

The fact that so many have voted yes to tabloid news may even pull us together a bit as a nation. Traditionally, men have broken down some of the barriers between them with talk of sports. Such modest bonding excludes most women—and men who aren't interested—but it brings American men together across lines of class and race and gives them something to talk about beyond the weather. This kind of common conversation is also now possible in the world of tabloid stories. At a loss for anything to say about Bosnia or health care, millions of men and women with nothing else in common could, this year, share a theory about what the Bronco ride really meant. The promise of a shared experience in an otherwise fractured culture may have even helped make these stories so big in the first place. Who wants to be left out of the conversation? This connection between people is not going to save the republic; it doesn't excuse the shoddiness, tawdriness or just plain excess of much of the coverage. But it's something.

The Power to Change What's "Cool"

—— 1995 ——

*One of the great untold stories of the 1990s
was the way public service campaigns helped change behavior.
Later in the decade, Jay Winsten, one source of this story,
used TV to popularize the concept of mentoring.*

FORGET BLABBY state troopers and razorback S&L operators in hot pants. The ultimate rim shot for Leno, Letterman and the rest is the United States government trying to be hip about sex. The new radio and TV public service announcements (PSA) on condoms constitute a Full Employment Act for Talk Show Hosts. If the debut is any indication, it's the feds who should be using some protection. One of the first spots announced and quickly withdrawn last week by the Centers for Disease Control and Prevention featured a rock star—Anthony Kiedis of the Red Hot Chili Peppers—who turned out to have once been convicted of indecent exposure and sexual battery. Another radio spot, in which a condom is noisily placed over a microphone, is a rip-off of a parody originated by Rush Limbaugh, the noted anti-condomite. It's a long way from "Don't Be a Litterbug."

The problem with all the snickering is not just that 200,000 Americans have already died of AIDS, but that unlike so many government programs, these ads—which also preach abstinence—may actually save lives. And even if they don't sharply change behavior among gay men and IV drug users (the main at-risk groups), they will likely help curb other sexually transmitted diseases and unwanted pregnancies. Because Republican administrations were so afraid of condom campaigns, the evidence isn't in yet here. But look at Africa, where nonprofit groups are entering the war against AIDS. According to the Washington-based Population Services International, 900,000 condoms were sold in Zaire in 1988. By 1991, with condom ads on TV, that number had reached 18 million, a twentyfold increase in three years.

If anything, Americans are more susceptible than Zairians to media-induced behavior modification, especially the at-risk kids who—conveniently enough—watch a disproportionate share of television. In recent years, attitudes toward smoking, drugs and drunk driving have changed more quickly in the United States than anywhere. Obviously, the words and pictures on the air must be complemented by organizational commitment on the ground. The press must be willing to set aside its world-weariness and join the crusade. And the country must be ready to hear the message, or it won't get through. But the potential of well-crafted media campaigns to blast huge holes in social problems is seriously underappreciated.

Perhaps the best-known model is the transformation of smoking behavior. It's easy to forget just how acceptable cigarettes were throughout the culture until the 1960s. Now it's a furtive habit. Television and Hollywood do their part, with only newspapers and magazine ads (including those in *Newsweek*) still playing the glamour game. Even accounting for slow progress among the young, the basic change is striking. We've gone from a country where roughly half of all adults smoked to one where less than one-third do.

One of the great untold success stories of recent years is the effect of a huge, coordinated media campaign on the use of illegal drugs. Between 1985 and 1992, the number of Americans who regularly used drugs declined 50 percent, from 23 million to 11.4 million. Drug use among blacks is down 58 percent. Many factors contributed to the decline, including the sudden death of basketball star Len Bias in 1986. But public service ads created and placed by the Partnership for a Drug-Free America clearly made a huge difference, not so much for the roughly 6 million hard-core drug users as for young recreational users influenced by definitions of what's cool.

The same is true of the "designated driver" campaign, which had little impact on alcoholics but proved tremendously successful overall. Since 1989, alcohol-related auto deaths are down a full 25 percent. after staying flat for a few years. (A raise in the drinking age in many states was also a large factor.) Unlike the traditional Ad Council PSAs, which are routinely preempted on local stations, the network ads on drunk driving were carried in prime time and widely absorbed. So were the designated driver themes inserted in popular TV sitcoms. The challenge now, says Jay Winsten, director of the Center for Health Communication at the Harvard School of Public Health (which spearheaded the campaign), is sustaining the success. As the anti-drug activists also find, when the campaign becomes old news, the bad numbers inch up again.

That's the real issue facing the media this year on violence. How to keep the momentum of outrage from fading? Daily or weekly death tolls in newspapers and TV newscasts are one way to institutionalize the crusade, just as Walter Cronkite once kept the Iranian hostage crisis front and center with a nightly sign-off ("The 346th day of captivity for the American hostages ...").

After attacking violence (even the verbs are tricky on this one), the nonprofits, the media and the government should move on to teen pregnancy, the root of so many other social pathologies. Then: stop. Or public service media campaigns, tremendously valuable if tightly focused, will expand to the whole litany of social causes and become a real joke, instead of just an easy one.

In the Time of the Tabs

*In the mid-1990s it looked for a time as if the
preoccupations of Americans were "beneath history."
I was hardly the only one who knew it wouldn't last.*

D URING WORLD WAR II, General Dwight D. Eisenhower, a
married man, "fraternized" with Kay Summersby, his army
driver. As the rumors spread widely, Ike, who had a few other things on
his mind, stonewalled, leaving even his friends to wonder about the
particulars. Today they would have their fill of the story and then some,
courtesy of *Extra*, or perhaps the *New York Times*. He lied! Book
Mamie! All that camera equipment would sink the D-Day landing
crafts. A half-century later, with Ike cashiered, the good people of
Minot, North Dakota, could be gossiping about Air Force Lieutenant
Kelly Flinn in German.

No wars? No news? No problem. We still have invasions today.
Of media hordes, tracking Tiger Woods's endorsements. We still have a
military. Its primary purpose in the 1990s seems to be to serve as a theater of war between the sexes. Strategy is what gets executed in court
and on TV. Espionage is the *Globe* supermarket tabloid setting up
Frank Gifford at a New York hotel. The front is a Marv Albert press
conference.

"People know that it is a small time," writes George W.S. Trow in
Within the Context of No Context, a short 1980 book republished this
year. "They assume that the small things they hear discussed are gossip
because they feel, correctly, that the things they hear and want to hear
and insist on hearing are beneath history."

Are we all beneath history, entertaining ourselves into a stupor?
Scandal-mongering is ancient. Men (and increasingly women) have
always thought too often with a part of their anatomy that is not their
brain. And the people around them have always loved to gossip about

human frailty, no matter how important the other events of the day. It makes life fun.

But the gulf between what intrigues us and what directly affects us is widening. Last week, for instance, the country had a choice: chatter about what Marv Albert and some woman might have done to each other in a Virginia hotel room—or about what President Clinton and Trent Lott did do to millions of uninsured American children across the river in Washington, D.C.* It was no contest. For now, anyway, Americans are fat, sassy and always hungry for more cheese.

Juicy stories can have fiber. Kelly Flinn's court-martial for having an affair with a married man may be more significant than— blast from the past— Joey Buttafuoco's. But we do have an Importance Gap, and it's worsened by the communication revolution. The "data smog," as author David Shenk calls our wired lives, wafts in on the same cable, modem, screen. Media blur: EddieMurphytransvestiteRussialoosenukes. When news oozes 24 hours a day it's not really news anymore. The TV becomes ambient noise. The newspaper becomes wallpaper. Finding the patterns of importance becomes hard. It's easier—and more profitable—just to make the consumer gape. Young men and women who went into journalism hoping to be Woodward and Bernstein find themselves ersatz Walter Winchells writing for an audience of ersatz rat packers.

To extend the shelf life of mainstream gossip, inquiring minds—from newsrooms to chat rooms—take refuge in debating "the rules," formal or informal. Last week alone we thrashed over how they applied in cases as diverse as adultery in the military, the New York Knicks' bench-clearing, and whether a girl who didn't want to wear a cup should be allowed to play catcher in Little League. The worst rule to break is the informal one against hypocrisy. The cackle, the frisson, the journalism lucre all come from exposing it. The message to celebrities is clear: if you say one thing and do another, prepare to be devoured. Kathie Lee Gifford promotes her family on her dopey show? Drop an H-bomb on her when her marriage breaks up. She and Frank and Cody and Cassidy asked for it.

So now we can all get our jollies following the story of the bite marks found on the back of the woman described as Marv Albert's friend. Can any story possibly compete with the vigorous denials and soon-to-come teeth molds of the man handling the NBA play-by-play?

*They failed to come to agreement on what later became S-CHIP.

The answer, of course, is Yesssss!! Michael Kennedy was rescued by Eddie Murphy, who was rescued by Frank Gifford (Michael Kennedy's father-in-law), who was rescued by Marv Albert. Celebrities in trouble can usually do nothing but pray for other celebrities to step in it, which doesn't take long.

Here things get trickier. Noncelebrities in trouble are well advised to try to become celebrities, as Kelly Flinn did with the help of her spinmeister lawyer, Franklin Spinner. Even *60 Minutes* is easier than a military tribunal. On the other hand, noncelebrities who aren't in trouble but become celebrities usually fall into trouble as a result. The man who rescued that baby from the well in Texas, one of the biggest news stories of the 1980s, later committed suicide.

In Chechnya not long ago, Lee Hockstader of the *Washington Post* found himself in a ditch with rifles pointed in his belly. Fearing for his life, he lied to his captors that he once interviewed Sylvester Stallone. "You really know Sly?" they asked with wonder, releasing him. His life saved, the reporter went back to filing the kind of foreign dispatches that too many people aren't reading. Should have filed on Sly—he'd have gotten better play.

The Uncertainty Principle

—— 2003 ——

I have a weakness for comparing the media to physics. After using a dim understanding of chaos theory in 1993, I moved on to Heisenberg in 2003, the week that Saddam Hussein was apprehended and Howard Dean seemed to be riding high. In later years, I should have been smarter about observing "The Law of Premature Predictions."

"**G**AME OVER," an Iraqi on the streets of Baghdad told CNN. Maybe. More likely, the game is just beginning, and not only on the ground in Iraq. The American presidential campaign, connected at the hip this year to foreign policy, will now move in a different direction. Toward a Bush landslide? Not so fast.

The biggest fallacy in forecasting of any kind is to take current conditions and extrapolate forward as if those conditions won't change. President Bush could still be vulnerable politically. Same for Howard Dean in the primaries, regardless of how positive the news climate may be for both of them right now. Even with good odds, the shoo-in doesn't fit.

That's because the media-political universe adheres to two strange laws simultaneously. The first is the Law of Premature Predictions. It's a dinner party or chat-room thing. "Stick a fork in him" sounds confident and smart. "Who knows?" sounds boring and lame. So people look at the latest news—Saddam captured, Al Gore endorses Dean—and ignore other inconvenient variables.

Then there's the Law of Media Oscillation. The process invites—no, demands—a series of sine curves to keep everyone interested. Up one week, down the next. The only safe prediction is that a static, unchanging political narrative is impossible. As we're seeing, stuff happens in war and politics, and when it doesn't, the media will half-consciously rearrange all the atoms of emphasis and particles of story choice to make it seem so.

Think of Werner Heisenberg's theory of physics, the Uncertainty Principle: "The more precisely the position is determined, the less precisely the momentum is known." In other words, the more we handicap, the more handicapped we are.

From here on, beating the ever-changing expectations spread gets tricky, abroad and at home. Bush must now show rapid progress toward security and democracy in Iraq, or end up worse off than he was before Saddam was apprehended. For all the value of the Gore endorsement in making Dean more credible with African-Americans and other core constituencies, the governor may be at his moment of maximum peril. The usual Democratic buyers' remorse (which hobbles every presumptive nominee in early summer) could set in early this time, as harsh antiwar declarations lose their appeal.

The only certainty of American politics is that its quantum physics will continue to confound us.

Behind the Obama "Madrassa" Hoax

—— 2007 ——

From the start of his campaign in early 2007,
Obama was dogged with bogus rumors. The way they were handled
offers clues about the impact of media bias and the Internet.

W HAT WILL the first full week of Campaign '08 be remembered for? That Barack Obama was under attack for his behavior as a 6-year-old. It's worth revisiting the Madrassa Hoax story for what it tells us about our warp-speed politics.

The subtext of the story was that Obama was some kind of Muslim Manchurian Candidate (or the Russian spy played by Kevin Costner in *No Way Out*)—trained in an Indonesian religious school to be a jihadist who would do Al Qaeda's work from within. Under the old media order, the whole thing would have made for a nice joke amid the somber mood surrounding President Bush's State of the Union address. But this is a different time, when every campaign lives in fear of being Swift-Boated. Even after the story was debunked, the folks at Fox News Channel wouldn't apologize, and in one case kept pushing a line on the air they knew was false.

The pathetic little saga begins on the Web site of *Insight Magazine*, a scandal sheet connected to the Reverend Sun Myung Moon's *Washington Times*. On January 17, *Insight* reported that "Hillary Rodham Clinton's camp" had conducted a background check that found Obama attended a madrassa (religious seminary) when he moved with his mother and stepfather to Jakarta in the late 1960s. The idea, according to *Insight*, was to show that Obama was deceptive about his "Muslim past." Clinton spokesman Howard Wolfson says flatly: "They made it up."

True or not, this bit of grade-school innuendo proved irresistible to Steve Doocy, know-it-all host of *Fox and Friends*, Roger Ailes's idea for a right-wing morning chat show. Doocy garbled the story into a reference to Obama "spending the first decade of his life raised by a Muslim father." After John Gibson of Fox repeated this yarn, which managed to slime two campaigns simultaneously, CNN dispatched a reporter to Obama's old school in Jakarta, where he revealed it to be a normal public school with religion classes only once a week and no indication of Wahhabism, the Saudi-inspired extremist philosophy. (Indonesian schools were even more secular 40 years ago than they are today.) The whole underlying tale was untrue.

But neither this solid reporting—later backed up by ABC News— nor a categorical statement from the Obama campaign that he "has never been a Muslim, was not raised a Muslim and is a committed Christian who attends the United Church of Christ in Chicago," killed the story. Fox was "unwilling to stop when they knew they were wrong or correct what they knew was a lie," says Robert Gibbs, Obama's communications director. Executives at the network claimed that their on-air "clarification" was enough, but Fox's own people didn't get the message. Gibson—once a respected correspondent and host—went on the radio to malign the CNN reporter, John Vause. He "probably went to the very [same] madrassa" as Obama, Gibson said.

On one level, the story ended up being a net positive for Obama. His supporters were glad he fought back hard, and the emphasis on his church attendance (he committed to Christ in his 20s) may help soften the concern about his troublesome middle name, "Hussein"—a family name given him by his atheist father, a Kenyan academic whom Obama met only once in his life. Even though Fox wouldn't apologize, at least the falsity of the story was not in doubt. The problem for the Obama team is that other such stories might not lend themselves as readily to being shot down. Without being black and white, they fester in gray. And where Hillary Clinton's vulnerabilities are all a decade or so old, Obama's are new. He's so green he deserves—and will receive—more scrutiny than politicians who've been around for a while. So even when the charges are false, they are imbued with a patina of "news" that will not apply to Hillary stories about Rose Law Firm billing records or cattle futures. Generally speaking, being fresh is an advantage in politics. But it makes any critical story fresh, too, when stale might be easier to squelch.

Political operatives on all sides are worried about the new rules governing their world. "We used to whine about round-the-clock cable in '96—that's child's play now," says Harold Ickes, a longtime Clinton aide getting ready to help Hillary. "The lesson of Swift Boat [the 2004 efforts to throw mud on John Kerry over his Vietnam service on a river craft] is you cannot let this stuff circulate unanswered." The implications for opposition research are only now coming into view. "If they [bloggers] can finger you trying to drop poison into the well, you'll be hurt by it," Ickes adds. "Stuff moves out so quickly that campaigns have to exercise much more control over their negative information apparatus." This could be good. When "oppo" goes transparent, it might shrivel, if it doesn't get "Doocy'd" first.

PART SIX

PEOPLE

Hillary and Rudy

—— 2007 ——

This article ran in late 2007 when both Clinton and Giuliani were still riding high in the polls.

W HAT IS IT with New York presidential candidates and the fake laugh? When Hillary Clinton unveiled her health care plan over the summer and went on television to answer probing questions about it, she began giggling, often uncontrollably, whenever the interviewer asked about critics who called the plan "socialized medicine." You knew she really thought it was about as funny as kidney stones.

Then, on Sunday, when Rudy Giuliani, who has dodged nearly every interview request (even one from the conservative bible, the *National Review*), finally relented and appeared on *Meet the Press*, he answered questions about his mistress and his poor judgment as if he had just inhaled laughing gas. Of course, it was obvious once he bared those fangs that Giuliani would have bitten Tim Russert on the neck and sucked every drop of blood from his body if he had the chance.

If a Bronx cheer is really a boo, maybe a Bronx laugh is really a glare.

This wasn't always the case with Empire State empire builders. Theodore Roosevelt played the blustery fool sometimes, but no one ever called him a phony. His fifth cousin Franklin wasn't always on the level; his laugh, like so much else, was a weapon of manipulation. But it sure made you feel better, "as joyous, hearty, rolling, thunderous laughter as ever was heard on this sorrowful globe," was the way the writer Fulton Oursler put it.

Nelson Rockefeller's gruff humor seemed genuine enough (though his wife Happy's happiness could be a bit forced). Mario Cuomo would sometimes smile to get himself over a rough patch, but his mirth gauge seemed in working order. I can still hear Pat Moynihan's fabulous

"Ha!" For all his blarney, humor resided in a zone of sincerity he could not bring himself to breach for political convenience.

Some non–New York presidents have been no slouches in the phony humor department. Jimmy Carter's famous toothy grin masked an essentially humorless man. Ronald Reagan's devastating "There you go again" jab at Carter in a 1980 debate was delivered with a rueful smile that was all craft. And George W. Bush's nervous "heh, heh, heh" is a sure sign he'd rather be somewhere else.

But Hillary and Rudy are in a fake-laugh league of their own.

Let's give her the benefit of the doubt and assume Clinton thought the "socialized medicine" question was funny because it was so predictable. But how about her tittering answers to the exact same question from Bob Schieffer, Harry Smith, Diane Sawyer and others? Was the question genuinely funny to her the sixth time it was asked? When she got YouTubed on it, her aides canned the laugh overnight.

By Chris Matthews's count, Giuliani laughed 15 times during his *Meet the Press* appearance, one of the great TV grillings of all time (e.g., Russert: "Would it be appropriate for a president to provide Secret Service protection to his mistress?"). Because certifiable phoniness is apparently preferable to looking wounded or overly defensive, we can expect to see Rudy circling the laugh track anytime anyone goes after him. It reminds me of the caption *Esquire* routinely used under a picture of a smiling Richard Nixon (the "new Nixon") when he ran in 1968: "Why is this man laughing?"

So we'd better get used to that google-eyed chuckle when reporters bring up his hostile attitude toward dissent in New York; his placing of the emergency command center in the World Trade Center after it had already been bombed in 1993; his use of on-duty police officers to take his mistress shopping and walk her dog; his attempted unconstitutional power grab when his term ended; his recommendation that Bernie Kerik, who was associated with people who themselves had suspected mob links, protect the nation from terrorism; his still-undisclosed profiteering off of 9/11; and whatever else might be relevant to predicting the temperament he would bring to the laugh riot that would be his presidency.

One of the questions that the 2008 handlers in both parties will likely discuss when they all get together is whether laughing works. Should it go into the damage-control toolbox with spin and counterattack?

Right now, the answer looks like no. Clinton actually has a nice sense of humor in private, but her fake laugh just reinforces the rap that she's inauthentic. Giuliani can also be funny with friends (especially if you like your humor with a nasty streak), but he's not a good enough actor to yuk his way through the muck.

John McCain

—— 2000 ——

*I spent the evening at John McCain's ranch in 2000 and
filed this column. In 2008, he's a different, less principled candidate.*

JOHN MCCAIN missed the 1960s. His captivity in Hanoi covered
the exact period—1967 to 1973—that we think of as that era. He's
a fun-loving '50s guy whose recreation consists mostly of hiking,
watching football and barbecuing. When he took a day off to recharge
at his cabin in the mountains near Sedona, Arizona, McCain spent most
of his waking hours cooking for guests. On the porch sit no fewer than
four "Turbo" gas grills. "You know where they put in that putting
green [at the White House]?" he asks. "I'd put in grills." His specialty
is spicy chicken, which he patiently grills for an hour and a half over
low heat without turning it, so as to "cook everything bad out of it—a
purifying thing."

For now, anyway, McCain embodies a familiar purification
ritual in American life. Great suffering can ennoble, especially if the
survivor emerges with his sense of humor. Reform crusades are about
cleaning the system of its toxins. As George W. Bush is learning, this
flame burns at a level beyond politics. A Democrat who agrees with
McCain on few issues stood up at one of his town hall meetings last
week at Sacramento State University and said she was ashamed to tell
her young son about the current president of the United States. She
asked if the boy could come forward and shake a hero's hand, which
he did. Just another McCain moment.

In South Carolina Bush winked at the bucket of sludge
right-wingers dumped on McCain's head and, after winning, said
once again he was "proud" of his opponent. Then, having lost
Michigan, Bush forgot his Andover manners and failed to call
McCain on primary night with congratulations, a standard political

courtesy McCain had extended to Bush after he lost South Carolina.

Even at his remote ranch, McCain has a taste for campaign combat—and little interest in solitude. "He's been alone enough. He doesn't need that," says his closest aide and coauthor, Mark Salter, referring to the two years his boss spent in solitary confinement. But McCain might do well to talk a little less and think a little more about what he would actually do with the presidency.

In his stump speech the candidate jokes that his wife says the only reason he's running is "that I received several sharp blows to the head while in prison." This is a good example of how McCain combines self-deprecation and the POW experience with a jab at the critics who challenge his mental fitness. His real, JFK-style reason for running—"to inspire a generation of young Americans to commit themselves to causes greater than their own self-interest"—is itself inspirational but still lacks a coherent second sentence. Any plans for expanding AmeriCorps (a program he once opposed but now embraces) remain unformulated, perhaps because the idea is too connected to Bill Clinton. Will he be commander in chief of an all-volunteer domestic Army that feeds the hungry, reads to the elderly and works with mental patients? He drops hints that he wants that kind of country, cautions that participants "can't be motivated by money" and—like so much of his other domestic policy—leaves the rest for later.

McCain's critics, on the left and right, say that as president he'd take us for a ride. In a sense, they're right. "I'm a romanticist and an adventurer," he said last week in answer to a voter's question about exploring Mars. He'd confront Congress and lose often (almost certainly more often than would Bush). Stylistically, McCain's presidency would be neo-Rough Rider: big-stick diplomacy, some class-bashing at home ("I don't think Bill Gates needs a tax cut right now," he says), a larger-than-life mix of bruised honor and bully-pulpit pounding. More risks; more potential rewards.

Sometimes Uncle Fun gets a little carried away. "I'm Luke Skywalker getting out of the Death Star!" he exults, giving the lie to his claim to be "the only grown-up" in the race. At a rally of several thousand in the rain in Bremerton, Washington, he got tangled up in his enthusiasm and told the crowd: "Get out and vote for me on Tuesday, and I promise you, you'll be happy." That's quite a pledge, and a perfect recipe for letdown later. But in this season of comfort, like John McCain's spicy chicken, it tastes plenty good.

Daniel Patrick Moynihan

—— 2003 ——

Knowing Pat Moynihan was a great pleasure.
I wrote this when he died.

T HE VOICE was a dandified stutter-step of mumbled allusion and exaggerated enunciation. Yet if you listened hard enough, the erudite policy references and blustery historical detours cohered into a twinkly and often brilliant flash of insight. Like the finest professors and provocateurs, Pat Moynihan consistently frustrated the foolishly consistent. In midlife this made him a magnet for predictable resentments. But when he died last week, from an infection after his appendix burst, Moynihan was revered across party lines as a statesman in the mold of the Founders. Ideas have consequences, and this man of ideas was one of the most consequential figures of American public life.

Before his 24 years representing New York in the Senate, Moynihan had several other storied careers. He was raised from infancy in New York City, the son of a hard-drinking former newspaperman who abandoned his family when Pat was 10. His mother ran a saloon in Hell's Kitchen, and young Moynihan shined shoes in nearby Times Square, enlisted in the Navy and graduated from Tufts. At 28 he was a top aide to Governor W. Averell Harriman in Albany, where he met and married Liz Brennan, without whose canny supervision his later political career would have been impossible. By 1963 he was breaking through as a public personality, remarking after the Kennedy assassination: "I don't think there's any point in being Irish if you don't know the world is going to break your heart eventually."

From the start, Moynihan understood how to create sparks at the intersection of academia (he taught intermittently at Harvard) and policymaking (he served four presidents, from JFK to Gerald Ford). He championed auto safety years before Ralph Nader, and his first of 18 books, *Beyond the Melting Pot* (with Nathan Glazer), challenged the shibboleth that ethnicity was fading in America. At the Labor Department in 1965, he was savaged by liberals for breaking a taboo and presciently pointing out the growing crisis of single-parent black families. Later the critics pounced even harder when he used the term "benign neglect" in a memo to President Nixon on urban problems. Moynihan wasn't arguing for neglect of blacks; he just wanted a pause in the superheated racial rhetoric of the day. In fact, the failed plan he was hatching for Nixon called for a guaranteed annual income for the poor that looks extremely liberal by today's standards.

By then Moynihan was increasingly identified as a neoconservative Democrat, especially on cold-war foreign policy. After serving as U.S. ambassador to India he took his tart tongue to the United Nations, where he denounced the U.N.'s notorious resolution equating Zionism with racism. Among Moynihan's proudest moments was that he was the first leader to predict the demise of the Soviet Union, writing in a *Newsweek* article in 1979 that the U.S.S.R. was coming under economic and ethnic strain neglected by analysts.

Until the end of the century, Moynihan was ensconced in the Senate, where his milestones included protecting Social Security and teaching hospitals. He moved left, calling for huge cuts in the defense budget, more respect for international law and limits on government secrecy. Despite his early work on welfare dependency, he opposed President Clinton's 1996 welfare reform and predicted—wrongly, so far—that it would have disastrous consequences.

But legislative victories are a small gauge of his influence. For nearly 50 years Moynihan's fingerprints were on every significant social policy—and the critique of that policy. He wrote more books, George F. Will remarked, than most senators have ever read. And he looked deeper. "The central conservative truth is that it is culture, not politics, that determines the success of a society," he wrote. "The central liberal truth is that politics can change a culture and save it from itself."

In 2000 Moynihan retired and backed Hillary Clinton for his seat. Had he been a British political intellectual, like Disraeli or Churchill, he might have run the country. But Moynihan was more monumental than most presidents. So it's fitting that New York's Pennsylvania Station, slated to move in 2008 into a beautiful old post office across the street (thanks to the senator's efforts), will be known as Moynihan Station. Perhaps someday a few commuters there will pause, look up for a moment, and, in the finest homage, think.

Ross Perot

*Ross Perot called me out of the blue in 2008
to dump on John McCain, who had once called him "nuttier
than a fruitcake." I wrote about that, but have instead included
this article from 1992, when Perot received an astonishing
19 percent of the vote for president as a third-party candidate.*

Ross Perot is not an actor, but he plays one on TV. He is essentially the same man he was before his strange campaign was born; his Chihuahua persona is so original that he's ridiculously easy to parody. But for reasons that even Marshall McLuhan didn't anticipate, the camera—and the country—keep casting him in a series of different roles. While Perot is famous as a control freak, he cannot usually control whose character the medium will make him inhabit, which makes predicting his television performance this month impossible. So far this year, he's played more parts than Dana Carvey:

Cincinnatus: In his April role, Perot re-created the appealing legend of the Roman general who reluctantly left his private labors when his country called. The billionaire seemed remarkably unselfish. He played hard-to-get in a medium where everyone's selling something. The fact that he was actually easy to get—a publicity hound who loves the talk-show circuit—didn't register.

Harry Truman: Unlike George Bush and Bill Clinton, Perot seemed to fit into the clothes from Truman's haberdashery. He spoke refreshingly plain language, free of the endless weasel words that cause so much distrust of politicians. Even if the deficit couldn't be fixed without breaking a sweat, as he claimed, the no-nonsense spirit shone through.

George Washington: By May, Perot was leading in polls, and serious people actually embraced the idea of electing the first president since Washington who belonged to no party. His riffs on the Founding Fathers, the pioneers and *The Sound of Music* ("Climb every mountain, ford every stream" was a favorite) made him seem the inspirational commander of a new American revolution. In Perot Land, politics would be shed of "politics" and the president would be elected without campaigning.

Hercule Poirot: There's absolutely nothing European about Perot, but beset by stories about his penchant to investigate people, he began to resemble the fictional detective. It was later charged that he even spied on his daughter's boyfriend because he was Jewish. He was so security-obsessed that he hired his own bodyguards because he thought the Secret Service would snoop on him for Bush and the CIA.

Joe Isuzu: The press eventually began to learn that straight talk also meant straight lies. He said, "I don't dig into people's private lives. I never have." (There are any number of cases.) He said reports of a company policy against beards were a "goofy ... myth." (A written policy existed.) He said he'd "never once" lobbied the mayor of Fort Worth on a family project. (Plenty of evidence proved otherwise.) Every day brought a new example. By the time Perot claimed he was getting out because he thought he would throw the election into the House of Representatives, he sounded like just another car salesman.

The Wizard of Oz: Once he withdrew, it was as if Toto had pulled back the curtain to reveal a silly little man, fruitlessly spinning dials and blowing smoke. And Perot's efforts to continue his petition drive looked a bit like the Wizard's efforts to get back to Kansas by balloon; with the spell of his power broken, the excursion was folly.

Gypsy Ross Lee: The September tease—was he in or out?—would have made a stripper blush. Democratic and Republican officials showed up in Dallas to catch the garters—bit parts in his burlesque. The press knew it was being conned into reporting that his decision was "up to the volunteers" but let the charade continue anyway because it made good copy.

Perot's next media incarnation is no more predictable than the last. He could come across as a Donald Trumpesque egomaniac, diverting but annoying. Or a chicken-fried Cassandra, confronting the economic future the other candidates ignore.

The risk for Perot is that the medium that created him may now trivialize him. But in any role, hero or villain, Perot breaks through. And on TV, how politicians play (who sounds good, looks honest, seems presidential) is usually more decisive than what they say. The only sure outcome on television is that impression triumphs over content. Whether Perot cheapens or deepens the drama depends on which of his characters show up—and which ones the audience wants to see.

Garry Trudeau

—— 1991 ——

In 1990, the great cartoonist Garry Trudeau was celebrating his 20th anniversary drawing Doonesbury. *Unable to grant interviews to all of the thousands of newspapers that run his strip, he gave me an exclusive—one of only two profiles he has agreed to since 1971.*

T HE SHOWER HELPS. Two or three ideas always strike as the nozzle in his Central Park West apartment pelts him on deadline day. He's been up late the night before, shoes off, writing and erasing, drawing and erasing. "I don't laugh when I'm writing. I don't even smile. It's very serious," Garry Trudeau says. The weekly crunch is coming, and those little synapses of inspiration had better be crackling. After breakfast, he drops his children off at school and strolls down Columbus Avenue to an ordinary studio apartment he keeps, where the real work gets done. "I create lives for everyone I pass on the street: 'That guy looks like a fool. This guy is unbelievably aware of how he is presenting himself'." He laughs, not cruelly, but with the sense that the human comedy is his to enjoy.

For weeks, Trudeau's mind has been somewhere in Saudi Arabia. "I've got characters stacked up, buzzing around, waiting to land," he says happily. Mike Doonesbury is designing an ad campaign for the greedy oil executive Jim Andrews, who is lovingly named after the late syndicator who discovered him at Yale (one of many in-jokes). ABC's Roland Burton Hedley Jr., who wears "epaulettes in his underwear," is lost and thirsty in the desert. "I thought, 'What could I do about the U.N.?' Then I remembered I had a character I'd completely forgotten. So you'll be seeing Phred [a former Viet Cong guerrilla turned diplomat] back in the strip." B.D., the character who launched his career, was dispatched to Saudi Arabia as an Army reservist, but not before having his famous football helmet surgically removed. "They freeze it and cut it away like an avocado. Strictly outpatient," B.D. explains, a procedure that his creator, the descendant of roughly eight generations of doctors, has been performing on squirming subjects since he was 20 years old.

Garry Trudeau is the premier American political and social satirist of his time. Of course this is exactly the sort of hype that he'd normally vaporize in a few short pencil strokes. But because it's about him, he's under no obligation to try. As he celebrates the 20th anniversary of the syndication of *Doonesbury* this month, Trudeau can be excused for agreeing to break his silence and take a single bow. By any reasonable expectation, his strip, which began as a riff on college life in the 1960s, should be as stale as a hash brownie. Instead, it's as funny and popular as ever, and better drawn.

In an age when every $3 bottle of perfume calls itself original, Trudeau has some genuine claim on the word. Jonathan Swift, Thomas Nast, Walt Kelly (whose *Pogo* strips he collects)—none of these comparisons work quite right. He is as much journalist as artist—an investigative cartoonist. Zeitgeist megaphone, flight attendant for his generation ... This is beginning to sound like a bad imitation of one of his baby-boomer strips. Editors long ago gave up trying to figure out where *Doonesbury* belongs in the paper. (About a quarter opt for the editorial page rather than the funnies.) Suffice it to say that Donald Trump doesn't "get" him, which makes it almost axiomatic that millions of others do.

This year has found Trudeau still stretching the form. His perfect-pitch series about a character dying of AIDS—risky business on the comics page—drew scores of letters from grateful patients, "the most moving I've ever received." The strips were written after three years of mulling the subject, but—astonishingly—without his personally knowing anyone with the disease.

Trudeau has savaged every American president since Richard Nixon, but he has a particular zest for George Bush. From the time during the 1984 campaign when he first placed the vice president's "manhood in a blind trust," Trudeau has all but owned Bush, even if his face never appears in the strip. His fine contempt for this president—partially rooted in their common prep school and privileged heritage—tends to embarrass the cartoonist's adoring mother, who moves in the same social circles as the Bush family. "That [blind trust] strip upset me. I said, 'Stay off Barbara and don't touch the children,'" recalls Jean Amory. Her son complied, until Neil Bush ran into trouble.

Unlike his thicker-skinned predecessors, Bush has admitted he has a history of going "ballistic" on the subject of Trudeau. ("He speaks for a bunch of Brie-tasting, Chardonnay-sipping elitists," he said in 1988.)

While he has tried to act more presidential lately, Bush still says privately that Trudeau and George Will, who compared him to a lap dog, are the only critics he will never forgive. Memorandum for the president: if you really want to insult Trudeau, try the word cynical. It makes the cartoonist wince. Even humor is too value-free for him as a description of what he does. Trudeau prefers the term satire.

Satire isn't about jokes: "I can't write a joke to save my ass," Trudeau says. And it certainly isn't about being fair: "Criticizing a political satirist for being unfair is like criticizing a nose guard for being physical." It's about, well, idealism. "It's propelled by a sense of moral indignation, which you hope doesn't slip into malice when you're executing. The critical difference is that you're not only against something, you're for something. It springs out of a sense of hope. The day I start writing from a scorched-earth viewpoint is the day I don't think I can justify my presence in the business."

Here he hesitates, and the sweet earnestness no longer seems quite so paradoxical. "I mean, I'm really one of the last people who still believe in the perfectibility of man."

Could this be the same Garry Trudeau who knows no mercy when it comes to the powerful, who makes Barbara Bush feel as if she has to take a swim after she reads him? Yes. "This is a guy who tries every day to do good things and be a good person," says writer Nicholas von Hoffman, an early Trudeau mentor. "Every so often I think of him and say to myself, 'You've got to try harder.'" "The thing that people don't understand about Garry," says David Stanford, his sometime assistant, "is that he's a patriot in the truest sense."

The question that arises is: what's wrong with this picture? The answer is: not much, frustrating as that might be to a reporter committed to finding the monster in anyone. Administering that deeply deserved taste of his own medicine isn't easy. One ex-roommate was reduced to making up faults: "Did he tell you about the embezzlement charges? How about the paternity suit?" Another friend remembers that after careful thought, the Trudeaus decided the kids should address their parents' adult friends as "Mr."—but the elevator operator remained on a first-name basis. Pretty slim pickings. When pressed for his faults, Trudeau admits he can be "obstinate." "I look out for my interests in an argument and I'm stubborn about conceding the other side."

Even that doesn't really hold up. The truth is that his quickness and gentle laugh make him almost as good a conversationalist as he is a cartoonist. Perhaps because he spends so much time working alone, the man is a talker. Sprawled across a chair in his cluttered home office, gabbing in a low-rent Chinese restaurant or trendy bistro, he talks in a cushioned, almost small-town voice completely devoid of world-weariness. "There are certain moral values and qualities that I aspire to in my life, and my faults lie in falling short of them," he says finally. And he means it. If he weren't a WASP, you'd call him a mensch.

This year, anyway, Trudeau is more likely to describe himself as "Joan of Arc's spouse." After 10 years of marriage, he and Jane Pauley woke up one day to find that she had become a pop-culture icon, a notion that seems to alarm her more than him. NBC's mishandling of her role on the *Today* show heightens some of the contradictions of her husband's job. "There's no way I wouldn't have written [in the strip] about *Today*. It had a formal Kabukilike quality, a nice symmetry, that would have been natural for me," he says.

With the exception of occasional speeches, plus a few interviews in the mid-1980s to promote one of his musicals, Trudeau has not talked on the record to the press in 17 years. He has not appeared on TV since *To Tell the Truth* in 1971 and plans to keep it that way, his wife's efforts to book him for her new show notwithstanding. Over the years Trudeau leaked a few scripted lines to explain it. "I've been trying to develop a lifestyle that doesn't require my presence," he'd say. Or: "This is the only country where failure to promote yourself is widely considered arrogant."

His real reasons are more prosaic, and closer to home. At first he complied with the requests of hundreds of client newspapers, each of which felt entitled to his time whenever some controversy broke. "But there was this process of reinventing yourself over and over again for public consumption that I found exhausting," he now says. He also "began to get the sense that I was getting in the way, that it was easier for me to speak more directly to readers if there wasn't the static of me coming at them as a public personality. I think what's terribly important is reputation as distinct from fame." Besides, he says with a laugh, wondering aloud why he consented this time, "one public figure in the family is quite enough."

His wife, facing the potential of hypocrisy, is unable to hide out: "I can't say, 'I don't stoop to interviews; by the way, will you be on my show?'" she says. But the two go to considerable pains to keep their family life (twins Rachel and Ross, and Tommy) genuinely private. He's also bashful about describing the half-day each week he volunteers his time at a Manhattan homeless shelter: "I take ribbing inside the family for polishing my halo."

Jane's canonization is always good for a few laughs around the house. "Such is the power of 'The Loved One,' as we call her," Garry jokes, referring to the title of a particularly fawning magazine cover story on her. Stuck to their refrigerator door is another cover, sent by Tom Brokaw. It's a *Ladies' Home Journal* image of Pauley with all of the headlines clipped away except: MY HUSBAND KEEPS CALLING THOSE SEX HOTLINES.

When it comes to his family, Garry is boyishly effusive. But the value of publicizing anything beyond the work still escapes him: "I would have been more comfortable being a 19th-century famous person, at a time when a president of the United States could walk down the street without being recognized ... Nobody cared 200 years ago what Thomas Jefferson's living room looked like or whether he was kind to his children or whether he worked late."

Garretson Beekman Trudeau is not the first caricaturist in his family. Back in the mid-19th century his great-great-grandfather Dr. James Trudeau was driven out of New York for creating statuette caricatures of medical faculty. He lit out for the territories with the naturalist painter John Jay Audubon, eventually living for a time with Osage Indians. "That's where Garry got his genes, and he looks just like him," says his father Francis. Near the turn of the century, Trudeau's great-grandfather Dr. Edward Trudeau contracted tuberculosis and moved to Saranac Lake, New York, to die. For some reason the fresh air made him feel better, and the sanitarium "rest cure"—the first known treatment of TB—was born. (Today's Trudeau Institute continues to do biomedical research, and Garry serves on the board.) Another ancestor, who gave his name to New York's Beekman Place, set up a trust to educate all of his descendants. On his mother's side, Trudeau is descended from a treasurer of the United States under Lincoln and one of Thomas Watson Sr.'s original colleagues in the founding of IBM.

Growing up in rural Saranac Lake, Trudeau avoided the life of a pampered rich kid. From the start he possessed unusual powers of concentration; as a toddler he could pound pegs into holes for a half hour without looking up. Theater, more than drawing, was his passion. At the age of 7 he arranged plays in the basement that went far beyond those produced by most children, complete with tickets, scripts and programs. The Acting Corporation, as he called it, stayed in business until he was 17. Michelle Trudeau, now a reporter for National Public

Radio, recalls that her brother's projects "were complete in every detail—there was a fullness to them. He could actualize whatever was in his imagination."

When he was 12, already dispatched to Harvey, a pre-prep school outside New York, his parents divorced with no warning. "He came into the room and said, 'What is it?'"his mother recalls. "I told him and said, 'You children are more important to me than anything.' And he looked at me and said, 'If you love me so much, why are you doing this?'" His parents, to whom Garry remains close, both say that he took the divorce harder than his two sisters did. That year Trudeau developed an ulcer, rare in teenagers. Like so much else in his life, though, it turned out well in the end. The condition went undiagnosed until 10 years later, when, bearing a low lottery number, he reluctantly submitted to an induction exam for the Vietnam War. "Little did I know it would turn out to be my salvation," Trudeau laughs.

Trudeau was so unhappy at St. Paul's, an elite boarding school, that he later declined invitations to speak there. "I was not the class clown. In fact, I was pretty shy. One of the reasons that adolescence was such a tortured time for me was that I was the second or third smallest in my class," Trudeau says. (He's now of average height.) One art teacher luckily saw his talent and encouraged it. Toward the end of prep school, he finally began to earn some popularity by drawing his first cartoon character, "Weenie Man," on a poster selling hot dogs for football games.

Until then, prep school epithets like "weenie," "zero" and "doone" (which Trudeau defines as a "well-meaning fool") were routinely tossed his way. Pigeon-toed at the time, he wasn't much of a jock. And if you weren't a jock at St. Paul's, you were nothing. "People say, 'Why does he have it in for Bush?' I'm sure he extrapolates part of it from boys he didn't like at St. Paul's," says his mother. (Bush was a popular jock at his own prep school and at Yale.) After all, Trudeau's main problem with the president is that he can identify no time when he had the courage to undertake something unpopular. "I would like somebody to point to an example of where [Bush] did something because he believed it, not because he thought it was the easiest way to go," he says.

Trudeau himself at first denies there's anything personal with Bush (the only public figure he will concede that about is Henry Kissinger, whom he still believes to be a "war criminal"). "I hate to sound like a low-level mafioso, but it's just business—you know?" he says of the president. This doesn't quite wash, and Trudeau eventually retreats.

"I've had a problem with authority ever since college that George Bush never did—both in terms of exercising it and being on the receiving end of it …. There may be some lingering antipathy, but I like to think that has simply melded into an understanding of what that culture breeds, for better or worse. I'm not striking back at someone who got me in the ninth grade." The antagonists are linked one other way: a friend says that Trudeau and Bush have the same "glass jaw" when attacked.

At Yale, where he coedited the humor magazine, his gifts first began to be appreciated. Almost all of his close friends today come from that period. Tapped by the secret society Skull and Bones, Trudeau chose membership in the rival Scroll and Key, which puts his Bonesman-bashing strips in a different context. This is exactly the kind of secret score-settling that so annoys members of the Bush family.

In September 1968, his junior year, Trudeau began drawing a cartoon for the *Yale Daily News* called "bull tales" that revolved mostly around the exploits of a character based on Yale's legendary quarterback, Brian Dowling, whom Trudeau only met once. (Dowling, now a sales VP, eventually used the character on his business card.) Within just one month, the strip caught the eye of syndicator Jim Andrews, who was searching the *Daily* for a column by theologian Malcolm Boyd. "UPS [Universal Press Syndicate] was essentially just a mail drop at the time, but I didn't know that," says Trudeau. It's now a powerhouse, "the syndicate that *Doonesbury* built," says UPS president John McMeel.

As he prepared to take the strip national Andrews suggested calling it "B.D." Instead, he and Trudeau settled on naming it after another character, loosely based on Charlie Pillsbury, a Trudeau room-mate, Minnesota flour-fortune heir (now a mediator of legal disputes) and, by his own admission, something of a "doone." Andrews got Trudeau to agree to clothe the naked coeds of "bull tales." But he also advised him in a 1969 letter that, "At this point, the strip would be better off as non-political." The college senior didn't take his advice.

Unlike Mike Doonesbury, America's first couch potato, Trudeau succeeded so fast that he never had to worry about selling out. He hedged his bets by attending Yale Art School for a master's degree, but from the time the strip debuted in 29 papers in October 1970, it was a hit. In the early years Trudeau sent an "inane questionnaire" to newspaper editors asking what subjects were appropriate for the strip. One editor wrote back, "It has nothing to do with subjects, it's how you execute it." The advice was simple, but it "opened up a world to me and I felt if you bring a certain amount of taste and judgment there's nothing that can't be addressed in comic strips."

While the characters are obviously hybrid works of imagination, there have been some clear inspirations. Hunter S. Thompson (who has never met Trudeau) still resents Uncle Duke, though the character's legend no doubt helps him book college lecture dates. While Trudeau claims Lacey Davenport was actually born before he knew of Representative Millicent Fenwick, the resemblance is clear. Less well known is that the cartoonist's first cousin left her husband and three children by the side of the road and went to live on her own. She inspired Joanie Caucus, "the closest correspondence between a character and a real person."

In the mid-1970s, a Pulitzer Prize in hand, Trudeau was still living in New Haven but dating people like Ronee Blakely (of the movie *Nashville*) and Candice Bergen. He says he slept too late to watch *Today* and wasn't much aware of Jane Pauley until being set up at a dinner party hosted by Brokaw and his wife. Brokaw, then Pauley's *Today* coanchor, remembers it differently. Sometime before the dinner, he says, "Garry came by the show where he couldn't stop staring—and it wasn't at me." On their first date, Jane—who wasn't a reader of the strip—had a cold, so Garry did all of the talking. He spoke affectionately about a recent fishing trip with his father, a choice of topics that impressed her.

Like everyone else in his life, Pauley has had almost no effect on the strip. She noticed before Trudeau himself that Mike and J.J.'s marriage was in trouble ("I told him he was setting up an unstable relationship"). But she says she has never seen material move from their personal life directly onto the comics page. Trudeau says he doesn't want "readers to feel I'm reporting on my own family, which is a violation [as well as] infinitely banal. The creators of [the TV show] *thirtysomething* and a lot of baby boomers think that nobody ever parented a child before they did, that they're the first ones to really tap into this miracle. That whole phenomenon is so repellent to me."

Trudeau prefers to work on his own terms, which hasn't always been easy. In 1983 he broke precedent in the cartooning business by taking a 21-month sabbatical. The experience eventually refreshed him creatively but it was not altogether pleasant. *Doonesbury*, the Broadway musical he wrote with Elizabeth Swados, received mixed reviews, which friends say he took hard. Hollywood has not been kind. Robert Redford and Jack Nicholson embraced him, but screenplays written over the years on campaign reporters and right-wing activists amounted to nothing. More recently, a TV sitcom pilot about white-collar criminals, called *Club Fed* also fizzled. "I found Garry a little innocent. He doesn't see this place for the snake pit it often is," says Jacob Epstein, his collaborator. Projects over which he has more control, like the rousing 1984 anti-Reagan musical revue, *Rap Master Ronnie* (produced partly with an NEA grant: "My dirty little secret!"), did far better; it ran for four years in different cities with Trudeau and Swados constantly adding new material.

He resumed the strip in 1984 to less than universal raves. In fact, *Doonesbury* was better than before the break, when the characters had been frozen in time for 12 years; now they could grow older and spread out. There had already been years of controversy, over Joanie Caucus and Rick Redfern sleeping together (1976), calling President Ford's son a "pothead" (1976), Tip O'Neill's and Jerry Brown's unsavory campaign contributions (1978, 1979), and much more. But now Trudeau turned up the heat even further. In 1986 Frank Sinatra threatened a lawsuit over a mob series and Trudeau's "Silent Scream" abortion strips became the only series his syndicate ever refused to distribute. (He happily had it printed in the *New Republic.*)

Unlike many of his readers, Trudeau bears no grudge against editors who occasionally refuse to run strips. "That's not censorship, it's editing. Each makes a daily judgment about community standards," he says, though he's puzzled by the absence of a pattern as to which papers drop him which weeks, and why. Most seem to be learning. In 1973, when radio host Mark Slackmeyer pronounced John Mitchell "Guilty! Guilty, Guilty, Guilty!!" of Watergate crimes before he was convicted, many papers dropped the series. In 1987 the same strip about Oliver North and John Poindexter raised barely a peep.

After his return, some editors thought Trudeau arrogant to insist that the strip run at a large size, or not at all. (The standard size had been uniformly reduced during his absence.) The cartoonist is proud that he convinced many newspapers they were harming the comics by shrinking them. Today, thanks to Trudeau's crusade, several other strips also run at the larger, more readable size.

One of the uncanny things about Trudeau is how well he anticipates which direction the news is moving. He must submit his Sunday strips about five weeks before publication. That means that the recent Sunday section on Mr. Butts selling cigarettes in the Soviet Union, for instance, was completed weeks before American tobacco companies announced that they would export cigarettes there. His daily strips must be submitted by Friday at 5 PM, nine days before publication. Even working right up to deadline, which he always does, he often relies on a combination of good instincts and his usual good luck. Trudeau writes and draws in pencil, which allows him to erase and rewrite. Then, to save time, he faxes the strips to an "inker" named Don Carlton who lives near his syndicate in Kansas City. The originals look almost identical to what Carlton traces in ink, except for filling some black backgrounds and minor technical instructions. This is common among cartoonists. (Many strips are far more collaborative than Trudeau's.) Carlton reproduces even Trudeau's signature, and these versions sell for $600, which goes to The National Coalition for the Homeless. Trudeau inexplicably destroys the true pencil originals.

With his Sunday section dispatched early in the week, he concentrates on the six dailies. "If I'm lucky there will be two or three ideas that kind of jockey for position in my mind through the week, which I will bone up on." (He's a rabid news consumer who keeps 200 to 300 open files of clips, plus workbooks for jotting down ideas.) "Somewhere around Wednesday or Thursday, I'll start making the final cuts and commit to one story line. The process for me is very much sitting down and holding a casting call to marry an idea with the right characters and the right story."

But his creativity is nonlinear. "It always amazes me that there are people who wander around with their receptors open to a direct flow between experience and productivity. I can't do that. I have to turn all the spigots on. I hold on to things I hear or read, but not consciously. If I go to a party and someone says something clever, it rarely translates into a strip."

Like Jules Feiffer, an early inspiration, Trudeau long downplayed the drawing in order to highlight the writing. But in 1987, he found himself "bored with the look of the strip. It was static. This is when the cartoonist decided to wake up." The critics had always been hard on his drawing (and he bad-mouths his own draftsmanship). But beginning with the classic tour inside "Reagan's Brain," the art improved dramatically.

For all that, the writing—particularly the politics—remains closest to his heart. Trudeau describes himself as a "Kevin Phillips liberal," who is getting "unabashedly conservative" on some social issues. He realized this last year when the right-wing *Wall Street Journal* editorial page ran an end-of-the-decade selection of his strips critical of New Age ideas. He even finds himself admiring Senator Sam

Nunn, one of "very few grown-ups in the Senate." Per his custom, he rarely socializes with the powerful; knowing them makes his work more difficult, he says. After he and Pauley were taken on a gracious tour of the Senate recently by John Glenn, he was pained to have to return home to do an acerbic "Keating Five" series. Another time he ventured out, he was introduced to Henry Kissinger, who pretended he had never heard of him—a "small social lie" he found telling.

Of late, Trudeau's great frustration creatively is that he has yet to find a handle on the race issue. "At a seminar I heard Spike Lee tell whites they should be wondering to themselves why they were frightened when they see a group of young black men walking down the street. I was thinking, 'Spike, if you were walking down the street in $150 Nikes, you'd be calculating your chances, wondering, "Will they recognize I'm Spike Lee?'" One problem with tackling race is that it's at odds with his normal approach, which is to choose targets—gun nuts, tobacco companies, presidents—who are up, not down: "I'm around underfoot, kicking in the shins, not the head." But he's thinking hard about it.

The cartoonist downgrades his role in American politics. "I don't think the media has any power. They have influence, which is not the same. The lowliest functionary in the federal government has more actual power over people's lives." True, he's never elected—or defeated—anyone; all he's done is get inside the brains of several million people.

When Garry Trudeau was a boy, his father told him that "life is not to be enjoyed, it's to be gotten on with." Francis and Garry both laugh about it now. Years ago, the judgment revised, these words were put into the mouth of Mark Slackmeyer's father, and the strip adorns Francis's Saranac Lake office. Beyond everything else in his charmed life, the cartoonist now feels "some serene sense of job satisfaction." With any luck, he'll still have it when Zonker starts living off Social Security.

Mario Cuomo

—— 1992 ——

*In 1992, New York Governor Mario Cuomo was
the frontrunner for the Democratic presidential nomination,
but he decided not to run.*

IN THE BLINK of an eye, Mario Cuomo looks as if he may have
lost his moment. The decision dance is boring. The Democratic state
chairmen, original peddlers of the Mario Scenario, are now blown
away by Bill Clinton. But Cuomo's at his best when embattled by the
white-bread establishment types he has loathed since the 1950s, when
they suggested he'd do better in the world as "Mark Conrad."

Is it really any surprise that he receives friendly letters from
Richard Nixon? Cuomo would be rightly disgusted by any comparison
of their ethics (or their senses of humor). But they share an esthetic: the
brooding intellectual, alone in a dark political world with nothing but
his instincts. As young lawyers, both were rejected by big Wall Street
law firms. Both nurse old resentments.

Without stretching the analogy to the breaking point, there's also
the sheer complexity of their combativeness, the layering of their identity as agonistes. It doesn't matter that one has a ski-jump nose and the
other a face for radio; it doesn't matter that their insecurities are always
in danger of blowing them up. They fascinate, and so they dominate.
The Adlai Stevenson indecisiveness model never really fit Cuomo,
because even when he is exasperating, he is always "in the arena," as
Nixon called it, quoting a much-despised former New York governor
named Theodore Roosevelt.

Actually, Cuomo doesn't like the boxing metaphors. When I questioned him at a press conference about the wisdom of "duking
it out" with Dan Quayle, he subjected me to the same third degree that
the thoroughly hazed Albany press corps has been putting up with for
years. "Where are you from?" he demanded. When I told him Chicago,

he responded: "You want to duke it out. I'm not a 'duker-outer.' That's your neighborhood. My neighborhood believes in the mind, poetry, books, the Queens Borough Public Library."

Mean? Funny? Both? Of course in the hothouse of a presidential campaign some Chicagoans would take note of the unintended slight against their fair city, and Cuomo might have to apologize a little for his provincialism. Multiply that a hundred times—there can be a hundred such vintage Cuomoisms in a single day—and you get some idea of what a Cuomo presidential campaign might be like. Imagine columnist Jimmy Breslin as an informal campaign adviser. (Breslin is one of Cuomo's closest friends.) I wondered aloud to a Cuomo aide about how his battles with the press would affect his candidacy. Would he seem exciting or exhausting? Does he do it because it's in his interest, or in his nature? The next day, my phone rang, at home. George Bush plays golf, Cuomo calls reporters. It's kind of a hobby.

I asked about his epidermis. "If by thin-skinned you mean very, very quick to respond—that's what I've done for a lifetime. I'd been a lawyer for more than 20 years. You can't let the comment from the witness pass. If there's a jury, everything is important." Life as courtroom: reporters are witnesses to be cross-examined; voters are juries. This much is irreducibly part of his nature. But he draws the line there, adding without irony: "If [by thin-skinned] you're talking about being personally sensitive to criticism, that's a lot of crap."

I had my perfect Cuomo sound bite now, but the question of his self-control was still at issue. Cuomo offered a familiar explanation for why the press highlights his explosiveness: "Because you're a big Italian, everyone thinks you have to be very volatile." At some deeper level, though, he knows that the biggest hurdle facing him is not his ethnicity or New York or his opposition to the death penalty. It's himself—his struggle to stay on close terms with what his idol Lincoln called "the better angels of [his] nature."

Cuomo assured me that he can calibrate his combativeness: "If a high school debater asks me a tough question at a gym in Chicago, I'm not going to answer her the way I answer Sam Donaldson." But even the pleasure and political gain that comes from watching him deck Donaldson on the *Brinkley* show ("That's silly, Sam, even for you") may wear thin. The long-term dynamic is wrong. Ronald Reagan used Donaldson as a foil, too, but he did so by suggesting to the public that the press was beating up on the president, not the other way around. The difference is hardly trivial.

Cuomo must calibrate. If he can't, the press will report only his theatrics and skip the substance of his powerful anti-Bush case. To win, Cuomo needs to be Cuomo without being too Cuomo. In other words, "The New Mario."

Newt Gingrich

—— 1995 ——

When Republicans took control of the
House of Representatives in 1994, Newt Gingrich became
Speaker of the House. I tracked his rise and fall.

WHAT STRANGE FATE befell Newt Gingrich this year? Entering 1995, he wore history's halo; now he's in its dust-bin, so astonishingly unpopular in the polls that he makes Bill Clinton look like Cal Ripkin. Gingrich is hardly finished. When he ends the public silence his backers have urged on him, the speaker will likely rise and fall and rise again in the normal yo-yo of American notoriety. But a year ago not even the most rabid Democrat dared to predict that Gingrich could be brought so low so quickly.

The most useful explanation goes beyond Gingrich's ideology and background to an American public still sorting out ambivalent feelings toward conflict and commonality in the 1990s. In that sense, the new speaker and the O.J. Simpson trial (you didn't really think you could read this far without a reference to it, did you?) are of a piece—blood sports that compel and repel at the same time. We listen for the clang, and wince at it. Today's brawling style titillates—then ultimately disgusts. This love-hate relationship with conflict might be expected to keep the divisiveness in check, but it doesn't. The adversarial excess that has tarnished our legal system is infecting politics and public life, with Gingrich as its most recognizable symbol.

The original idea undergirding American law was that Marcia Clark versus Johnnie Cochran adds up to the truth. Translated to politics, it's that Newt Gingrich versus Bill Clinton yields understanding of the stakes the country faces. But we all know it isn't working out that way. Loud conflict—built into the structure of TV-driven debate—doesn't yield truth in politics any more easily than it does in the courtroom. What remains are the recriminations, reverberating endlessly through the process. Adversary infinitum.

Gingrich must be aware that the screaming and scheming he did for 15 years as a lowly backbencher doesn't work in the speakership. But he no doubt comforts himself with the fact that he remains, by general consensus, the most powerful speaker of the era, enforcing a degree of party discipline almost totally absent under the Democrats. He knows that he has transformed the terms of the debate—both practically and philosophically—and forged a new generation of radical Republicans. And he knows that whatever happens to him personally, the antigovernment revolution he masterminded cannot be rolled back completely, and will most likely advance. While the speaker may have a weakness for pseudo-intellectual blather, he can be rightly proud of how early he understood the tides of political history.

Yet Gingrich's understanding of social tides—the way the American people relate to each other and to their leaders—remains impaired. This is why his problems go deeper than rule-breaking by his PAC, pettiness on Air Force One or even the story of how he presented divorce terms to his first wife when she was in the hospital with cancer. Send a message, Johnnie Cochran says to the jury. Send a message, Newt Gingrich says to the public. At first, this feels good to any audience—like the contact high one gets from watching boxing or the *McLaughlin Group*. But the buzz wears off, leaving only a longing for something larger and more ennobling.

Politics has been famously described as the mobilization of resentments, yet even Richard Nixon paid at least some lip service to unity and common interest. (Remember that placard, BRING US TOGETHER?) At the beginning of this year, Gingrich set his sights high, too. He talked eloquently, for instance, about the need to explore the idea of bringing back orphanages. While liberals yelped, the public was intrigued. But when the GOP budget appeared the speaker had not earmarked one penny to test whether his grand idea might actually work.

Even if the public didn't hold Gingrich accountable for this in particular, a general impression of hardness set in. "The Devil has taken his heart," Jackie Gingrich once told her Georgia church congregation, in explaining why she needed charity to get by after her husband left her. While Americans today are unusually unsympathetic to the underprivileged, we want our politicians to convey compassion. "Message: I don't care" is a sure loser, especially when the budget is so tilted against the poor. Were Gingrich a more pleasing, Reaganesque figure, he might have been able to fight back better against the obvious demagoguery of the Democrats' attacks on his modest Medicare reform.

Perhaps Gingrich is simply tone deaf. He laces nearly every sentence with the word "frankly," which must be the single most off-putting Orwellian expression a voter can hear. More broadly, a politician dedicated to preventing the government from telling citizens what to think and do cannot himself lecture them so often on what to think and do. It's as if he's saying, "To get the government off your back I have to climb on it." What he fails to understand is that, for many voters, he is the government, or part of it.

When we drive, we like to honk. But we don't like those big trucks leading us down the highway to honk at us. Gingrich doesn't get that each American is proud, too proud, of his or her particular anger, but not of anybody else's. When he lowers his voice and lays off the horn, he'll win more credit for changing the country.

Paul McCartney

—— 2003 ——

In 2003, I interviewed Paul McCartney.
Among the topics we discussed was the role the
Beatles played in the fall of communism.

EDWARD TELLER and Paul McCartney didn't know each other, but maybe they should have. The nuclear physicist and father of the H-bomb, who died last week at 95, was the model for Dr. Strangelove. A fierce anti-communist, his advice to Ronald Reagan to launch Star Wars is credited by some conservative analysts with sweeping the Soviet Union into the dustbin of history.

And the connection between Teller and the Beatles would be ... what? That Ringo starred in a movie with Peter Sellers? Actually, many Russians themselves believe that the Western cultural forces symbolized by Beatles music helped hollow out communism, slowly eroding its authority until it collapsed. That it disintegrated without a huge war is the greatest blessing of the last half of the 20th century. In other words, "hard power" (Western strength and resolve) and "soft power" (Western ideas of freedom) worked together, with plenty of help from brave refuseniks, a pragmatic, bumbling and ultimately peace-loving Mikhail Gorbachev—and the numbing effects of vodka.

The A&E network will soon air *Paul McCartney in Red Square*, a concert film that chronicles McCartney's first-ever trip last May to Russia, where he was greeted like a conquering hero. McCartney's first world tour in a decade was surprisingly big—close to half a million turned out for him in Rome—but the rapturous throngs of Muscovites below the onion domes at sunset were there to celebrate more than just the music. "The only person in Red Square who wasn't moved was Lenin," one Russian critic reported. As he sang "Back in the U.S.S.R.," originally a spoof, "that's when the volts went through them," McCartney told me. The song plays to a Russian national pride that is no longer frightening.

The film explains how young fans in the mid-1960s would spend half a month's salary on contraband albums, or disassemble public telephones to build "electric" guitars. Old pictures of the Fab Four were passed around like icons. Gorbachev turns up to recall how the Beatles "taught the young that there was another life." Defense Minister Sergei Ivanov says that as an ambitious young party member he was "moderated" by the music. Prime Minister Vladimir Putin, attending the concert flanked by goons who boogie like crazy, says the Beatles gave people "a gulp of freedom." (He might consider giving them a few more gulps now.)

Even discounting the usual exaggeration in these films—and the fact that other bands toured the Eastern bloc while no Beatles ever did—there's something instructive here. McCartney makes no claim to being a geopolitical thinker, but suggests, "When somebody comes in with an alternate idea that's just a little looser—that's powerful ... [The people] are thinking 'If only, if only ...' And it starts to spread." Periodic Soviet crackdowns on rock fans, including the confiscation of memorabilia, continued into the 1980s, each one creating yet more "inner immigrants"—Russians fleeing Lenin for Lennon without leaving home.

The music was more important to them than it was to us. I remember visiting Moscow in 1987 and seeing hippies still there more than a decade after the whole thing disappeared in the West. It was a way of rebelling without becoming a full-fledged dissident. Songs of love and freedom helped make ordinary Russians ideologically undependable in the eyes of their rulers. The Red Army's pathetic failure in Afghanistan showed a certain lessening of the old Russian fighting spirit. By the end in 1989, victory for the West was like walking through a door that was already open.

So what does any of this have to do with today's challenges? On one level, nothing. "I don't think they smuggled Beatles records into the Arab world," McCartney says. In fact, today's Islamic fanaticism is in part a reaction *against* Western popular culture. In the Middle East, unlike in the U.S.S.R., young rebels are the enemies of the West. Bin Laden's picture is the forbidden icon, not some Western rock star. And the whole "soft power" bit can be overdrawn in other ways. In Canada last week, the *National Post* editorialized that the soft focus has become a handy excuse for the Canadians to avoid the hard work of helping the United States catch terrorists. It doesn't sound promising in North Korea, either, where if anyone smuggled in CDs, the strange imports might get used as tiny plates on which to serve their tiny food portions.

None of which is to suggest that soft power can't work today. But perhaps McCartney's most important observation was that "we did it without knowing it ... It all begins with whispers and then ideas are launched and spread on the wind." Cultural and even political ideas are more appealing, particularly to the young, when governments are not trying to push them on people. The Russians' second-favorite song in Red Square was "All You Need Is Love." Yet if the Bush administration were sponsoring the show—or if the Johnson and Nixon administrations had been big rock-and-roll fans—the Beatles' reception would have been very different, even back in the U.S.S.R.

Jimmy Stewart

—— 1997 ——

Jimmy Stewart was a huge movie star before my time.
But I thought he represented something important.

W HEN *MR. SMITH GOES TO WASHINGTON* premiered
in the capital in 1939, about a third of the audience of
dignitaries stormed out. "Not all senators are sons of bitches," fumed
one senator. "It stinks," said another. Senator George Norris, himself a
Mr. Smith type, said of Jimmy Stewart's character: "I've been in
Congress for 36 years, and I've never seen a member as dumb as that
boy." In his memoirs, Frank Capra recalled how "hopping-mad
Washington press correspondents belittled, berated, scorned, vilified
and ripped me open from stem to stern" for having portrayed them as
"too fond of the juice of the grape." Joseph P. Kennedy tried to keep the
movie from being released in Europe. Bad for morale, he said.

When Capra first pitched Stewart on the role of George Bailey for
It's a Wonderful Life, the director was briefly seized by self-doubt: "This
is the lousiest piece of cheese I ever heard of," he thought. Ticket sales
in 1947 were so lackluster that Capra had to place his production
company in bankruptcy. James Agee compared the movie to *A
Christmas Carol*, but many other critics savaged it. "A figment of pure
Pollyanna platitudes," said the *New York Times*. The *New Republic*
accused the film of trying "to convince audiences that American life is
exactly like the *Saturday Evening Post* covers of Norman Rockwell."

A half century later, at Stewart's death, these movies lie deep in
the marrow of America. For all his acting brilliance in Hitchcock films
and Westerns, Jimmy Stewart's most lasting contribution lies in two
unforgettable roles. Senator Jefferson Smith changed how we view our
politics; George Bailey of Bedford Falls changed how we view ourselves.

Mr. Smith is now the premier allegory for idealism in Washington.

That's good for inspiring integrity and resistance to special interests. Unfortunately, sanctimonious showboats pretending to be Mr. Smith now use the once rare filibuster as a parliamentary gimmick to defend pork at home. And the film's cartoonish qualities make it harder to see that complexity plays a larger role in politics than venality. Even so, Jeff Smith holds out the promise of using smarts (in the form of Jean Arthur) and shame to reclaim innocence. That's a powerful idea in a cynical world. By emblazoning those terms of debate on the consciousness of the American public, Capra and Stewart at least give virtue in politics a fighting chance.

It's a Wonderful Life is far darker than any Norman Rockwell picture and, with its dissection of the local power structure, far more socially conscious than most movies today. And it's not truly sentimental, a word that suggests a cheap, easy way into the heart. Like Jeff Smith, George Bailey is a much angrier man than the casual viewer may remember. "Will I ever get out of this crummy Bedford Falls?" he laments, as he sacrifices his ambitions for college and travel to fulfill responsibilities at home. He's prone to self-pity, not to mention the selfishness of suicide. But with the help of Clarence the angel, George comes to the central insights necessary for living happily in this country: a good man is a great man, friendship is the real wealth, no one is born a failure.

Most art challenges middle-class values. That is one if its important functions. But art can also illuminate and make precious what we take for granted. Jimmy Stewart managed to inhabit abstract ideas like democracy and community and make them real for millions. This didn't just tell us about ourselves; it made us try to be better, which is no small legacy for any man.

Jerry Falwell

—— 2007 ——

*The kind tributes to Reverend Jerry Falwell when he died
left me feeling the historical record was being distorted.*

I MEAN NO DISRESPECT to the dead, but I take the British view
of obituaries, which is to try to capture the true public significance
of the person who died, not just his good qualities. The truth about
the Reverend Jerry Falwell is that he was a character assassin and
hype artist who left little positive impact on the United States—and little negative impact either, for that matter. Besides founding Liberty
University, he won't be remembered as nearly as influential as he's
made out to be.

First, his real legacy: Falwell built the Thomas Road Baptist Church
in Lynchburg, Virginia, from scratch into a mega-church with a 6,000-
seat auditorium. And he built Liberty University into a formidable
institution that attracts over 20,000 students from around the world and
a qualified faculty. Last year, Liberty's debate team won the national
championship. It's not easy to create a university and Falwell deserves
credit as an institution-builder. He will also be remembered through
a famous Supreme Court case he lost, *Hustler vs. Falwell*, which
established that public figures cannot recover damages when depicted
in parodies. (The story of the lawsuit is told in the film *The People vs.
Larry Flynt.*) In that sense, he inadvertently helped bolster the First
Amendment.

But Falwell's political legacy is much less impressive. He started out
as a segregationist who harshly attacked Martin Luther King through
the 1960s and later called Archbishop Desmond Tutu of South Africa
a phony. He was a strong supporter of Israel but openly anti-Semitic,
announcing on many occasions that the anti-Christ would return as a
Jew. He said repeatedly that those suffering from AIDS deserved it.

On September 13, 2001, Falwell said this on Pat Robertson's show *The 700 Club*: "The enemies of America give us probably what we deserve." When asked to elaborate, Falwell added, "When we destroy 40 million little innocent babies, we make God mad. I really believe that the pagans and the abortionists and the feminists and the gays and the lesbians who are actively trying to make that an alternative lifestyle, the ACLU, People For the American Way—all of them who have tried to secularize America—I point the finger in their face and say, 'you helped this happen.'" Robertson replied, "Well, I totally concur." Falwell later apologized, unconvincingly, for offending anyone.

It was fitting that this was said on Robertson's program, not Falwell's. That's because Falwell never had great success as a broadcaster or televangelist. His *Old Time Gospel Hour* was never the most popular religious program. While he claimed 20 million viewers, the real number was a tiny fraction of that, usually below one ratings point. In the November 1980 Nielsen ratings, for instance, *Old Time Gospel Hour* was watched by 1.21 million people—well behind not just Oral Roberts and Jimmy Swaggert but Rex Humbard and James Robison.

According to lore (and much of the coverage of his death), November 1980 found Falwell at the peak of his powers. That was the month Ronald Reagan was elected president, after having met with Falwell and other members of his brilliantly named organization, the Moral Majority. While Falwell might have contributed slightly to Reagan's margin of victory, he was not even close to being instrumental in his election. With incumbent Jimmy Carter bogged down with the Iranian hostage crisis and double-digit inflation and interest rates, Reagan won with 57 percent of the vote—a huge landslide. At best, the Moral Majority added a point or two to Reagan's totals. More likely, it contributed nothing. Exit polls showed that Carter bested Reagan among Southern Baptists, 50–46 percent. And abortion ranked well behind foreign policy and economics among issues that mattered most to voters that year.

The Moral Majority claimed to have registered eight million new voters but could never provide any hard figures, and many smaller evangelical organizations said they operated independently of Falwell. (In fact, there was considerable tension within the religious right.) The real political muscle was provided by Robertson and his protégé, Ralph Reed. Their Christian Coalition was far more powerful than the Moral Majority, whose voter guides were never credited with winning any particular election.

From the 1980s on, Falwell existed mostly as a media creation, not a real player in national politics. He missed the cable TV revolution, which deprived him of a platform. He took over Jimmy and Tammy Faye Bakker's PTL after it collapsed in scandal, but by then its revenues were a modest $13 million. The related theme park, Heritage USA, went into Chapter 11. His monthly magazine, *National Liberty Journal*, became a modest success, with an unaudited circulation of 250,000.

Falwell's power was hyped not just by him but by a media establishment that needed a consistently conservative voice—not to mention a "guest" who could usually be counted on to show up at the studio on time and say something provocative. On shows like *Nightline* and *Larry King Live*, Falwell became a spokesman for the religious right and "good TV." Who can forget when he claimed that the Teletubbies character Tinky Winky was actually a hidden symbol of the homosexual agenda? Ironically, he may have loomed larger among secular audiences than religious ones.

In 1994, Falwell paid for a documentary called *The Clinton Chronicles* that supposedly implicated Bill Clinton, Vincent Foster, Ron Brown and Jim McDougal in a cocaine-smuggling operation. A man shown in the film in silhouette claimed that President Clinton ordered several of his critics killed. Falwell never repudiated the film, though he later admitted, "I do not know the accuracy" of it. Some of the characters featured in the film became involved in the Paula Jones lawsuit that led to Clinton's impeachment, though Falwell was not central to that story either.

The rise of the religious right was an important development in late–20th century American history. Falwell's name is among those associated with the movement. But just because someone is famous doesn't make him significant. Jerry Falwell wasn't.

Norman Borlaug

—— 2007 ——

*This column, about a world-changing figure known
to few outside the fields of agriculture and hunger prevention,
generated hundreds of letters from readers grateful for
a positive and inspiring story. The headline was "He Only Saved a
Billion People." Borlaug's daughter later told me he liked
the column but has no idea who Angelina Jolie is.*

IT'S A TRIFECTA much bigger and rarer than an Oscar, an
Emmy and a Tony. Only five people in history have ever won the
Nobel Peace Prize, the Presidential Medal of Freedom and the
Congressional Gold Medal: Martin Luther King Jr., Mother Teresa,
Nelson Mandela, Elie Wiesel ... and Norman Borlaug.

Norman who? Few news organizations covered last week's
Congressional Gold Medal ceremony for Borlaug, which was presided
over by President Bush and the leadership of the House and Senate. An
elderly agronomist doesn't make news, even when he is widely credited
with saving the lives of one billion human beings worldwide, more than
one in seven people on the planet.

Borlaug's success in feeding the world testifies to the difference a
single person can make. But the obscurity of a man of such surpassing
accomplishment is a reminder of our culture's surpassing superficiality.
Reading Walter Isaacson's terrific biography of Albert Einstein, I
was struck by how famous Einstein was long before his role in the atom
bomb. Great scientists and humanitarians were once heroes and cover
boys. No more. For Borlaug, still vital at 93, to win more notice,
he would have to make his next trip to Africa in the company of
Angelina Jolie.

The consequences of obscuring complex issues like agriculture
are serious. Take the huge farm bill now nearing passage, a subject
Borlaug knows a thing or two about. Because it seems boring and
technical and unrelated to our busy urban lives, we aren't focused
on how it relates directly to the environment, immigration, global
poverty and the budget deficit, not to mention the highly subsidized

high-fructose corn syrup we ingest every day. We can blame the mindless media for failing to keep us better informed about how $95 billion a year is hijacked by a few powerful corporate interests. But we can also blame ourselves. It's all there on the Internet (or in books like Daniel Imhoff's breezy *Food Fight*), if we decide to get interested. But will we? Sometimes it seems the more we've got at our fingertips, the less that sticks in our minds.

Born poor in Iowa and turned down at first by the University of Minnesota, Borlaug brought his fingertips and mind together in rural Mexico in the 1940s and 1950s to develop a hybrid called "dwarf wheat" that tripled grain production there. Then, with the help of the Rockefeller Foundation, he attracted agronomists from around the world to northwest Mexico to learn his planting and soil conservation techniques. "They [academic and U.S. government critics] said I was nutty to think that it would work in different soil," Borlaug told me last week. The resulting "nuttiness" led to what was arguably the greatest humanitarian accomplishment of the 20th century, the so-called Green Revolution. By 1965 he was dodging artillery shells in the Indo-Pakistan War but still managed to increase Indian agricultural output sevenfold.

The experts who said peasants would never change their centuries-old ways were wrong. In the mid-1970s, Nobel Prize in hand, Borlaug brought his approach to Communist China, where he arguably had his greatest success. In only a few years, his ideas—which go far beyond seed varieties—had spread around the world and disproved Malthusian doomsday scenarios like Paul Ehrlich's 1968 best seller *The Population Bomb*. Now the Gates Foundation is helping extend his innovations to the one continent where famine remains a serious threat—Africa.

Borlaug, who launched the prestigious World Food Prize, has little patience for current agricultural policy in the developed world. "The claims for these subsidies today by the affluent nations are pretty silly," he says. So far, Congress isn't listening. The octopus-like farm bill does little to curb the ridiculous corporate welfare payments to a tiny number of wealthy (and often absentee) "farmers" who get more than $1 million a year each for subsidized commodities that make our children obese. (Did you ever wonder why junk food is cheaper than nutritious food? Because it's taxpayer-funded.)

Borlaug scoffs at the mania for organic food, which he proves with calm logic is unsuited to fight global hunger. (Dung, for instance, is an inefficient source of nitrogen.) And while he encourages energy-conscious people to "use all the organic you can, especially on high-end crops like vegetables," he's convinced that paying more for organic is "a lot of nonsense." There's "no evidence the food is any different than that produced by chemical fertilizer."

In 1960 about 60 percent of the world's people experienced some hunger every year. By 2000 that number was 14 percent, a remarkable achievement. But as Borlaug cautioned at the ceremony in his honor, that still leaves 850 million hungry men, women and children. They are waiting for the Norman Borlaugs of the future to make their mark, even if they aren't likely to get famous for it.

Tom Delay

—— 2005 ——

It still amazes me that a man this radical in his right-wing views was essentially running the House of Representatives for 12 years.

A DECADE AGO, I paid a call on Tom DeLay in his ornate office in the Capitol. I had heard a rumor about him that I figured could not possibly be true. The rumor was that after the GOP took control of the House that year, DeLay had begun keeping a little black book with the names of Washington lobbyists who wanted to come see him. If the lobbyists were not Republicans and contributors to his power base, they didn't get into "the people's House." DeLay not only confirmed the story, he showed me the book. His time was limited, DeLay explained with a genial smile. Why should he open his door to people who were not on the team?

Thus began what historians will regard as the single most corrupt decade in the long and colorful history of the House of Representatives. Come on, you say. How about all those years when congressmen accepted cash in the House chamber and then staggered onto the floor drunk? Yes, special interests have bought off members of Congress at least since Daniel Webster took his seat while on the payroll of a bank. And yes, Congress over the years has seen dozens of sex scandals and dozens of members brought low by financial improprieties. But never before has the leadership of the House been hijacked by a small band of extremists bent on building a ruthless shakedown machine, lining the pockets of their richest constituents and rolling back popular protections for ordinary people. These folks borrow like banana republics and spend like Tip O'Neill on speed.

I have no idea if DeLay has technically broken the law. What interests me is how this moderate, evenly divided nation came to be ruled on at least one side of Capitol Hill by a zealot. This is a man who calls the Environmental Protection Agency "the Gestapo of government" and favors repealing the Clean Air Act because "it's never been proven that air toxins are hazardous to people"; who insists repeatedly that judges on the other side of issues "need to be intimidated" and rejects the idea of a separation of church and state; who claims there are no parents trying to raise families on the minimum wage—that "fortunately, such families do not exist" (at least Newt Gingrich was intrigued by the challenges of poverty); who once said, "A woman can't take care of the family. It takes a man to provide structure." I could go on all day. Congress has always had its share of extremists. But the DeLay era is the first time the fringe has ever been in charge.

The only comparison to DeLay & Company might be the Radical Republicans of the 1860s. But the 19th-century Radical Republican agenda was to integrate and remake the South. The 21st-century Radical Republican agenda is to enact the wish list of the tobacco and gun lobbies, repeal health and safety regulations and spend billions on shameless pork-barrel projects to keep the GOP at the trough. Another analogy is to Republican Speaker Joe Cannon, who ran the House with an iron fist a century ago. But Cannon had to contend with Progressive Republicans who eventually stripped him of his power. DeLay's ruling radical conservative claque remains united, at least for now.

Comparisons with fellow Texan Sam Rayburn fall short, too. Rayburn was respected on both sides of the aisle for his rock-solid integrity. He and most other House speakers carefully balanced their support for corporate interests like the oil depletion allowance with at least some sense of the public good. And they had to share much of their power with committee chairmen. Today, seniority is much less important. Chairmen are term-limited (six years) or tossed if they displease DeLay. And this crowd views "the public interest" as strictly for liberal pantywaists.

The only reason the House hasn't done even more damage is that the Senate often sands down the most noxious ideas, making the bills merely bad, not disastrous. What next for the House of Shame? If DeLay's acquitted, he'll be back in power. If he's convicted, his protégés will continue his work. Reform efforts by fiscal conservatives determined to curb their borrow-and-spend colleagues are probably doomed. The only way to get rid of the termites eating away the people's House is to stamp them out at the next election.

Jim McGreevey

—— 2004 ——

When New Jersey Governor Jim McGreevey was forced to resign amid a sex scandal, it got me thinking about politicians as human beings. I wrote this from my bed in Memorial Sloan-Kettering Cancer Center, where the next day I underwent a bone marrow transplant.

I DON'T KNOW Jim McGreevey well, and the few times I met him he didn't interest me much. He seemed like just another super-ambitious student-body-president type; the clichéd glad-handing style and well-scrubbed-policy-wonk personality brought to mind a very minor-league Bill Clinton, without the cool. I found that he was smarter than I first thought, but not smart enough to make himself an especially successful governor, even before last week. And yet despite the scumminess of what he did (giving an important six-figure state job as head of homeland security to one's totally unqualified lover, gay or straight, is inexcusable), his story raises a couple of useful questions that go beyond the enduring confines of the closet: Why are the most ambitious so often the most self-destructive, willing to jeopardize everything (Clinton again) for some sex? And can we learn anything from their folly to bring better balance to our own lives?

To all appearances, McGreevey was the quintessential outer-directed person. From the time he was in high school, he was obsessed with getting ahead in politics, first in Middlesex County, then as governor of New Jersey, and someday, he hoped, as president. Of course in the business he chose, normal private life—with marriage and family—is thoroughly public, the more so nowadays with so much media crawling over everything. The microscope intensifies the human need for some space that can be truly private. "Were there realities from which I was running?" McGreevey asked in his honest speech. "Which master was I trying to serve?"

The master he chose for most of his life—what he called the "acceptable reality"—was a set of expectations generated from without. This role-playing, which went far beyond his double life, is hardly unique to the governor of New Jersey. Too many of us increasingly live our lives according to some external narrative that we think represents "success" or "acceptance" but has little to do with who we really are. In other words, ordinary Americans are becoming more and more like politicians. That's right—the very profession we claim to despise has turned into one of the templates for modern life. It's not just that we occasionally make promises we can't keep and tell convenient white lies and are a little too eager to please those who might do us some good. That has always been true, which is why our elected officials may represent us better than we know. What has changed is that the outer-directedness of politicians—their relentless need to be in touch and feed off other people—is now leeching into the larger culture.

Technology is shaping the change. When I was in college in the 1970s, my roommates once played a practical joke on me. They knew how much a political-reporter type like me enjoyed talking on the telephone, so they disassembled our room phone for a couple of days, cutting off my access to the outer world. I went nuts, but they didn't miss the phone at all. Today, with cell phones and instant messaging like umbilical cords, the whole dorm would riot if someone managed to cut the connection. Even the meek have inherited the BlackBerry. I remember chuckling with bemusement in the 1980s, when I would travel with politicians and they used newfangled car phones to call a dozen friends and contacts en route. This was part of what defined them as politicians. These days, it helps define all of us.

It used to be that only people in professions like politics, show business and sales dealt with scores of people each day. Now anyone with e-mail does. And because Americans frequently change jobs, they are constantly selling themselves—just like politicians. And undergoing image makeovers—just like politicians. Much of this outer direction is fine; the coiled ambition helps productivity and brings at least some people the sense of connection they crave in their lives. But these are different lives than led by earlier generations—stretched thin between outer and inner selves, self-absorbed without being self-knowing. The search for spirituality and meaning now underway in so many places must be some reaction against the soullessness of the backslap and the speed dial, the impossibility of "multitasking" what really matters.

The character flaws that allowed Bill Clinton or Jim McGreevey to exercise such appalling judgment are particular to them and ultimately unfathomable. All we know for sure is that neither Clinton's shame, nor McGreevey's, will prevent others from making their mistakes over and over again; human folly (or cries for help) trumps rationality on a regular basis, especially if we manage to stay in touch with everyone except ourselves. When life spins ever faster, the odds increase of its spinning out of control. Whatever his personal psychodrama, the governor's predicament was, by his rare admission, worsened by the tension between a life led for the approval of others and one led for himself. When the balance between the two is lost, so is any sense of mastery. The best politicians—and best-adjusted people—know how to strike that balance before it strikes them down.

Rush Limbaugh

—— 2003 ——

The conservative dominance from 1994 to 2006 was due in no small part to Rush Limbaugh, who turned out to be just another hypocrite.

IF YOU LISTEN HARD, you can hear the booming radio voice: *Look, the Clinton liberals and feminazis won't tell you, but here's the problem with this big talk-show host who turns out to be a prescription-drug junkie. You have a guy who finally stops spinning and fesses up for his actions. Fine. He says he won't play the victim. Good. He's off to rehab. God bless. But what he and his apologists want you to forget is that he broke the law—yes, the L-A-W. Some of us around here still have respect for it.*

Folks, this guy didn't just use drugs, he put another person in harm's way to feed his own habit. He repeatedly sent his maid out into a parking lot to score for him. Thousands of pills. Talk about cowardly. The housekeeper was being set up by her big celebrity boss to take the fall if they got busted. Now, that's the problem with these famous people who develop the wrong '60s values. The little person—the kind of average American who listens to this program—takes the risks, while the celebrity gets the slobbering praise for overcoming his "problems." That's the world these liberals have brought you. Unforgivable.

Perhaps you can do a better Limbaugh imitation. But you have to admit that if the shoe were on the other foot, he would be banging it on his microphone. So why have almost all of his conservative talk-show friends rushed to Rush's defense? Why will he, undoubtedly, get a long-standing ovation at his first public appearance after he returns from rehab? Why will both conservatives and liberals show him the compassion he routinely denies to other people?

Because the sad case of Rush Limbaugh is also about the sad state of American politics. Things have reached a point where the health problems of a radio commentator might genuinely affect the outcome of the 2004 election. Most of Limbaugh's 20 million listeners are diehard Republicans, but millions are not. These non-dittohead independents are critical in the election. They have rightly concluded that he is a first-rate communicator and entertainer. They don't follow him slavishly but give him a hearing, which is a huge asset in politics. You can drive almost anywhere in the United States on any weekday and get a three-hour, undiluted, un-rebutted and often persuasive advertisement for President Bush and the Republican Party. If Rush goes, so does the biggest megaphone in the GOP's elephant echo chamber.

This conservative "free media" is worth even more than Bush's war chest in delivering the message, stigmatizing the Democrats and turning out the base at election time. It consists not just of Rush, of course, but of other radio talk shows and the Fox News Channel, all of which have a big stake in the continued success of the much-revered leader of their product category. For several years, they have succeeded not because of some right-wing conspiracy in network-executive suites but because their "production values" are simply superior to those of liberals. They know how to grab and hold an audience.

The Democrats have only two ways to compete. The first is by building their own radio and TV outlets. The second hope for Democrats is that every political phenomenon eventually burns out. It hasn't been a good year for bully boy (or girl) conservatives. Their critics—including me—are ready to give them a taste of their own bitter medicine. Smirking William Bennett got his hand caught in a slot machine. Shrewish Ann Coulter hit the best-seller list but her charge that liberals are all guilty of "treason" makes her look like a wacko. Bill O'Reilly urged Fox to sue Al Franken, then denied having done so. Conservative books still sell but, for the first time, they have company. Sharp-elbowed liberal books by Franken, Michael Moore, Paul Krugman, Molly Ivins and Joe Conason (not to mention Hillary Clinton) cram the best-seller lists. It's not exactly a liberal renaissance, but at least they are finally fighting back.

Liberals, believers in tolerance and drug treatment, treat Rush with insincere sympathy. Conservatives have the nerve to blast the liberals for playing too rough, the better to rally the faithful. The big guy himself could help the dialogue if he returns to the airwaves after rehab with a more tolerant and less vitriolic message. But then he wouldn't be Rush Limbaugh anymore.

Roone Arledge

—— 2002 ——

For seven years, I covered the media and got to know all of the great correspondents, editors, and producers of the era, including Roone Arledge.

H E W A S F A M O U S for it at ABC—not returning your phone calls for months, then suddenly having you to Café des Artistes for a charming four-hour lunch. Or maybe you spent six months working on a new set for your show, only to have him stroll in the night before the premiere, change everything and tell you with that Zen calm to fix it by tomorrow. Or you felt your heart thump at the ringing of the "Roone phone" in the control room—the one connected directly to his house. Was the strawberry-faced sun god beaming in on some small, but brilliantly observed, mistake? Or calling to deliver the only meaningful praise that Jim McKay or Ted Koppel or Peter Jennings or any of a thousand sports and news producers who saw him as their leader ever yearned for: "Good job"?

"He was impossible, he was exasperating. If you wanted to reach him, it was very hard," remembers Barbara Walters, who credits Roone Arledge with saving her career. "But no one ever had a greater 'vision thing' than Roone."

Arledge, who died at 71 last week after a long struggle with cancer, was the most innovative TV producer ever, with only Don Hewitt even in the same league. First, Arledge revolutionized not just sports on TV, but the whole idea of sports. Slow motion, instant replay, handheld cameras, big salaries for athletes, the nighttime World Series, Howard Cosell—all his legacy. He figured out how to magically transport the viewer to some Tyrolean ski jump in *ABC's Wide World of Sports* or the skyline of Dallas on his *Monday Night Football*. ABC paid $200,000 for his first Olympics; they now go for half a billion. The Olympics that Americans see are still largely Arledge's.

From the day Edgar Scherick (who also died last week) hired him to help a lagging ABC in 1960, Arledge always used the newest and most expensive technology. But his secret was the ancient art of personal narrative that he learned to appreciate studying English at Columbia. "The thrill of victory and the agony of defeat" and "Up Close and Personal" were hackneyed when he coined them, but they had simply never been properly applied to television. "He showed that you can marry the best fictional storytelling to nonfiction," says Neal Shapiro, now president of NBC News.

After his path-breaking coverage of the Palestinian terrorism at the 1972 Munich Olympics, Arledge wanted to run news, too. But when he took over ABC News in 1977, he was viewed as a flashy and egotistical barbarian carrying entertainment values into the temple. There was some truth in it, but news has been theatrical and breathless since the battle of Thermopylae. And the notion of big salaries for big stars is simply the market speaking.

Arledge once told me that he thought his major contribution was *Nightline* (though he wrote off Koppel at first as an "Alfred E. Neuman" who couldn't carry a show). It wasn't just that he used the 1979 seizure of American hostages in Iran to carve out a new half hour of news. Arledge's creation, now 5,500 shows down the road, has covered a score of topics long thought too complex for TV. His greatest legacy might be his fundamental seriousness: the safari-suited man once seen as too showbiz for news almost single-handedly kept foreign affairs on network television for the last 20 years.

As Arledge lay dying, Jennings was among those ministering to him, playing father to a difficult father figure. One of his last coherent conversations was with Walters; he complained that TV was chasing away viewers with too many ads, once more siding with the audience over the bean counters. He ended their talk the way he did with every-one: "Great to see you." No, Roone, it was great to see you change the way we see the world.

Ralph Nader

—— 2000 ——

This column was written two weeks before the 2000 presidential election, when I feared Ralph Nader might be a spoiler.

W HEN I WAS 10 years old, growing up in Chicago, I heard the demonstrators in town for the 1968 Democratic Convention chanting, "Dump the Hump." That fall, they and millions of other supporters of Eugene McCarthy believed there was "no difference" between Hubert Humphrey and Richard Nixon. They were deeply mistaken, as we learned the hard way. When I was 22 years old, I spent the summer of 1980 working for Ralph Nader. My job was to write part of a book about the campaign that year. (I was responsible for chronicling third-party candidate John Anderson.) For all of our lacerations of Jimmy Carter, we understood that a vote for Anderson was a vote for Ronald Reagan. Even then, I disagreed with Nader on several issues (starting with his unshakable faith in lawyers and regulators). But I developed a deep respect for his leadership of the consumer movement. Last year, when several lists were published of the most important Americans of the 20th century, Nader's name was rightfully included. Bill Clinton's was not.

In recent years, Nader ambled the streets of Washington unrecognized. He wasn't quite a has-been (his groups still do some important work), but he seemed a figure from the 1960s and 1970s. Now he's cool again—mobbed by young supporters—and don't think he doesn't love it. When I saw him recently, his beef was with the press— particularly the *New York Times*—for not covering him more. Fair enough. And he and Pat Buchanan should have been allowed into at least one of the debates. (It was idiotic to bar Nader even from the audience.) But my beef with him was bigger. By refusing to admit that there are deep differences between Al Gore and George W. Bush, by clinging to this emotionally satisfying but factually inaccurate notion of a "DemRep Party," Nader is squandering his most precious asset—his intellectual honesty.

Start with the environment, which the Green Party is supposed to be about. Beyond his support for gun control, why is Gore in such trouble in a state like West Virginia? Because he won't roll over for the coal and chemical industries that run the state. They know he is the most serious environmentalist ever to run for president. It's Gore who negotiated the Kyoto Accords on global warming and got Clinton to set aside the most acres for conservation since Teddy Roosevelt. The Sierra Club and Friends of the Earth believe Clinton has fallen short on getting some things through (as would, needless to say, a President Nader), but these and other environmental groups have enthusiastically endorsed Gore over a GOP candidate who argued in Texas that compliance with clean-air standards should be "voluntary."

Or take campaign-finance reform, the signature issue of many Naderites. A recent poll showed that voters actually thought Bush would be better on that issue than Gore, though Bush *opposes* reform and Gore *supports* it. This cockeyed notion is a result of all of the coverage of the Democrats' 1996 irregularities. Much of that coverage was justified, but in combination with the endless GOP slurs on Gore's honesty and integrity, it created the phony impression that Gore is: (a) in someone's pocket and (b) not for cleaning up the system.

Nader has fed these canards. The fact is, President Bush would veto the McCain-Feingold bill banning soft money, while President Gore would work with John McCain and quite likely get it passed. That wouldn't solve the problem of money in politics forever, but why make the perfect the enemy of the good?

Nader voters might consider what's being called "the Ivins strategy" (after columnist Molly Ivins). She urges "voting with your heart where you can and your head where you must." New York mayoral candidate Mark Green, who backs Gore despite having once been Nader's closest associate, last week privately urged his old boss to embrace that approach, which would mean campaigning in states like Texas and New York, where the outcome is preordained, but not in Oregon, Washington, Minnesota, Wisconsin, Pennsylvania, Michigan and other swing states, where he could truly cost Gore the election. So far, Nader is not complying. He's looking past the campaign toward building a movement.

But he's going about it the wrong way. An ascendant Green Party (whose zany platform of abolishing the Senate and other left-wing idiocies has been renounced by Nader himself) would simply guarantee Republican presidents for the foreseeable future. Naderites should have persuaded their man to run in the Democratic primaries; he might well have won a few, scared Gore and pushed the party to the left on trade. That is the way real change occurs in American politics, and it would have given Nader the genuine influence he craves. Instead, he risks being marginalized by angry fellow progressives and remembered by history as a spoiler. That would overshadow all he has accomplished.

Nader voters are under the illusion that a Bush era is somehow harmless to them—a mere interlude to rally their cause. Many were in grade school when Reagan was president and forget the consequences for progressive causes. It would be one thing if Bush were brilliant but lazy—or thick but hardworking. But he is neither brilliant nor hardworking, which means that the presidency will be essentially subcontracted to exactly those corporate interests that Naderites believe are threatening our democracy. That reminds me of the logic of those who extended the Vietnam War, courtesy of Nixon and his unwitting allies on the left: "We had to destroy the village in order to save it." America has tried that, Ralph. It doesn't work.

John Kennedy Jr.

—— 1999 ——

*I met Caroline Kennedy and John F. Kennedy Jr. in the 1970s
when we were students, so this one was personal for me.*

WHEN CAROLINE KENNEDY married Edwin Schlossberg
in the summer of 1986 at Hyannis, her brother made a toast.
John Kennedy spoke in far more moving words than I can remember
about three people: his "mummy" (Jacqueline Kennedy Onassis), his
beloved sister and himself. As he welcomed Schlossberg to this most
golden of circles, John conjured a family like no other. This was not the
big, sprawling Kennedy family of lore but a much smaller unit, huddled
together against history, trying to make a difference in the world but
mostly just looking for a normal life.

The three could never fully find it. Years would pass when they
could laugh and live like everyone else: Kennedys, yes, but not so
terribly different from the rest of us. Then the fabric would tear again.
The clichés they fled—"cursed," "tragic" and so on—pursued them
like some Shakespearean ghost, pulling them ceaselessly into the past.
But they refused to live there, preferring always to look ahead, even
as they kept an eye out for those left behind. I remember John Kennedy
Jr. as a man with an astonishing psychological balance for someone in
his position, with an easy, self-effacing sense of humor and a genuine
social conscience. With the help of his mother and sister, he wore his
royalty lightly.

Think about other aristocratic offspring in other parts of the
world, perhaps none as famous as Kennedy. Most fit a predictable
playboy mold, cutting a ribbon or two but more often racing speed-
boats, playing polo, mixing with a certain set. Superior and oblivious.
Kennedy was unfocused for a time, but was fundamentally decent.
Perhaps he will turn out to have been careless in choosing to fly that

night, too willing to tempt fate. But he was unburdened by the constant need to test his manhood that afflicted some of his cousins. The one child of the 1960s who had the greatest chance of growing up strange and insecure turned into one of the most centered and easygoing guys around.

President Kennedy once said that life is unfair; his family's pain—and that of the Bessettes—is bracing proof of that. Caroline has grown to adulthood mostly in peacetime but has endured the unending funerals associated with war. Unlike John, she clearly remembers her father, who was assassinated when she was nearly 6. Caroline was in Palm Beach, Florida, when her cousin David died of an overdose in 1984 and with her mother when she died of cancer in 1994. Her aunts and uncle lost four siblings to war and assassination. But they came from a family of nine children; Caroline has a husband and three kids, but her original nuclear family, once made up of five (brother Patrick died in infancy in 1963), now consists of her alone. To say that John and Caroline were close does no justice to their relationship.

Consider this poem that Caroline wrote for her Grandma Rose when John was 11:

He paints his bathroom walls in the middle of the night,
He comes into the room and unscrews every light ....
At four in the morning you can find him making glue
In the back hall near his guinea pig zoo ....
I love him not because I oughter
But because blood is thicker than water

John Kennedy inherited much else from his father beyond astonishing looks: a graceful way of working a room that made everyone he greeted feel at ease; a gently teasing, droll sense of humor that would have been charming even had the name been John Fitzgerald; a canny way of slipping away or avoiding scrutiny when it served him; an insouciance about risk. During World War II, John F. Kennedy had no business piloting a PT boat, given the condition of his back; his son probably had no business piloting a plane, given the condition of his foot. But they both grabbed life by the lapels.

Young Kennedy was routinely asked by New York Democrats to be a candidate for public office. A close friend confided to *Newsweek* after his accident that Kennedy might well have run for the U.S. Senate in 2000, if Hillary Clinton had not; he was very quietly exploring a campaign before the First Lady expressed interest. It was only a matter of time before he ran for something. Kennedy lacked the obsession so often necessary today for success in politics, but he would have brought obvious assets of celebrity, money, wit and a compelling presence on television. There was a complexity to him that wasn't apparent at first glance, when he seemed a kind of playful man-child. At some moments, Kennedy didn't care what people thought; he refused to be constrained by who he was or feel forced to live up to expectations. When he was criticized for auctioning off many of his parents' possessions, he shrugged impishly, then laughed privately at the idea of his cousin Maria's husband, Arnold Schwarzenegger, paying a fortune for golf clubs that Kennedy would have given him free if he had asked.

But the security and self-confidence masked a need to prove the doubters wrong. If Kennedy was driven by anything, it was to show that he wasn't a dilettante—that he was a serious person, even if he didn't take himself too seriously. He was immensely proud of having insisted on an idea people dismissed as foolish—*George*, a glossy magazine about politics—and making it work.

Kennedy seemed to have both more and fewer social graces than other people. He was almost always warm toward well-wishers, especially if they seemed down on their luck—extraordinarily accessible for someone so seemingly inaccessible. But he was happy to take the privileges that came with what he and friends jokingly called "the JK factor"—the willingness of everyone from tennis coaches to store clerks to do him favors. Kennedy's charm came in part from his guilelessness, even about this: taking a subway to Yankee Stadium last week while on crutches, he was surprised that passengers stood up to give him their seats. "See," he told a friend, "New Yorkers aren't so rude." When reminded that the JK factor was at work, he just laughed.

My own last conversation with Kennedy was about his magazine; *George*'s focus on history and politics made it a tough sell in the ad world. But Kennedy skillfully exploited his own name to keep it afloat, and the magazine's comfort with the intersection of celebrity and politics was a reflection not just of its editor but of the times.

George, which will almost surely die now after four years of publication, is an underrated magazine—easy to brush off because it rejects the normal cynicism about American politics. In his June 1999 editor's note, Kennedy explains why he helped select Senators John McCain and Russell Feingold, sponsors of campaign-finance reform, for this year's Profiles in Courage Award. "While we at *George* share your skepticism about many in Washington, we've always believed that political leaders can inspire a sense of pride and possibility. These two men have done just that." After mentioning this summer's *Star Wars* (which he later walked out of), Kennedy concluded: "But don't walk out thinking heroes exist only in movies."

This kind of talk is seen as almost quaint now, terribly out of fashion. In his own light way, Kennedy was trying to bring it back—to make idealism important and fun again. After visiting India and later South Africa as a young man, he returned knowing that he would use his wealth and fame to do his part. He helped some old friends start Exodus House, a school for Harlem kids. His efforts on behalf of the Robin Hood Foundation have helped spur innovative, community-based poverty organizations that actually produce results. For a time he was heavily involved with a program called Reaching Up, which aided mental-health workers. Each social commitment was done quietly, but with the intent of conveying to other wealthy people that they aren't truly successful if they lack a sense of public service.

The Kennedy family will play a role in American public life in the next century. But we will never see a figure quite like John F. Kennedy Jr. again. He was more than our "Prince Charming," as the New York tabs called him. We etched the past and the future on his fine face.

Eli Segal

*Eli Segal was unknown to the public but beloved
within Democratic politics. When he died, I wanted people
to remember how he changed the country.*

"*E*ACH TIME *a man stands up for an ideal, or acts to improve the
lot of others, or strikes out against injustice, he sends forth a tiny
ripple of hope, and crossing each other from a million different
centers of energy and daring those ripples build a current which can
sweep down the mightiest walls of oppression and resistance.*"
Those stirring words, uttered by Robert F. Kennedy in South Africa
40 years ago, were heard again at a huge funeral this week in
Massachusetts. They were among the favorite quotations of Eli Segal,
an extraordinary public servant who died February 21 of mesothelioma
(an asbestos-related disease) at age 63. Segal gave meaning to RFK's
line. Although he was almost unknown to the American public,
he deserves credit for two tiny ripples that became the most lasting
accomplishments of the Clinton presidency.

I met Segal in 1992, after he had run several successful toy and
crafts businesses and become chief of staff for Bill Clinton's now-
legendary campaign. He was, as Jack Lew (later Clinton's budget
director) put it, "the most beloved person on the campaign"—a
soft-spoken organizer always ready with a smile or helpful piece of
advice. While James Carville and George Stephanopoulos got the glory
for strategy and communications in the "war room," it was Segal who
managed the operation day-to-day. Had someone less talented been in
charge, the campaign might well have imploded under the weight of
scandal and dissension. Clinton would have ended up an obscure
ex-governor teaching law at the University of Arkansas.

Before Clinton, Segal backed only losers. He had major roles in the
campaigns of Gene McCarthy, George McGovern and Gary Hart. But

he changed history even then, co-writing the key report that reformed party nominating rules to take power away from bosses in smoke-filled rooms and give it to primary voters. In the 1972 campaign, he hired Clinton, just out of law school, to run Texas for McGovern, who won just 17 percent. When Clinton hired Segal in 1992, Segal said, "The only thing I can promise you, Bill, is that I'll do better for you than you did for McGovern in Texas."

He did, but I remember having dinner with Segal in Little Rock not long after Clinton's victory and learning to my surprise that he had no interest in a major post in the new administration. Instead, he wanted to use his entrepreneurial skills to help Clinton fulfill his campaign promise to create a national service program. He was given a tiny office and no money, but within months he established the Corporation for National Service, which became AmeriCorps. By structuring the program with local control and managing it carefully, Segal built a base of political support and gave an idea loathed by Republicans a fighting chance of success.

Today, AmeriCorps is no longer controversial. About 400,000 young people have been enrolled so far (more than the number of soldiers who have gone to Iraq). They, in turn, have touched and changed the lives of millions. Segal took a particular interest in City Year, an urban community-service non-profit he later chaired. At the request of Nelson Mandela, he helped launch City Year in South Africa. The idea of young people engaging in community service is now deeply embedded in school curricula throughout the United States and much of the world.

This accomplishment—greater than any by a Clinton Cabinet member—would have been enough on its own, but it was only the beginning for Segal. When Clinton signed welfare reform in 1996, many liberals were up in arms. They believed the president had sold out the poor, who would never be able to find jobs as required by law. Instead of whining about it, Segal got to work. Operating once more without a high-level job, he set about enlisting American businesses to commit to hiring former welfare recipients. His "welfare-to-work partnership" began with only five companies; the rest were afraid that those coming off welfare would be unreliable employees.

I remember when Segal told me that companies willing to take the risk actually found welfare recipients were so grateful for jobs that they made better workers than those who had not been on the dole. Still clinging to stereotypes, I didn't believe him at first. But slowly and with little publicity (I traveled with Clinton and Segal to a few welfare-to-work events but, like the rest of the media, did not cover them nearly as much as I should have), the program expanded.

Eventually, 20,000 companies committed to hiring welfare recipients. They put them through a workplace training program that is now standard for all entry-level employees at major companies. Partly through Segal's efforts, welfare reform became one of the most successful social programs of the late 20th Century.

The Yiddish word mensch is overused nowadays, but it fits Segal, who was devoted not just to his family but to hundreds of young people inspired by his upbeat personality and example of how to meld careers in business and public service. When he got sick (no one knows where his asbestos exposure took place), scores weighed in on caringbridge.org, a terrific Web site that links the family and friends of the ailing. He was modest about his contributions, but the record for historians is clear: The economic growth, balanced budgets and foreign policy initiatives of the Clinton years have evaporated under George W. Bush. National service and welfare reform remain, the legacies of a president known by everyone and of his friend, who occupied what Harry Truman called the highest office in a democracy—citizen.

Warren Beatty

—— 1998 ——

Warren Beatty's film Bulworth *was a noble*
if not terribly successful experiment that reflected liberal
dissatisfaction with the politics of the 1990s.

BOUNDING UP the long flight of stairs at Moomba, New York's
downtown club of the moment, Warren Beatty is living his
contradictions. One of his old flames, Madonna, is on the way over, as
well as Leonardo DiCaprio, looking for some career advice. But friendly
chats with other stars won't bring to Beatty's eyes the same ironic
twinkle as the man waiting at the top of the stairs.

"Ron Perelman's here," Beatty explains. "Old friend. Not exactly
a communist." Over a drink, the billionaire tells the movie star he can't
wait to see *Bulworth*, the subversive, hilarious and important new
Molotov cocktail that Beatty is set to explode at 1,800 theaters by
Memorial Day. Perelman doesn't know what he's in for. The film evis-
cerates plutocrats like him, not to mention complacent blacks, violent
white cops, craven political operatives, schlocky Jewish movie moguls,
corporate lackey reporters, vile insurance companies and gluttonous
media conglomerates like the one owned by Rupert Murdoch, whose
studio Beatty essentially tricked into making the movie.

Later that late April night, another well-wisher thanks Beatty
for "everything you've done for the Democratic Party," referring to his
years of campaigning for the Kennedys, George McGovern, Gary Hart
and many others. The fan is unaware of everything Beatty
does *to* the party (especially Clinton Democrats) in the film, which represents the breaching of a long relationship with elective politics. But
Beatty still moves easily in that world. The following weekend, making
the rounds in Washington, he warmly greets Henry Kissinger, Senator
Dianne Feinstein, John McLaughlin and the other big wheels of the
American political-media-industrial complex. After they see *Bulworth*,

of course, many powerful people will tell Beatty they loved it. They're either lying or perversely pleased by the celluloid shiv he has shoved deep into the heart of their status quo.

Bulworth is Beatty's baby, and he says it's really made for the three babies he produced with his wife, Annette Bening, 6-year-old Kathlyn, 3-year-old Ben and 1-year-old Isabel. "I wanted to do something that would mean something to them in the future," he says. The language is so vulgar and the racial politics so raw that Beatty, now 61, will be well into his 70s before his kids are old enough to hear their father's message about the disparities of wealth and opportunity in American life. Those disparities—and the way politicians have sold out to big-money interests—are "the real obscenities," he says, both on screen and off.

Beatty has always been a risk-taker. As the old studio system collapsed in the late 1960s, he revived the idea of actor as auteur, with his own money on the line. But *Bulworth*, a story about a senator who goes bonkers and ends up in hip-hop clothes wooing a black girl less than half his age (Halle Berry), is a gamble of a different magnitude. Instead of trying to restore some of his luster as a screen icon, Beatty exposes himself as never before—to ridicule, racial recriminations and the all-too-real odds of failure at the box office. The man about whom Carly Simon supposedly wrote "You're So Vain" admits his age and spends most of the film in a shirt soiled with cocktail sauce. And he raps. About campaign-finance reform.

But even if you reject the politics and the premise, it's hard not to laugh—and to admire Beatty's guts. Radical isn't chic anymore, even in Hollywood. And even when it was, liberals mouthed off publicly but usually checked their political views at the editing-room door. The choice between money and ideology has been no contest. In mainstream film, few beyond Oliver Stone ever muster the creative courage of their political convictions.

When filmmakers do use political settings, it's almost always for esthetics, not substance. Politics serves as a backdrop for stories either about character (*Primary Colors, The Seduction of Joe Tynan*) or the emptiness and hypocrisy of the process (*The Candidate, Wag the Dog*). Even Frank Capra films, as Beatty notes, never identified anyone's party.

Sometimes the symbols in *Bulworth* clang. His plot seems to suggest that brutal honesty would be rewarded by the voters, which Beatty himself is too sophisticated to believe. The nostalgia for the destructive Black Panther politics of Huey Newton is not just dated but unwarranted. And a recurring assassination theme, while useful in dramatic terms, seems more than a tad grandiose.

But the sincerity is so old it's new. To spread his message, Beatty is practically selling *Bulworth* like a bootleg video out of the back of a car. The normally stealthy actor is serving as his own publicist on the movie, and he's amping up his protean charm on any reporter or young rapper in earshot.

Beatty says the origins of *Bulworth* go back to *Shampoo* (1975), when he briefly considered having his character, George, open a beauty parlor with Richard Pryor in a black neighborhood. He wasn't ready to tackle race yet. But by the mid-1990s, Beatty launched *Bulworth*—and began spending time late at night with Suge Knight, Tupac Shakur, Dr. Dre and other gangsta rappers. "He was just a pest sometimes—hanging on my porch when I got home, trying to get into the black world," Knight told *Newsweek* from prison. While he's not much of a hip-hop fan himself, Beatty insists "they are poets, and must be heard."

With his usual Hollywood cunning, Beatty went to Twentieth Century Fox, which he says still owed him $35 million from a pre-Disney deal involving *Dick Tracy*. Instead of suing for it, he offered to make a film for less, but only if it gave him total control. He says he told the studio only the barest plot outlines, with the politics and racial dimension left out. "I don't think anyone would have financed this with *anyone* in it if they'd known what it was," Beatty says. When he turned in the script, "Fox hated it, though at least they were honest enough to say so."

Beatty needs a hit. His last film, *Love Affair*, tanked in 1994. But he's realistic about what has happened to the movie business. "The same thing that has stagnated politics has stagnated movies—this incredible ability to evaluate public opinion, to look in the rearview mirror."

In balancing art and commerce, Beatty makes plenty of concessions to the younger movie marketplace; he's got a rap soundtrack featuring all the hot artists that's already climbing the charts, and Halle Berry could lure anyone to the 'hood. But *Bulworth* is essentially a 1970s film, as if from the era before movies were focus-grouped and special-effected to death. The first question asked of Paddy Chayefsky's *Network* or Robert Altman's *Nashville* was not: "What will they gross the first weekend?" It was, "What are they trying to say?"

Bulworth is a wonderful throwback to that golden age of modern

filmmaking when movies could be scabrous and messy and "unsatisfy-
ing" (a major insult nowadays) in their plot resolution as long as
they fulfilled the demands of real art—to provoke the audience and
challenge our settled view of the world.

Beatty's own view of the world has hardened. For decades, he was
a highly active liberal Democrat; he says he turned down leading roles
in both *The Godfather* and *The Sting* to work for McGovern in 1972
and became a close adviser to Hart in 1984 and 1988. He and Hart
remain good friends, though Beatty says Hart rejected his advice to
campaign heavily in the inner city and thus had "no hard-core con-
stituency" to fall back on when the Donna Rice sex scandal hit.
Through the years, Hollywood was a major source of money for the
Democratic Party, and Beatty a major draw for donors.

Not anymore. Like Jay Bulworth, "I know what it feels like to be
a suicidally depressed Democrat," Beatty says. The disillusionment set
in slowly under Clinton. "His sin has nothing to do with interns—it's
the sin of not honoring the mission of the party." By mission,
he means the old Democratic goals of fairer distribution of income and
help for the least fortunate first. "Clinton had a window to really do
something. What's the point of winning if you aren't going to try?" The
name Bulworth, he says, is partly a play on Bull Moose, Teddy
Roosevelt's 1912 break from the two-party system. "The parties
have melded; they both represent the top 20 percent who have all
the money."

Speaking of which, Ron Perelman is on the phone. He's seen
Bulworth and pronounces it "fabulous." He's laughing now: "Warren's
a capitalist, a feeling capitalist."

A Bulworth capitalist. The movie star's politics are not America's
politics in 1998, but that's not the point. "This is about leading, not
winning," he says, a sentiment even rarer in Hollywood than it is in
Washington. Beatty knows that it's really about both: if he doesn't
"win" at the box office, he'll have a harder time getting the studio
financing to "lead" again any time soon. Yet by keeping faith with his
ideas, he's already won, even if the throngs don't show up to vote.

Frank Sinatra

―― 1998 ――

I only met Frank Sinatra once but was struck by how his journey across the political spectrum was typical of many white men.

JANUARY 19, 1961. The lavish "gala" on the eve of John F. Kennedy's Inauguration is produced by the 43-year-old president-elect's friend Frank Sinatra. His song "High Hopes" is adapted for the Kennedys. Because of a snowstorm, the event, featuring Sir Laurence Olivier and Nat King Cole, doesn't end until close to 3 AM. It is widely hailed; the *New York Times* notes that the party "may have been the most stunning assembly of theatrical talent ever brought together for a single show."

January 19, 1981. The lavish "gala" on the eve of Ronald Reagan's Inauguration is produced by the 69-year-old president-elect's friend Frank Sinatra. His song "Nancy with the Laughing Face" is adapted for the Reagans. Because of a skit in which the actor Ben Vereen dons blackface, the event, which also stars Donny and Marie, is controversial. It is widely derided; one critic calls it "a cross between Dial-a-Joke and *Hee-Haw.*"

But who cared about the critics? Sinatra always knew his audience—musically and, offstage, politically. In the 1940s, the crooner symbolized the emergence of immigrants into the mainstream. In the 1950s and early '60s, his swagger mirrored that of his country at the height of the Cold War. By the late '60s, he was the anti-Beatle—the reaction against the counterculture. And by the 1980s and '90s, he represented restoration. The singer who started in swing became the embodiment of the swing voter, journeying from New Deal liberal to Agnew reactionary. It was a trip that a lot of his fans—lunch-bucket Archie Bunker Catholics—made with him.

Sinatra forever changed the relationship between Hollywood and

Washington. He luxuriated in proximity to power; politicians coveted his glamour. Before him, most entertainers and officeholders steered clear of each other. Stars feared their fans would be upset by partisanship, and politicians thought show business undignified. Sinatra helped to fuse the two cultures, and connect them to a third—organized crime.

Politics ran in Sinatra's blood. His mother was a local Democratic leader in Hoboken, New Jersey, and Sinatra remembered campaigning with her before he could read. In 1944, he stumped for an ailing Franklin Roosevelt. At Sinatra's concerts, some fans wore buttons: "Frankie's for FDR, And So Are We." By the 1950s, he was "Madly for Adlai"—and falsely listed as a communist in documents collected by the House Un-American Activities Committee. But even big-time Democrats could feel the sting of Sinatra's temper. At one Democratic National Convention, House Speaker Sam Rayburn put the arm on him to sing "The Yellow Rose of Texas." Sinatra's reply: "Take the hands off the suit, creep."

Senator John F. Kennedy gravitated to Sinatra. His sister Patricia was married to "Pete" Lawford, part of the Rat Pack. The "Chairman of the Board" called Lawford "Liaison Man with the Other Government of the Country," but some of the liaisons were of a different nature. JFK and the Rat Pack had similar notions of a good time—lounging poolside, smoking Havanas and chasing "broads."

In 1959, Sinatra had a fling with a young woman named Judith Campbell. On February 7, 1960, at the Sands in Las Vegas, Sinatra introduced Campbell to Kennedy. By mid-1960, Sinatra knew that JFK and Campbell had begun an affair, but in Miami he introduced Campbell to a man called "Sam Flood." His real name was Sam Giancana, and he was the chief of the Chicago Mafia. For more than a year, the president and the mob boss shared a mistress—courtesy of Frank Sinatra.

These relationships exposed Kennedy to potential blackmail, and eventually caused Sinatra great pain. By 1962, he had hatched plans to make his Palm Springs home a kind of Western White House. He built guest quarters and outfitted them with extra phones and teletype machines for the press. JFK was scheduled to visit in June for some of the old fun in the sun. But on March 22, J. Edgar Hoover gave Kennedy a memo on Giancana, who had been working with the CIA to assassinate Fidel Castro. The memo, based on wiretaps, outlined Giancana's affair with Campbell and closed with a mention of Sinatra's referring to her as the girl "shacking up with John Kennedy in the East." The president ended up staying with Bing Crosby. Soon, Sinatra was spotted with a sledgehammer, breaking the helicopter pad he'd built for the president.

Sinatra remained a down-the-line Democrat until 1970, when he supported Reagan's bid for re-election as governor. Sinatra forged a strong bond with Vice President Spiro Agnew, another up-from-the-streets ethnic who had made good. During this period, Agnew visited Sinatra 18 times in Palm Springs, including Thanksgiving, Christmas and Easter. Sinatra had never been fond of either Richard Nixon or Reagan before; friends had quoted him as saying the Gipper was "dumb and dangerous." But now Reagan defended Sinatra publicly on some of the Mafia charges, and Nixon began inviting him to fly on Air Force One, which Kennedy never had.

The Reagan years were a kitschy second act for Sinatra and his style. Nancy Reagan adored him. When he was unable to attend a Friars' Club roast, Sinatra sent a telegram saying: PRESIDENT REAGAN DOESN'T LIKE ME AND GEORGE SHULTZ TO BE ABSENT FROM THE WHITE HOUSE AT THE SAME TIME. Reagan gave him the Presidential Medal of Freedom, which outraged critics who noted his ties to murderers. More telling, the president asked Sinatra to campaign for him in 1984. He did, including a stop with Reagan seeking Italian-American votes in Hoboken: the Reagan Democrat had come home. "The Leader," as he was sometimes called by the rest of the Rat Pack, always managed to sing to the tempo of his times.

Diana Trilling

―― 1997 ――

When I began spending afternoons visiting with Diana Trilling in her apartment—unchanged since the 1950s—my wife got a little jealous of a woman nearing 90. But I loved getting her to write for Newsweek *and listening to her stories of long-dead legendary New York intellectuals.*

W HEN SHE WAS in her late 80s, Diana Trilling, one of the very last of the great mid-century New York intellectuals, began to write for *Newsweek*. She told me once that she now realized how all of those book reviews and essays she wrote starting in the 1940s for the *Nation* and the *Partisan Review* did not reach enough people. And so she wrote for *Newsweek*—and brilliantly—about the excesses of McCarthyism and the shortcomings of feminism. Still astonishingly sharp and relentlessly judgmental, she wrote on O.J. Simpson for the *New Republic* and on her summer camp of 75 years ago for the *New Yorker*. She completed an insightful memoir of her storied marriage to the critic Lionel Trilling, *The Beginning of the Journey*. At the time of her death at 91, Trilling was finishing a book on a visit to the Kennedy White House.

Why would a woman that age, too blind to read, still polish her stiletto every day from her ancient apartment near Columbia University? Part of the answer is that she started late. The daughter of immigrant Polish Jews, she experienced severe phobias as a child and endured an anxious adulthood. She didn't even begin to write the piercing book reviews for which she became known until she was in her late 30s. Even then, she wrote no original nonfiction books until she was in her late 70s (when she tackled the Jean Harris story) and no fiction or poetry at all. Motherhood and marriage came first, not out of old-fashioned subservience to Lionel, who died in 1975, but based on an informed insistence on the larger importance of family.

The deeper reason that Trilling kept writing was that she believed something essential was dying in America. Her circle of intellectuals could be a petty, pretentious lot, as Trilling herself never tired of explaining. But they believed in what they called "a life of significant contention"— arguing politics and culture in a deep, broad and serious way.

Trilling saw not only the demise of that life but the loss of standards everywhere. Although she moved from being a Communist sympathizer in the 1930s (Whittaker Chambers once tried—unsuccessfully—to recruit her) to an early, liberal anticommunism, she rejected simplistic thinking of all kinds. Trilling's impatience with careless standards was such that when I once mentioned that my young daughter had drawn a beautiful picture, she said that if it wasn't genuinely beautiful, I shouldn't say it was. The woman that the poet Robert Lowell once called "a housekeeping goddess of reason" didn't want our everyday critical furniture to grow soft and comfortable.

Lady Diana

—— 1997 ——

*The September night Lady Diana died in a car accident,
Newsweek had just "gone to bed" and so had I. Along with other
editors and writers, I rushed into work and we stayed up all night
putting together our extensive coverage.*

S HE DIED for a blurry picture, a pointless snap from a speeding
motorcycle that might have appeared on an inside spread of *Hello!*
or *Paris Match* or some other glossy of no consequence. It is unfair to
the real Diana Spencer, by all accounts a nice person who used her fame
well, that her death so symbolizes the emptiness of celebrity worship,
the false faith of the end of the 20th century. Dodging tabloid photographers, she was doing her bit not just to preserve some privacy but to
hold back forces that she helped unleash—forces of media intrusion
that will now be subjected to an unprecedented backlash. In a twisted
way, she died in the line of duty, not to country but to the age she came
to represent.

Historians are likely to judge that Diana's reign—and reign she
did—owed its brilliance to the tranquillity of the times. With no
global wars or cataclysm, no Hitlers or Churchills to dominate the
public realm, we could turn our full attention to diversions of gossip
and fantasy. We now routinely view image and spectacle as large with
meaning, with old-fashioned substance suddenly the boring trifle.

The irony is that with the end of her short life, Diana may well
achieve a political goal more substantial than that of all but a few
politicians. The shock of her death is being likened to the Kennedy
assassination in 1963. The analogy seems overdrawn, their forever-
young influences on popular culture notwithstanding. Diana wasn't
president, and her death leaves no creative vacuum like that of an Elvis
Presley or John Lennon. But just as Kennedy's memorial was the Civil
Rights Act, Diana's could be ratification of a treaty banning land mines,
not just in Britain (where her focus on this issue achieved results before

277

her death) but in the United States, where skeptical senators may now have to contend with a new public groundswell. This could yet yield for her a reputation as a humanitarian as well as immortal icon of style.

If Helen of Troy was the face that launched a thousand ships, Lady Di launched at least a thousand covers, and hundreds of millions of newspaper and magazine sales. In the 16 years since her marriage, she became not only the most famous woman in the world, but the only personality who consistently sold big in the global marketplace. While paparazzi are not a new phenomenon, Diana-as-prey took the game to a new level. Instead of three or four photographers trailing a celebrity, it could, in her case, be 30 or 40, each hoping for that six-figure shot. This created a strange and perhaps emblematic protocol of coverage: the president of France can stroll down the Champs-Elysées undisturbed; a divorced ex-royal couldn't leave a restaurant without a high-speed chase.

Diana came to understand that the tabloids were simultaneously the bane of her existence and the source of her strength. In recent years, she not only developed working relationships with tabloid editors but learned to exploit publicity for her cause, be it skewering Charles or raising money for charity. One reason for her popularity was that the public essentially shared her splurge-and-purge attitude toward celebrity news. Readers buy it and bemoan it without fully confronting the contradictions. They want to inspect the clay feet of their heroes— then cry for the head of the sculptors.

Will this global hypocrisy market still work as it always has? In the short run, only a foolish publication would pay for gory pictures of the accident. To do so would risk a boycott. The more difficult question is whether Diana's death might change the tabloid culture permanently. In recent years, with global news proliferating, photographers have gone from being a minor annoyance that came with the territory of fame to being a major source of anxiety for public figures. As their private loathing of the press boils over publicly, it will likely find a ready audience among millions already fed up with the news media—any news medium. The distinction between tabloids and so-called respectable news organizations will be difficult to uphold in the recriminations that lie ahead, and for good reason. If there had been no accident and the motorcycle paparazzi in the Paris tunnel had obtained a good shot of Di and Dodi kissing, most of the world's newspapers would have tsked-tsked over the price paid for first rights to the shot— then published it themselves.

The pressure will mount now to tighten privacy laws, though they were not relevant in this case. The French already have strict privacy laws on the books, but they did not—and cannot—apply to what happens on a public Paris street. Or can they? There's a chance that the fallout from Diana's death will be a series of press restrictions never seen before in Western democracies. Voluntary codes of press behavior have failed miserably. Expect to see legislative efforts to make it easier to sue for invasion of privacy and perhaps some proposals for outright bans on pictures of minors without their consent.

Ultimately, nothing much can change because media coverage is the oxygen of modern public life. Watch now as celebrityhood is transmogrified into secular sainthood, courtesy of a publicity machine that will turn even its own remorse into just another story. Perhaps that's appropriate, for it is the mighty communications culture that made Diana and shapes the world she left. The princess will never be queen, but maybe the titles don't mean much. The England in which she lived will never be remembered as Elizabethan. It will be The Di Era. So sad she had to die for it.

The Sopranos

—— 2001 ——

The Sopranos was my favorite television show ever, and midway through its run I wanted to explain why it was personal for me.

HEADING INTO its season finale on Sunday, *The Sopranos* has more loose ends than a plate of angel hair pasta. The beauty of the show is that David Chase won't tie them all up, and not just because he needs something for next season. Chase and his writers are dedicated to breaking every cliché of TV drama. That makes waiting for Sunday all the more suspenseful. Predicting some hackneyed resolution (Jackie Jr. gets whacked; the Russian blows Paulie's walnuts off) is like disrespecting the Bing.

I can't remember investing even a fraction of this much interest in any other TV show—ever. I won't answer the phone on Sunday nights between 9:00 and 10:00 and shoo away the kids—a fine signal to send when you're trying to get them to watch less TV. At the candy rack the other day, I even considered buying some Tic-Tacs. Never know when a spare one will come in handy down in the Pine Barrens.

Part of the appeal for me is that I live in Montclair, New Jersey, home of Yogi Berra, Bill Bradley and a large chunk of the staff of the *New York Times*, but now principally known as the town where Dr. Jennifer Melfi lives and works. It's also where she was raped, and Tony, in an early episode, was shot. I'm ashamed of the number of times I've bragged about this to out-of-town friends and colleagues. The amazing thing is that they actually seem impressed—even those who regularly interview real-life famous and important people. In a miraculous status turnaround, this newfound respect is directly attributable to my living in ... New Jersey.

I went to an Italian restaurant in nearby Little Falls last weekend and every five minutes another Christopher or Ralphie walked in, looking for an Adriana at the bar. I could have sworn I saw Carmela and Rosalie having dinner in the corner and Artie and Charmaine exchanging words. The Bada Bing is actually a bar on Route 17 in Lodi called Satin Dolls, where, to the chagrin of tourists, they have no nude dancing. Satriale's is in Kearny, but the pig on top is all Hollywood.

Jim Treffinger, our local Essex County executive, bears a passing resemblance to Assemblyman Zellman, the corrupt local politician played by Peter Riegert. And Treffinger made a mistake when he wouldn't let *The Sopranos* shoot (film or guns) in the beautiful South Mountain Reservation because he thinks the show slurs Italian Americans. (They had to film that wonderful episode where Paulie and Christopher get lost in the snow in Westchester County, New York, of all places.)

It's just a guess, but I bet those who are offended aren't regular viewers of the show. In any event, it was a boneheaded political move, and not just because Italians make up a shrinking portion of Essex County. The show is so popular locally that tryouts for extras were cancelled because hundreds of Italian-Americans showed up, overwhelming the casting directors. My plumber, perfect for a part, was among them.

Unfortunately, Joe the Plumber doesn't know any better than anyone else what's going to happen this week. But the truth is, it doesn't much matter. The exquisite pleasures of "The Sopranos" lie in the little character moments that have nothing to do with who gets whacked next: Junior and the blender; Meadow and her roommate; Carmela and the girls discussing Hillary Clinton.

Oh, and Ralphie in the kitchen showing Jackie Jr. how to make the tomato sauce cling better to the pasta? My wife tried it last night. Delicious.

PART SEVEN

IDEAS

From the Prison of the "Isms"

—— 1999 ——

At the turn of the century, this represented a
short reflection on the big ideas and ideologies of our time.

MISTER DOOLEY, a fictional newspaper character at the last turn of the century, described a fanatic as someone who viewed himself as "doing what the Lord would do—if He only had the facts." The century that followed was beset by just such grandiose fanaticism, and it became the bloodiest in all of human history. Will we see a sequel in the century to come? Communism and Nazism are gone, but their suffixes remain. The biggest of the big political questions is whether other malignant "isms" can be held in check. The health of the new century hinges on the answer.

The mother of all isms is utopianism, the belief that some belief structure can bring a perfect world. This has proved to be history's greatest mirage. We've learned the hard way that ideologies imbued with great certitude tend to be dangerous. That's not an argument against firm convictions or even against spreading them. But it does suggest that the world is safer when we are moderating ideology rather than imposing it, when we think for ourselves rather than submit to what the historian Robert Conquest calls "mindslaughter."

The big struggle ahead is between globalism and nationalism, with fundamentalism the wild card. So far, the best logic for the eventual triumph of global thinking is technological: cyberspace knows no borders. Just as 19th-century national technologies such as the transcontinental railroad aided nationalism, so 21st-century international technologies such as the Internet will aid internationalism. To be successful, bad ideologies need to seal off dissent; that's the idea behind totalitarianism. As technology breaches the old self-contained vessels of information, the whole notion of mind control will be much more difficult. It sometimes seems the only big ideology of the future will be what might be called "dot-comism," which, given its endlessly pluralistic nature, is not really an ideology at all. In this century, Marxists and Freudians depended on elaborate and exclusionary hierarchies of expertise. In the new world, big-thinking theoretical experts can expect to die a death of a thousand e-mail cuts.

As the Internet expands, some even believe that nations will eventually be replaced by cybercommunities. Or perhaps the struggle will be between artificial intelligence and what we still think of as the real thing, with "humanism" or "bioism" representing a preference for people over machines. In the meantime, technology is essentially neutral—an amplifier of existing ideologies that spreads all modes of thinking: hate and human rights, extreme capitalism and extreme environmentalism, dogmatism and moral relativism.

The isms that would seem most directly threatened by the Internet are nationalism and its economic face, protectionism. If history has proved anything, it's that the economic case for erecting barriers is weak. But for many nations, the political case remains strong. In fact, the more globalization takes hold, the stronger the nationalist reaction is likely to be. This is partly the result of convenient resentment against the United States. If you're trying to hang on to power, from China to Russia to the Middle East, stirring up nationalist fervor is still a good strategy.

And there's a deeper psychological pull. "The need to sanctify our ancestors or leave something for posterity is just not satisfied by global networks," says the writer Jim Sleeper. "They don't satisfy that longing precisely because they're instantaneous." No one has yet picketed in favor of "globalism" (which spellcheck still doesn't even recognize as a word). The war over Kosovo was a setback for sovereignty, but it still has plenty of kick left in it. In fact, the more international the world becomes, the greater the odds of what Sleeper calls "reactive retribalization." Still-incoherent glimmers of that are present in the emerging backlash against free trade. We may find soon that the speed of light is blinding us to powerful older visions.

If nationalism reflects the urge to preserve common heritage, fundamentalism is about spiritual longing in a sinful and materialistic world. While Jewish and Christian fundamentalism are growing, the most potent form is Islamic, dating back to the rise of the Ayatollah Khomeini in 1979. Terrorism remains a major threat in the new century, but many of the fears of Islamic fundamentalism are overblown. The vast majority of the world's 1 billion Muslims are not extremists, and even the extremists are too badly split for a worldwide movement. The doctrinal disputes within Islam, which have already led to political crises in Iran, Algeria and elsewhere, won't end any time soon. Even so, the pace of modernization will keep fundamentalism alive and potentially dangerous.

The second half of the 20th century was less bloody than the first in part because a healthy reaction against communism, nationalism and militarism set in. Racism, which was once a proud and aggressive ideology, has been pushed into the closet. Perhaps the century's most important movement—feminism—has, in the United States, been largely transformed into careerism, while Freudianism has gone pop. Across the world, major ideas are in retreat. The biggest isms in Russia nowadays are alcoholism and cynicism. The latter will, if left untreated, leave societies open to far more malevolent ideas. The best antidote can be found in two more isms—skepticism and idealism. Properly blended, they offer the best hope of charting a well-balanced middle course through the tumult ahead.

The Moral Equivalent of Apollo

—— 1995 ——

*This was written during the Gingrich Revolution of 1995
when faith in government's ability to solve problems had sunk
to a new low. We're there again now.*

"**F**AILURE IS NOT AN OPTION." These are the words of
Gene Kranz, the Apollo 13 flight director played by Ed Harris, and
they deserve to linger in the minds of moviegoers at least as long as the
superb technical re-creation of the American space program. The film
is tightly focused on the immense drama of the aborted mission; beyond
astronaut Jim Lovell's daughter in a hippie costume, it pretends to no
social comment at all. And yet I couldn't help thinking about the
larger ideas this movie's heat shield reflects—not about 1970, but 1995.
The real heroes of *Apollo 13*—on screen and in life—are today's
villains, namely federal bureaucrats. The paper-shuffling government
geeks who (we're informed daily from the House floor) couldn't handle
a three-car funeral not only put men on the moon; they rescued
them against all odds. Twenty-five years ago, failure was not in their
vocabulary. Today, we're told, failure is their first name.

Unless there's an American soldier or airman in danger. Then
we briefly suspend our disbelief about the federal government, and
remember the miracles. In recent years, this impulse has become a kind
of tiny rescue asterisk in our otherwise deep skepticism about what we
can accomplish as a nation. When Americans are lost in space (or
Bosnia) we pull together and get the job done. But when Americans are
lost in America—through terrible education, say, or a broken welfare
system—then it's hopeless. Let them come home under their own
power. Let the private sector save 'em. Let the states do it.

Ironically, this loss of faith in Washington coincided almost
exactly with the staggering accomplishment of the federal Apollo
program. The Vietnam War soured the public on the government just

as that same government was making history that will be remembered 500 years from now. The emerging bias against government solutions has been plenty justified by horror stories of unconscionable waste. But the bias is also impervious to evidence of success. The formulation went: "If we put a man on the moon, why can't we [fill in the blank]?" The assumption behind the question was that nothing ever filled in the blank: the moon was a glorious exception. In fact, in the years since, the U.S. government essentially ended hunger (through food stamps), cleaned up polluted air and water (through federal regulation), transformed the role of women and blacks (with routes for upward mobility). Almost no one stopped to notice.

It's true that today's problems are less amenable to NASA-style big fixes than yesterday's. The American family module is much easier to break and harder to repair than the lunar module. Even for technical problem solving, mainframes and command-and-control hierarchies are being replaced all over the world by PCs and decentralized systems, which work better.

But this development is not at odds with the message of Apollo 13. In fact, the small quality-circle teams of Houston technicians on the ground anticipated 1990s-style problem solving. At one point they saved the crew from fatal carbon dioxide poisoning by feverishly improvising a device with duct tape, then asking the astronauts to replicate their experiment. It worked. They literally fit a square peg into a round hole.

Social problem solving is often just a variation on these challenges. Simplistic as it was, Ross Perot had a point when he argued in 1992 that we need to get under the hood, identify what's wrong with education, welfare and the rest, experiment with pilot programs, then apply the workable solutions nationally. In the case of Apollo 13, this took the form of grounded astronaut Ken Mattingly (Gary Sinese) and others experimenting under extreme time pressure with solutions in the Houston flight simulator, then telling Jim Lovell (Tom Hanks) to apply the ideas in space.

Such thinking is light-years removed from today's debate, where replicating an idea nationally has become unfashionable. Newt Gingrich's approach is to eloquently conjure the problem, but offer no solution, His favorite sound bite is: "You cannot maintain civilization with 12-year-olds having children, with 13-year-olds killing each other. with 17-year-olds dying of AIDS, with 18-year-olds getting diplomas they can't even read." Then he argues that Washington simply can't figure out how to change those conditions. National goals for education? No way. And don't dare compare them to JFK's goals for space. If the states want to try, fine, but forget the idea of a national mission.

If this kind of thinking applied to the space program, Apollo 13 would still be orbiting with three dead astronauts. Texas was not about to rescue Lovell while Colorado figured out another way to get Jack Swigert back to earth. The private sector could not have handled the problem. Gingrich understands this; space exploration is an exception to his thinking about the role of the federal government. He supports it.

It's the implications of that distinction that are so troubling. Are Lovell, Swigert and Haise somehow more American, more deserving of heroic national efforts, than the rest of us, just trying to get prepared for brutal re-entry into the global work force? Of course, struggling Americans ultimately have to make their own way back from the dark side of the moon, just as the crew of Apollo 13 did. But they, too, could use a little help from those imaginative federal bureaucrats on the ground. To William James's moral equivalent of war, add the social equivalent of Apollo. If the plastic doesn't work, try the duct tape. That's our nation up there, and as the clock ticks down, the mission has not been completed. Failure should not be an option.

A Question of Anti-Semitism

—— 2002 ——

*As a Jew, I have a particular interest in the problem of
anti-Semitism and various events have prompted me to write
about it over the years. This one was occasioned by the
comments of a powerful member of Congress.*

D ICK ARMEY, the retiring House majority leader, told a Florida
audience last week that he sees "two Jewish communities" in
America—smart conservative Jews in the sciences, and dumb liberal
Jews in the arts. I don't know how this distinction accounts for liberal
Albert Einstein, conservative Saul Bellow and a few million others, but
never mind. Armey says he saw in college that conservatives are smart
and "liberals are just not very bright people." I guess that would make
him ... a liberal.

But not an anti-Semite. In this case, skull thickness is a mitigating
factor. The virus of true anti-Semitism is so strong in so much of the
world—where synagogues are burned and people cheer suicide
bombers—that garden-variety stupidity doesn't rate, even for the Anti-
Defamation League.

Yet suddenly the old Howard Stern game—"Who's a Jew?"—
has been replaced by "Who's an anti-Semite?" (defined by *Webster's*
as hatred of Jews, not Arab Semitic peoples). Daniel Pipes, a Mideast
expert, created a furor last week when he posted a Web site
(campus-watch.org) to monitor what he calls anti-Semitism in Middle
Eastern Studies programs on campus. Or how about Amiri Baraka, the
black activist and poet laureate of New Jersey, who recently read a
poem repeating the intercontinental lie that 4,000 Israelis stayed home
from the World Trade Center on September 11? Baraka's excuse
was that he wasn't anti-Semitic, just anti-Israel, thereby proving the
limitations of that oft-used distinction.

But that's an easy case. The harder calls are in the thick of the
policy debate, where some people sincerely believe their positions don't

amount to anti-Semitism, and others sincerely do. Take the issue of divestment. In a recent speech, Harvard president Lawrence Summers upbraided those who signed a campus petition that calls for universities to divest their endowment portfolios of any company doing business with Israel. You've got to respect Summers's guts in moving past the namby-pamby neutrality of most college presidents and actually saying something. But how about his argument itself? Summers posits that "serious and thoughtful people are advocating and taking actions that are anti-Semitic in their effect if not their intent."

Intent and effect. Summers's distinction is critical. Most of those who sign the divestment petitions at Harvard and several other campuses aren't anti-Semites. (Some are even Israeli professors.) They see a divestment strategy as a way of pressuring Ariel Sharon to change his policy in the West Bank. On one level, this is well within the bounds of legitimate debate. Criticism of Israeli policies is not anti-Semitic; in fact, it is arguably philo-Semitic—an upholding of noble Jewish traditions of scrutiny and self-examination.

But there's a dark side to divestment. In the case of Israel, the movement suffers from a careless use of analogy and a poor reading of the Middle East. The analogy used by signers of the divestment petitions is, of course, South Africa. You can understand why Jews might resent the comparison. The apartheid regime was a pariah state recognized by almost no one. Israel—lest we forget—was recognized even by the Palestinians in 1998. South Africa was the source of moral evil in the region; the good guys and bad guys weren't hard to sort out. In the Middle East, blame is more evenly shared, and more recently attributable to the Palestinians, who have rejected the homeland offered them two years ago at Camp David and repeatedly send suicide bombers to kill the innocent and provoke Sharon. Divestment directed against Israel when it was so clearly wrong in invading Lebanon in the 1980s might have made sense. Today it's just strange, and suspicious.

Some argue that the blindness to Palestinian blame is merely misplaced romanticism, not anti-Semitism. The students and professors on campus with a weakness for this kind of politics also champion other oppressed peoples fighting entrenched power, and overlook their abuses. But at a certain point, persistent double standards start to smell of something more malignant. Funny how campus activists never seem to mention, say, Syrian occupation of Lebanon. They bemoan capital punishment in the United States but say nothing when the Palestinians routinely execute suspected collaborators, including the mothers of young children. They single out Israeli human rights abuses that pale next to those of their Arab neighbors, which we know less about because of press restrictions. Anti-Zionism isn't anti-Semitism—until it reaches a certain pitch.

Divestment may be only a fall fad on college campuses, but it's political nitroglycerin. It raises unrealistic hopes that Palestinians might eventually get all of Palestine with the help of sympathizers in Europe and the United States. It undermines any progress toward a two-state solution, the only practical and moral path to peace. It displays a willful obtuseness about the world that, anti-Semitic or not, is clearly something else. Call it Armey-esque.

Charter Schools: Attack of "The Blob"

—— 2002 ——

Education is one of those areas where I have
consistently departed from Democratic Party orthodoxy.

THERE'S NO SILVER BULLET. That's what everyone in education says, and it's true. But certain types of schools are what might be called silver arrows in the quiver of reform. The charter school movement, which began ten years ago this fall with just one school in St. Paul, Minnesota, is quietly changing public education, especially in inner cities. With 2,400 such schools in 40 states, charters represent a workable and often inspiring form of public school choice. So of course mindless boards of education and reactionary teachers unions are trying to smear them.

This month, for instance, the Illinois Board of Education released results showing that the state's 23 charter schools had performed no better than the state average on tests. But many of those charter schools are for troubled kids who fail in regular public school settings, so the comparisons are meaningless. That didn't stop the teachers unions in that state from telling the press that this was some kind of black eye for charter schools.

Charters don't always hit their target. More than 150 of them have been shut down, the victims of poor fiscal management or even criminality. Maybe you heard about the Los Angeles principal who took $90,000 in taxpayer money meant for kids and used it to buy a sports car.

Forget the horror stories. Despite this year's Supreme Court decision legalizing them, vouchers are too toxic politically to have a real impact beyond talk TV. Charter schools, by contrast, go down much easier. They offer choice and healthy competition in a public setting.

The whole idea of charter schools is still confusing for most people (sort of like "fast-track authority" or "tort reform"), in part because the rules governing these independent public schools vary so much state by state. Basically, we're talking about a genuine grass-roots movement for small, non-religious, taxpayer-funded alternative schools. They're sponsored by idealistic educators, parents, non-profits, or businesses that win the freedom to try something different and avoid silly union work rules—all in exchange for accountability.

Instead of creaming the best students from the top, admission in most states is by lottery. More than half are in poor areas, where waiting lists are especially long.

The critics make sure you hear about the failures, but the successes receive less attention. Boston boasts the Academy of the Pacific Rim that gets some of the highest test scores in town using Asian instruction techniques with black kids; Mesa, Arizona, opened an Arts Academy in a Boys and Girls Club that has local gangs on the run and academic results surging. Whenever I visit Newark, New Jersey's North Star Academy, I'm amazed by how much learning is going on. The level of enthusiasm and commitment by teachers and students is phenomenal.

Charters represent a good compromise between status-quo mediocrity and vouchers. But fearful of losing control, "The Blob"—the education establishment—is trying to strangle the movement. Some states are refusing to expand the number of charters they grant in certain areas. (Chicago, for instance, is allowed only ten.)

School boards have conned pliant legislatures in 18 states into stipulating that they (the boards) alone can sponsor charters, thereby defeating the purpose. "It's like letting McDonald's decide where Burger King can open," says Joe Nathan, director of the Center for School Change at the University of Minnesota.

Now the American Federation of Teachers (AFT), whose late president, Albert Shanker, once championed charter schools, has launched a vicious frontal assault against them. I'm not sure why anyone would believe a report on charters by a teachers union, but this one deserves some kind of chutzpah award. The report complains that not enough charter schools have been closed for poor academic performance. (More than 150 have been shut, mostly for financial mismanagement.) Funny, the AFT doesn't say that about the thousands of lousy conventional schools where their members teach. And as the Center for Education Reform notes, the report neglects to mention that charters usually have to raise their own money for their buildings (covered by the public in conventional schools), which contributes to their financial shakiness.

Instead of judging by results, some states (under pressure from "The Blob") have started heavily regulating charter schools, trying to make them more like the ordinary schools they are meant to challenge. Republicans nationally are generally more open to the movement than Democrats, who remain in bed with teachers unions. But at the state level, GOP lawmakers are also thoroughly compromised by the vested interests of the "educrats."

"The Blob's" new game, at work now in Illinois, is to pay lip service to charter schools by allowing them for special ed or disruptive students. Then the school boards get to boast that the test scores of their own conventional schools have gone up (because they don't have to average in the weakest kids who've been put in charters), but the charter school scores have not. When some of these charter schools close, the establishment can say, "See! They don't work!" Of course the fact that six percent of charter schools have been shut down, cited by critics as a sign of failure, is actually an indication that the idea is working. Unlike most conventional schools, charters actually have to perform to survive.

The critics aren't completely crazy. Like all social movements, this one has had growing pains. Arizona added charters too quickly and got several shoddy ones; Texas and California didn't screen the founders well enough and have ended up with some crooks. Most states need better auditing of the financial performance of charters, a process that could weed out the poorly conceived ones more quickly. The next phase is to figure out why some charters work and others don't, and improve the batting average. (The Gates Foundation and other non-profits are investing in that process.) Then charter schools can make the leap from intriguing reform to major American social movement.

A decade ago, just 90 students at St. Paul's City Academy comprised the first charter school in history. Now, there are 650,000 students in charters. But that's out of 46 million school-age children in America. Fortunately, the groundswell will likely continue in the next decade. Charter schools are modern-day barn raisings. They tap something deeply democratic in the culture: local citizens, fighting the power structure, taking matters (legally) into their own hands, committed to market choice but in a public sphere, still dreaming the ancient dream of a better life for their children.

Cop-Out on Class

—— 1995 ——

At the time I wrote this, my children were in public school.
After seven years in public school, they went to private school,
but I still cling to the idea that private schools are the draft
deferments of my generation and that parents who send their
children to them still owe a debt to public education.

I'M A PART OF this so-called overclass—and so are my bosses
and many of my colleagues at *Newsweek* and elsewhere in the
national media. There's no point in denying it. Whether by birth, effort,
ability, luck or some combination, we are more successful and have
more options than most Americans, and that inevitably pulls us away
from the lives they lead. Neither eating pork rinds (George Bush)
nor boasting of humble origins (Bill Clinton) can erase that fact for
politicians any more than it can for the rest of the overprivileged. The
object should be to achieve consciousness of class, then work hard to
make the divisions it creates smaller instead of larger.

Until the 1970s, race was the rage in public debate. Class remained
almost a secret—discussed in private and delineated by taste but
subsumed in the assumption growing out of World War II that everyone except the very rich and the very poor was part of the great
American Middle.

Exposing the existence of an overclass began in places like the
Washington Monthly, a little political magazine. One day in 1970, the
wife of the editor, Charlie Peters, was in a bookstore and overheard
a hip-looking young man discussing the Vietnam draft. "Let those
hillbillies go get shot," he said. When Beth Peters told her husband
about the comment, Charlie turned the line into a cause: to convey to
American elites the emergence of an unthinking and dangerous class
bias in their ranks. Working-class Americans knew that Vietnam,
unlike earlier wars in this century, had become a rich man's war and a
poor boy's fight. But the people who ran the country hadn't yet faced
up to the price of that division.

Five years later, a young *Washington Monthly* editor named James Fallows drove home the point by graphically describing his feelings of guilt after he starved himself at Harvard in order to flunk the physical for the draft. The widely reprinted article, entitled "What Did You Do in the Class War, Daddy?" angered many veterans, but it kicked off some serious soul-searching among baby boomers about their anti-military, anti-blue-collar bias.

Unfortunately, the chasm remained. I was too young for Vietnam (and never enlisted). But by the time I joined the *Washington Monthly* in 1981, my generation was beginning to face its own less bloody yet no less serious class issue: public education. To deny the existence of a class problem in the United States is to ignore the flight from public schools by perpetually anxious, upwardly mobile parents trying to cover their bets on their children's future.

I know the feeling, as my parents did before me. Starting in kindergarten, I attended the finest, most diverse private schools and have good memories of them. Yet the fact remains that private schools stand apart from society. They can compensate for that separation with scholarships and good works but never fully bridge the gap from what America, in its Jeffersonian ideal, is supposed to be. I heard recently that at the tony St. Albans School in Washington, D.C.—alma mater of Vice President Gore—some teachers will tell a badly behaving student that if he doesn't shape up he may have to ship out to public school. They make it sound almost like going to Vietnam.

My wife and I have chosen public schools for our children, in part because of the eagerness with which other parents we know are abandoning them. Instead of organizing to fix the public schools, they nearly bankrupt themselves escaping, often without even personal visits to see whether their assumptions might be wrong. Here's where race comes in. When they say "bad," they usually mean "black," even if they won't admit it. The result is often overclass children who aren't educated in a larger sense—who don't know their own community and country. They are what my wife calls "under-deprived" kids. They think the world owes them a nice vacation. I know. When I was 12, I was like that, too.

Does this mean our three children will never go to private school? No. Children should not have to sacrifice their education to their parents' principles. If the public schools in our area fail—either generally or for our particular children—we'll be gone. But in the meantime we should stay awhile and fight—for high standards, for choice and for accountability. (Beyond safety, a great advantage of private schools is that they can more easily fire bad teachers and administrators.) The single biggest reason for the decline of American public education is that so many capable and committed parents have opted out. That in itself is a bad lesson for their children.

Even if they don't send their kids to public schools, successful people should invest time there. Call it the case for Overclass Hypocrisy. "If you feel the public schools can't be changed in the time your kids are that age," says Charlie Peters, "you should take on an extra burden to make sure that the next parents coming along don't have that excuse." My own parents anticipated that point. After putting their children through private school, they now volunteer in Chicago's inner-city public schools.

To really break down class divisions, we need a draft that would require every young person to serve either in the military or in the community. John F. Kennedy went to private schools, but he shared a PT boat during World War II with a mechanic and a fisherman. That doesn't happen much today. While some overclass parents make a commendable effort to see that their children meet people from different backgrounds, this risks being just another resume entry. And many others actually believe that it is supremely important to introduce their children to more People Like Us—to create social shelters instead of real communities.

Ambition for yourself and for your kids is good; it's what makes the country go. But what really matters is how you view the rungs below, and how you use all of the extra choices you have for a purpose broader than getting into Princeton. The best answer to American elites is not to bash them or indulge in reverse snobbery. It's to pull them (us) into the great work of the country.

An Education in Giving

—— 2002 ——

*In the six years since this appeared, DonorsChoose has become
a large national organization that serves millions of public school
students and has been repeatedly cited as a transformative
philanthropic model. I joined the board in 2003.*

AMERICANS ARE a generous people, but the sad truth is that
charitable giving is just not keeping pace with income. Why? For
many potential donors, the biggest obstacle is lack of faith. They aren't
confident that the money they give will actually end up helping people.
"Donors are sick of writing that $200 check to the Red Cross and not
knowing whether it goes for the executive director's salary or the office
rent," says Charles Best, a 26-year-old Phi Beta Kappa from Yale who
now teaches at a public school in the Bronx.

Best decided to do something about that. His new Web site
(DonorsChoose.org) is not just directly helping New York City kids, it
may eventually change the face of philanthropy. I know, because I tried it.

Like all revolutionary ideas, Best's is deceptively simple. His site—
a model of user-friendliness—asks New York City public school teachers to write a one-page summary of class projects and the amount of
money it would cost to fund them. Potential donors scan the list and
decide which project to fund. No contrived grant applications.
No fancy buildings full of grant reviewers and well-paid foundation
executives. No grant-making process at all.

So far, more than 130 teacher projects have been funded, in
amounts ranging from $70 for some books to $12,000 for laptops
for students in an economics class, funded entirely by a Seattle entre-
preneur. The tax-deductible money goes through Best's registered
501[c](3) (until recently run out of his lower Manhattan apartment).
Unless the donor specifically chooses to contribute 10 percent extra for
administration, not a penny goes for overhead. That compares to 35
percent for many charities. After the books, equipment, field trips, etc.,

(I'm not doing justice to the creativity of the projects) are purchased, the teacher sends a receipt to DonorsChoose, plus thank-you notes from the kids and photographs of them using the gift. All of this is then forwarded to the satisfied donor.

"Our mission is to help students in need and to democratize philanthropy," says Best, who has partnered with Teach for America and other groups focused on improving education in poor districts. "We've established a free marketplace of teacher ideas and donor interests." Best still teaches social studies full-time at the Wings Academy public school in the Bronx; he explained his program to me by phone last week during his lunch hour. But the idea, hatched two years ago, is now growing fast.

So far, donors in 23 states have funded everything from sports programs for schools displaced by the attack on the World Trade Center to oxygen meters for a science class measuring pollution in the Bronx River to life-size "Baby Think It Over" dolls designed to show preteens what they're in for if they get pregnant. DonorsChoose screens the teachers' proposals and won't post any that are too outlandish, like the one from a teacher who sought $50,000 for a culinary excursion to Paris.

I logged on to DonorsChoose.org with the idea of doing something in the arts and humanities. At first I thought about contributing a portion of the cost of establishing an architects-in-residence program, but I decided I wanted to start out trying to fund something all by myself. Some bookbinding equipment for an art class looked intriguing but was too pricey. After an enjoyable tour of the teachers' proposals, I settled on buying a class of students at Theodore Roosevelt High School in the Bronx copies of a moving and important chronicle of World War I that I first encountered in high school—*All Quiet on the Western Front.*

Best's concept is beginning to spread to other cities. Teachers in Washington, Los Angeles and Cincinnati are starting their own versions of DonorsChoose.org, and there's interest in using the technology to build international understanding. Recently, Muslim students at a school in Kuwait received a stack of books on New York City to supplement their reading of the Koran.

DonorsChoose reminds me a little of eBay in its early stages; it's a great fit for the Internet. Bad imitators are already emerging, and the idea will no doubt be perverted by someone hawking phony needs with weeping kids. But in the meantime, this site does the nearly impossible— it takes away our last excuse for being stingy.

Affirmative Action: What Merit Really Means

—— 2003 ——

The landmark Supreme Court decision in the
University of Michigan affirmative action case offered
an occasion to reflect on the larger issue.

A NYONE WITH half a brain knows that grades and test scores aren't the only way to define "merit" in college admissions. Sometimes a good jump shot or batting average is "merit." Or a commitment to a soup kitchen. Or the ability to overcome an obstacle in life. Conscientious admissions officers take a wide variety of factors into account and make rounded, subtle judgments about the composition of the incoming class. The debate over affirmative action in education boils down to whether universities should be free to make that judgment or be told by the government how to choose.

The problem with affirmative action is not, as some conservatives suggest, that it has eroded standards and dumbed-down elite institutions. The level of academic achievement among freshmen at, say, Yale is far higher than it was when George W. Bush entered in 1964. With his high school record, he probably wouldn't be admitted today, even if he were black. No, what's wrong with affirmative action is that it has too often been routinized and mechanized, and has thus begun to resemble the very thinking it was supposed to replace.

Conservatives, trying to stand on principle, argue that affirmative action is simply reverse discrimination. In certain realms, like the awarding of federal contracts, that may be true. But college is different. The college experience is partly about preparing students for adult life, which increasingly means learning to deal with people of many different backgrounds. To hear the Bill Bennetts of the world, whites and Asian-Americans rejected by the colleges of their choice are like blacks rejected by the lunch counters of their choice in the Jim Crow South. It's a lame analogy. Lunch counters (and other public facilities) have no right to discriminate; neither do nonselective colleges, about 80 percent of the total. But exclusive institutions, by definition, must exclude.

The basis on which they do so should at least be consistent. You either favor weighing immutable nonacademic preferences or you don't. Some conservatives want to continue preferences for alumni children and end those for minorities. Some liberals want the reverse—to keep affirmative action but end legacies. Both sides ace their hypocrisy boards. Personally, I go for preferences, within limits, because I want the smart alumni kid from Pacific Palisades to sit in the dining hall and get to know the smart poor kid from Camden. Neither the University of Michigan policy nor the Bush administration challenge to it are likely to take us closer to that end.

The larger problem is that exclusive colleges too often use that worn-out crutch of a word—"diversity"—to cover for their lack of genuine integration (in dorms, for instance), and a lack of progress on socioeconomic affirmative action. Only 3 percent of students in top universities come from the poorest quarter of the American population. A Harvard study last year found that colleges are too often "recyclers of privilege" instead of "engines of upward mobility." Harvard itself falls short on this score, with fewer than 9 percent of its students coming from families eligible for Pell grants (i.e., of modest means). Princeton and Notre Dame are among those that don't do discernibly better.

Ironically, colleges like these with nice-sounding "needs-blind admission" policies consistently admit fewer poorer kids because, as a James Irvine Foundation report discovered, "they feel like they're off the hook." They're so proud of themselves for not calculating students' ability to pay in making admissions decisions that they do less than they could to recruit poorer students—and thus fail to take enough "affirmative action" (in its original, beating-the-bushes sense) to redress socioeconomic disparities. It's easier to go with familiar, relatively affluent high schools they know will produce kids more likely to succeed.

Recently, Berkeley, UCLA and USC have done twice or three times better than every other elite school in enrolling economically disadvantaged students. Why? Because California has abolished racial preferences, which forced these schools to adopt economic affirmative action. Richard Kahlenberg of The Century Foundation says that's the only way to get more poor kids admitted. A forthcoming study from that foundation will show that substituting economic preferences for race at the top 146 schools would lessen the black and Hispanic representation only two percentage points (from 12 percent currently to 10 percent).

But I still think it makes sense to allow both class and race to be considered—and to let 1,000 other factors bloom, as good colleges do. Just don't make it mechanical. The anti-affirmative-action forces have to abandon the notion that GPAs and SATs add up to some numerical right to admission; the advocates for the status quo have to give up the numerical awarding of points for things like race, because sometimes being African-American or Hispanic or Native American should be a big plus, and sometimes it shouldn't. It depends on the kid. All of which means that no matter what happens in the Supreme Court, the University of Michigan and other large schools should spend the money needed for a more subtle and subjective quest for true merit.

Time to Think About Torture

—— 2001 ——

I've written many weak stories and made plenty of little mistakes over the years, but this piece, written a few weeks after 9/11, is the only column I'd like to have back—that makes me wince when I read it. I now know enough about torture to know that it doesn't work, and that it undermines American values. The fact that I wasn't advocating physical torture doesn't make it any better. I've included it to symbolize all the times I've been wrong.

IN THIS AUTUMN of anger, even a liberal can find his thoughts turning to ... torture. OK, not cattle prods or rubber hoses, at least not here in the United States, but *something* to jump-start the stalled investigation of the greatest crime in American history. Right now, four key hijacking suspects aren't talking at all.

Couldn't we at least subject them to psychological torture, like tapes of dying rabbits or high-decibel rap? (The military has done that in Panama and elsewhere.) How about truth serum, administered with a mandatory IV? Or deportation to Saudi Arabia, land of beheadings? (As the frustrated FBI has been threatening.) Some people still argue that we needn't rethink any of our old assumptions about law enforcement, but they're hopelessly "September 10"—living in a country that no longer exists.

One sign of how much things have changed is the reaction to the antiterrorism bill, which cleared the Senate last week by a vote of 98-1. While the ACLU felt obliged to quibble with a provision or two, the opposition was tepid, even from staunch civil libertarians. That great quote from the late Chief Justice Robert Jackson—"The Constitution is not a suicide pact"—is getting a good workout lately. "This was incomparably more sober and sensible than what some of our revered presidents did," says Floyd Abrams, the First Amendment lawyer, referring to the severe restrictions on liberty imposed during the Civil War and World War I.

Fortunately, the new law stops short of threatening basic rights like free speech, which is essential in wartime to hold the government accountable. The bill makes it easier to wiretap (under the old rules, you had to get a warrant for each individual phone, an anachronism in a cellular age), easier to detain immigrants who won't talk and easier to follow money through the international laundering process. A welcome "sunset" provision means the expansion of surveillance will expire after four years. That's an important precedent, though odds are these changes will end up being permanent. It's a new world.

Actually, the world hasn't changed as much as we have. The Israelis have been wrestling for years with the morality of torture. Until 1999 an interrogation technique called "shaking" was legal. It entailed holding a smelly bag over a suspect's head in a dark room, then applying scary psychological torment. (To avoid lessening the potential impact on terrorists, I won't specify exactly what kind.) Even now, Israeli law leaves a little room for "moderate physical pressure" in what are called "ticking time bomb" cases, where extracting information is essential to saving hundreds of lives. The decision of when to apply it is left in the hands of law-enforcement officials.

For more than 20 years Harvard Law School professor Alan Dershowitz has argued to the Israelis that this is terribly unfair to the members of the security services. In a forthcoming book *Shouting Fire*, he makes the case for what he calls a "torture warrant," where judges would balance competing claims and make the call, as they do in issuing search warrants. Dershowitz says that as long as the fruits of such interrogation are used for investigation, not to convict the detainee (a violation of the Fifth Amendment right against self-incrimination), it could be constitutional here, too. "I'm not in favor of torture, but if you're going to have it, it should damn well have court approval," Dershowitz says.

Not surprisingly, judges and lawyers in both Israel and the United States don't agree. They prefer looking the other way to giving even mild torture techniques the patina of legality. This leaves them in a strange moral position. The torture they can't see (or that occurs after deportation) is harder on the person they claim to be concerned about—the detainee—but easier on their consciences. Out of sight, out of mind.

Short of physical torture, there's always sodium pentothal ("truth serum"). The FBI is eager to try it, and deserves the chance. Unfortunately, truth serum, first used on spies in World War II, makes suspects gabby but not necessarily truthful. The same goes for even the harshest torture. When the subject breaks, he often lies. Prisoners "have only one objective—to end the pain," says retired Col. Kenneth

Allard, who was trained in interrogation. "It's a huge limitation."

Some torture clearly works. Jordan broke the most notorious terrorist of the 1980s, Abu Nidal, by threatening his family. Philippine police reportedly helped crack the 1993 World Trade Center bombings (plus a plot to crash 11 U.S. airliners and kill the pope) by convincing a suspect that they were about to turn him over to the Israelis. Then there's painful Islamic justice, which has the added benefit of greater acceptance among Muslims.

We can't legalize physical torture; it's contrary to American values. But even as we continue to speak out against human rights abuses around the world, we need to keep an open mind about certain measures to fight terrorism, like court-sanctioned psychological interrogation. And we'll have to think about transferring some suspects to our less squeamish allies, even if that's hypocritical. Nobody said this was going to be pretty.

Flag-Burning Phoniness

—— 2006 ——

Amending the Constitution to ban flag burning is
one of those bad ideas that doesn't ever seem to go away.

T HE PHRASE "LITMUS TEST" is in bad odor for good reason: politicians should be judged on a variety of positions, not just one. But deep down, nearly every voter has at least one litmus test—an issue so personally important that a politician who fails the test is forever tainted, or at least excluded from consideration for the presidency.

I inherited my one litmus test from my father, Jim Alter, who flew 33 harrowing missions over Nazi Germany during World War II. My father is not just a veteran who by all odds should not have survived. He is a true patriot. His litmus test is the proposal to amend the Constitution to ban flag burning, which will come up for a vote next week in the U.S. Senate. For dad—and me—any member of Congress who supports amending the Bill of Rights for the first time in the history of this country for a non-problem like flag burning is showing serious disrespect for our Constitution and for the values for which brave Americans gave their lives. Such disrespect is a much more serious threat than the random idiots who once every decade or so try (often unsuccessfully) to burn a flag.

Our understandable outrage at flag burning shouldn't turn our brains to mush. "I feel the same sense of outrage, but I would not amend that great shield of democracy [the Constitution] to hammer a few miscreants," Colin Powell said when the issue last came up (his position has not changed). "The flag will be flying proudly long after they have slunk away." Powell argues that a constitutional ban on flag burning is a sign of weakness and fear. Note: The other countries that have banned flag burning include Cuba, China, Iran and Saddam Hussein's Iraq.

John Glenn, another of the thousands of combat veterans against the amendment (they have banded together in a group called Veterans Defending the Bill of Rights), notes that "those 10 amendments we call the Bill of Rights have never been changed or altered by one iota, not by one word, not a single time in all of American history. There was not a single change during any of our foreign wars, and not during recessions or depressions or panics. Not a single change when we were going through times of great emotion and anger like the Vietnam era, when flag after flag was burned or desecrated. There is only one way to weaken our nation. The way to weaken our nation would be to erode the freedom that we all share."

Actually, even during the Vietnam War, flag burning was rare. By one count, there have been only 45 such incidents in 200 years, and fewer than half a dozen since it was outlawed in 1989. Should the Constitution be amended, however, the incidence of flag burning is expected to surge as a form of civil disobedience. What began as a phony issue designed to prove patriotism (usually on the part of those who never served, the primary sponsors) could become a real concern.

The flag-burning amendment, which already passed the House, is apparently just short of the 67 needed in the Senate. With one or two absences, the amendment would be approved. It would then go to the states for ratification, where its chances for approval appear good.

On the Republican side, all senators except Robert Bennett of Utah, Lincoln Chafee of Rhode Island and Mitch McConnell of Kentucky favor the amendment. The rest (including those who should know better, like John McCain and Chuck Hagel) are apparently in favor of trivializing the document they swore to uphold. Banning flag burning, in the words of Justice Antonin Scalia, "dilutes the very freedom that makes this emblem so revered."

Democrats mostly oppose the amendment. But at last count, 13 will support it: Max Baucus of Montana, Evan Bayh of Indiana, Mark Dayton of Minnesota, Dianne Feinstein of California, Tim Johnson of South Dakota, Mary Landrieu of Louisiana, Blanche Lincoln of Arkansas, Ben Nelson of Nebraska, Bill Nelson of Florida, Harry Reid of Nevada, Ken Salazar of Colorado, Jay Rockefeller of West Virginia, and Debbie Stabenow of Michigan. Bob Menendez is on the fence and leaning toward supporting the amendment, even though his constituents mostly oppose it. That's a twofer: Wrong on the merits. Wrong on the politics.

Senators afraid of being seen as soft on flag burners should just adopt the Hillary Clinton dodge: support for a statute, but not an amendment. Another law is a dopey idea (an earlier one was struck down by the Supreme Court), but it's politically safe and better than perverting the Constitution.

The assumption has always been that the politics of flag burning cut only one way: A "no" vote opens you up to attack ads saying, "Senator X voted against protecting our flag." This may still be true in some Red States, though even there it hasn't proven to be a killer campaign issue. But in Blue States—and especially in Democratic presidential primaries—the issue could ripen in a hurry. Once the consequences are fully aired, no liberal (in both the classic and modern definitions of the word) will vote for a candidate who wants to trivialize the Bill of Rights. And no candidate can be nominated by the Democratic Party without liberals.

To make matters worse, the amendment is vaguely worded, which led to fatuous debate in the Senate over whether a woman wearing a skimpy bathing suit patterned with stars and stripes was guilty of desecration. Bloggers wondered the same thing about President Bush's new habit of autographing flags when he shakes hands on rope lines. Unconstitutional? With a war on and a hundred other pressing problems, it's nice to see our elected representatives focused on what really counts.

The usual litmus tests—abortion, gun control, Iraq—shouldn't be. Reasonable and sincere people can disagree, with at least one or two principled arguments on each side. The flag-burning amendment is in a category by itself: the only argument for it is based on pure emotion. But ours is supposed to be a government of reason, not emotion, especially when it comes to the most precious repository of our rights. The American Constitution, the apogee of reason in the history of self-government, is real; the American flag, for all of its beauty and deep meaning, is symbolic. For more than 200 years, we've occasionally used the amendment process to expand rights. This would be the first time we would enshrine their restriction. Polluting the Constitution is far more dangerous than burning the flag.

Intelligent Design: Monkey See, Monkey Do

—— 2005 ——

*When President Bush endorsed the teaching of
"intelligent design" it was another sign of what came
to be known as his "war on science."*

A TEACHER IN KANSAS, where war over Darwin in the schools is still raging, calls the theory of intelligent design "creationism in a cheap tuxedo." Great line, but unfair to the elegant tailoring of the Discovery Institute, the Seattle-based think tank that has almost singlehandedly put intelligent design on the map. Eighty years after the Scopes "monkey trial," the threat to science and reason comes less from fundamentalists who believe the earth was created in six days than from sophisticated branding experts and polemical Ph.D.s who are clever enough to refrain from referring to God or even the Creator, and have now found a willing tool in the president of the United States.

Lest you think this is merely of academic interest, consider the stakes: the Pentagon last week revealed that it is spending money to train certain scientists how to write screenplays for thrillers related to their specialties. Why? Because the status of science has sunk so low that the government needs these disciplines to become sexy again among students or the brain drain will threaten national security. One of the reasons we have fewer science majors is the pernicious right-wing notion that conventional biology is vaguely atheistic.

Now President Bush has given that view a boost. When Bush was asked about intelligent design last week, he answered, "Both sides ought to be properly taught ... so people can understand what the debate is about." This sounds reasonable until you realize that, as the president's own science adviser, John H. Marburger III, admits, there *is no real debate*. "Intelligent design is not a scientific concept," Marburger told the *New York Times*, committing a bit of candor that will presumably earn him a trip to the White House woodshed.

Stephen Meyer of the Discovery Institute claims ID uses a scientifically valid "inference to the best explanation" to back up its theories. That might be good enough for a graduate course in the philosophy of science (and the ACLU should not prevent it from being discussed in high school humanities and philosophy classes), but the idea of its being offered as an alternative to evolution in ninth-grade biology is a cruel joke. Its basic claim—that the human cell is too complex to be explained by natural selection—is unproven and probably unprovable. ID walks like science and talks like science but, so far, performs in the lab worse than medieval alchemy.

It's not God who's the problem but ID's assault on Darwin. Brown University biologist Kenneth Miller (who attends mass every week) says the "unspoken message" peddled by the Discovery Institute is that evolution is the single shakiest theory in science. In fact, despite its flaws, it remains among the most durable theories in all of science.

Even as the president helps pit faith against science in the classroom, popes and other clerics have long known that religion and evolution are not truly at odds. Evolution does not, for instance, challenge the idea that the universe began with a spark of divinity. Darwin himself wrote movingly of God. Only the scientific process—not the scientist—must be agnostic. Long before Darwin, enlightened Christians understood that religion and science are best kept in separate realms. In the fifth century, for instance, Saint Augustine criticized other Christians who "talk nonsense" about the laws of nature.

The most clever thing about intelligent design is that it doesn't sound like nonsense. It conjures up Cambridge, not Kansas. The name evokes Apple software, the MoMA gift shop or a Frank Gehry chair. The scholarly articles are often well written and provocative. But the science within these papers has been demolished over and over by other scientists. As Miller explains, science is perhaps the last true marketplace of ideas. After a decade in circulation, intelligent design has failed the market test. So now its backers are seeking the equivalent of a government bailout, by going around their scientific peers to Red State politicians trying to slip religious dogma into the classroom.

While the Discovery Institute calls God the "designer" to appear less creationist, some of its biggest funders are serious fundamentalists. An internal fund-raising memo leaked in 1999 laid out its theological agenda and intention to use ID as a "wedge" to triumph in the culture wars.

Last week Fox News lent a hand. Bill O'Reilly says that the National Academy of Science is guilty of "fascism" for arguing that ID should not take up valuable class time in high school biology. (Not to be outdone, Dr. James Dobson compared embryonic-stem-cell research to "Nazi experiments.") These are the same modest gents who decry relativism and curricular inclusiveness in the humanities, where it is far more justifiable than in the sciences.

Bush's policy of politicizing science—retreating from the field of facts and evidence on everything from evolution to global warming to the number of cell lines available to justify his 2001 stem-cell compromise—will eventually wreak havoc with his legacy. Until then, like his masquerade-ball friends, the president will get more clever at harming science while pretending to promote it. Monkey see, monkey do.

PART EIGHT

PERSONAL

My Life with Cancer

—— 2007 ——

I TOOK THE CALL on my cell phone at the Starbucks in New York's Penn Station. It was from a doctor I barely knew telling me that a CT scan—ordered after three weeks of worsening stomach pain—showed a large mass in my abdomen, with what she said was "considerable lymph node involvement." I rubbed my eyes and sensed the truth instantly: cancer and not one that had been detected early. I was 46 years old and had not spent a night in the hospital since I was born. Nonsmoker. No junk food beyond the occasional barbecue potato chips. Jogged a couple of times a week. I was not remotely ready for this.

It was Super Tuesday, March 2, 2004, the day voters would select most of the delegates to the Democratic National Convention. Although the complete diagnosis was still several days off, the intense abdominal pain meant that my wife Emily and I had no time to stop, absorb and adjust to our twisted new world. We immediately began negotiating the endless round of doctors' appointments and insurance hassles that mark a cancer patient's life. With my head on fire, I quietly endured a festive lunch with political reporters and anchors, then went back to work. My job that day was to analyze the end of John Edwards's presidential campaign.

Three years later, I'm in remission and, strangely enough, thinking once more about the future of Edwards and his family. Like the 10.5 million other cancer survivors in the United States, I experienced a bit of extra stress last week. When Elizabeth Edwards's breast cancer recurred in her bones and Tony Snow's colon cancer recurred in his liver, the cold fear that many of us live with every day crept a little closer. The good news is that the candor of Edwards and Snow (who is recuperating from surgery but has been open about his situation from his perch as White House press secretary) has helped stimulate a useful national conversation about how people handle a cancer diagnosis. It has also exposed the foolishness of a few busybodies who don't have cancer, but feel free to judge the complex choices made by those who do.

My own story isn't typical, because none is. Every patient reacts a little differently, both biologically and psychologically. The only constant in cancer is inconstancy; the only certainty is a future of uncertainty, a truism for all of modern life but one made vivid by life-threatening illness. According to the latest projections, a third of all Americans will be diagnosed with cancer at some point during their lifetimes, most likely when they're old. Many will never achieve remission at all, while the lucky ones like me get to live with a sword of Damocles hanging over our heads. A friend compares his semiannual scans to visiting a parole officer. When the scans are clean, it's worth another six months of freedom, though with no guarantee of extra time for good behavior.

In my case, the news went from bad to worse. To calm my nerves before the laparoscopic surgery (they cut my colon into a semicolon and removed my appendix while they were at it), I heard some happy talk about how the bowel obstruction might be benign. As I recovered and watched the slow gait of my internist down the hospital corridor I knew otherwise. "Time is an illusion," he told me cryptically, explaining that after a certain age, a few years could seem like many, and many could seem like few. I was informed that I had non-Hodgkin's lymphoma, a blood cancer that would likely shorten my life without ending it any time soon.

But we didn't yet know the all-important cell type. The day after being discharged, I grew impatient with the slowness of the pathology report and had the hospital lab fax it to me directly. Big mistake. After Googling "mantle cell lymphoma," I learned it was a rare and nasty form of the disease with a terrifying prognosis.

By this time I was in mental free fall. Friends later said I handled it courageously, but they were wrong. American culture rewards cheerful stoicism, a quality that cancer patients usually display in public but find difficult to sustain in private, especially at the beginning. I collapsed in tears only briefly, but retreated into a fog of unshakable misery. My detachment alarmed Emily, who wisely resisted many well-intentioned efforts by family and friends to coddle me. She understood that their instinct to be protective was making me into a weaker person than I needed to be. So she lovingly but firmly pushed me back into some semblance of normal life. "Get off the Internet and get back to your real work!" she insisted on more than one occasion.

I slept only with the help of sleeping pills. After taking too many, I botched the disclosure of my condition to our three kids, then ages 14, 12 and 10, stumbling so badly over my words that Emily finally sent me to bed. Our family freely discusses everything but in this case we only told them the extent of the problem when we had a plan in place to try to fix it. They didn't want to know the details, and their self-protective lack of curiosity on this subject (and this subject alone) was a relief to me. We rarely talked about it with them thereafter, an unfashionable approach I would recommend. Physically, I felt OK; emotionally, I was in hell. A woman I knew who was dying of breast cancer told me that none of the pain she was suffering at the end of her life compared with that first month and the daze of diagnosis.

I fell back on what I knew—reporting and analysis—and undertook a furious round of investigative phone calls. Everyone agreed that it was critical to be examined at a major cancer center, where doctors would have seen my disease much more often than at other hospitals. (I was even told of studies showing the farther one travels for treatment, the better the chance of survival.) With the help of friends, I finally got an appointment at New York's Memorial Sloan-Kettering Cancer Center. It happened on my wife's birthday, the only present she wanted.

After receiving a second opinion on the lab results, the brilliant doctor who became my oncologist administered an excruciating bone-marrow biopsy, which felt as if I were on a medieval rack. The results confirmed that I was Stage Four, the most advanced, though the systemic nature of lymphoma may have made that less dire than in other cancers. He told me that my two-year odds of survival were essentially a coin toss, and that my best chance to improve them lay in four months of accelerated chemotherapy, followed by a bone-marrow transplant, an aggressive regimen previously used mostly for relapsed patients.

Many patients place full trust in their physician and never second-guess them. I was constitutionally incapable of that, so I hit him with a barrage of questions. Why this chemo protocol and not another used by a different hospital? Why not enroll me in a clinical trial? Why couldn't he tell me more? Even though I admired him, I continued reporting. With no standard of care for this disease, each expert I managed to get on the phone had a slightly different take on how it should be treated, which I later discovered is common with cancer.

I vacuumed up everything I could. (Cancer is unbelievably complex:

lymphoma alone is made up of more than 30 different types.) I even became capable of decoding some of the doctors' medical jargon, which is like picking up a foreign language. The more I knew, the more frustrated I grew at the Catch-22 of oncology, which is that the most cutting-edge therapies are used only for the sickest patients, when it's often too late. Newly diagnosed patients get the old stuff, unless they get much sicker, when it's often too late for them, too.

But a little knowledge can be a dangerous and depressing thing. The Internet is a fantastic resource for patients, who increasingly use it to ask pertinent questions of their doctors. It can also baffle and disorient. Some of what I read about mantle cell lymphoma was out of date or even wrong, and logging on began to make me feel anxious. I thought Emily was in denial and she thought I was an easy mark for every cancer "cure." We quarreled about it. When I tasted the rank "noni juice" I'd ordered on the Internet, I knew she was right.

One Web resource, however, was indispensable. My sister set up an account with a nonprofit site called caringbridge.org that brought order and even pleasure to my communication with the outside world. Instead of having to repeat my story endlessly on the phone or in individual e-mails, I could offer periodic updates, then watch in amazement and gratitude as the good wishes, parodies and embarrassing stories about me from fourth grade rolled in. The site kept practically everyone in my universe informed while easing their sense of helplessness—and mine. The postings of my children and my mother-in-law became particular crowd-pleasers and before long the idea spread through parts of the media world. Even B.D. from *Doonesbury*, home from Iraq and hospitalized at Walter Reed, got a caringbridge site.

I decided early not to keep my cancer a secret. I felt enough stress already without trying to figure out who knew and who didn't. One morning on the radio, Don Imus, sensing something in my voice, asked in his inimitable way why I sounded awful. I blurted out to a few million listeners that I was headed for chemo that day. But I kept the prognosis under wraps for fear that people would pity me or write me off. By then I knew that for all the new openness about cancer, sick people still get sidelined.

The idea of joining a support group held no appeal for me, in part because my disease is so rare and I had little interest in hearing about other kinds of cancer. ("My sister-in-law's cousin had prostate cancer and he's doing fine," I was once told, unhelpfully.) But we mantle cell survivors found each other by phone and e-mail. Unfortunately, many hospitals still do little or nothing to connect newly diagnosed patients with those who have survived the same disease for several years, though this is what we crave.

Most people I know—and many I don't—were unbelievably supportive, offering prayers and comfort when I needed it most. I can't even conceive how people without close family (my brother even shaved his head in solidarity), friends and co-workers can survive the ordeal. Millions of Americans live alone and fight the disease mostly alone. They are the heroic ones.

The experience changes your relationship with friends, as some who were once mere acquaintances step up magnificently and others who were closer fade away. The long faces and doleful "How are you, *really?*" false intimacies were less welcome than the cheerful ribbing and sense I was being viewed normally. Emily and I got a laugh out of those people so interested in my initial symptoms that we concluded the inquiries into my health were more about them and whether the indigestion they were experiencing might be cancer. Others just wanted to know whether I had "beaten" it so they could check me off as one less person to worry about. Even now, it's just inaccurate to say that I have.

As my chemotherapy continued through the spring, my spirits lifted a bit. One of the worst parts of cancer is the loss of control, the sense that you have no recourse when your body betrays you. That's why nutrition and hygiene became so important to me in that period. For the first time, I actually understood how someone could develop an obsessive-compulsive disorder involving repeated handwashing. My own insistence on it was beginning to drive my family nuts. But I was determined to stay free of infection when my immunity was down during treatment. Chemo brought out the warrior in me, and the obedient servant. If the doctor suggested drinking a gallon of fluids on the first day after treatment, I didn't drink three and three-quarter quarts. I drank the full gallon, for maximum control, or the illusion of it.

My luck began to turn when I found I was avoiding the worst side effects, with the help of a dozen pills a day. I suffered fatigue, bone pain, anemia, total hair loss (my family said I looked like an egg), hemorrhoids, numbness and foot cramps, but thanks to anti-nausea drugs, which I popped prophylactically at $70 a pill, no vomiting. I missed my 25th college reunion but made the 2004 Democratic Convention, with syringes in my bag and a catheter in my chest that my wife nervously learned to clean and dress. Cancer tests any marriage, trying to work tiny cracks into fissures. But as I slowly checked out of my fog, ours prospered.

By this time I had fashioned my own daily recovery plan, which I dubbed *Herman*. The H stood for humor, a few minutes each day with *Curb Your Enthusiasm* or Will Ferrell or an Ian Frazier story or a friend who would make me laugh. E was—and is—for exercise, which may not fight cancer but clears my head. R represented religion. At the depths, I tried to read something about Judaism or talk to God a little every day, though like a soldier escaped from the foxhole, I've backslid since. (Religion often morphed into superstition, as I avoided the sweater I had worn on the day of a bad test result and refused, long after remission, to refer to my cancer in the past tense for fear of tempting a recurrence.) M was for meditation, which with the help of my friend Barbara helped calm me for a time. A was for attitude. Studies show no connection between a good attitude and reducing tumor size and I can't stand the way our therapeutic society makes people feel that cancer is their own fault because they weren't more chipper. But mind-set is important. By chance, I was already at work on a book about Franklin D. Roosevelt, and the writing offered a useful distraction from cancer. His upbeat attitude after being stricken with polio was inspirational for me, and made me wonder, What would Franklin do? N stood for niceness to my family. They bore the brunt of my irritability, which I tried to reduce, not always successfully.

As I learned about myself, I also learned a lot about medicine. Most cancer doctors are awe-inspiring in their humanity and dedication. They make, say, hedge-fund billionaires (not to mention journalists) look puny and insignificant. But I also found oncology full of the same mammoth egos and petty jealousies that plague any high-powered field. Doctors from competing institutions are often so competitive that they talk to each other only a couple of times a year at conferences. They do lab work on parallel tracks instead of collaborating. And under pressure from hospital lawyers, they frequently even refuse to share cell lines with other qualified researchers, which retards progress toward cures and is clearly unethical. Thanks to a wealthy mantle cell lymphoma survivor, ours is one of the first subsets of cancer to establish a consortium to get top experts in the field to exchange ideas regularly. Every cancer should have a consortium.

And every cancer doctor would do well to recalibrate on occasion the balance he or she strikes between science and hope. While the survival odds they offer might be technically accurate (X percentage with Y cancer will survive five years), they are often misleading and sometimes unnecessarily cruel. Patients and families obsess over these survival-rate statistics, but they reduce the countless variables of a person's genetic makeup and environmental exposure to a number, which is cold and often phony. Depending on the individual (whose age is usually not even factored into the statistics), a 50 percent chance of survival could easily be 80 percent—or 20 percent. Moreover, few patients understand the meaning of the term "median survival." That simply means half live less time and half live more—perhaps much more.

Dr. Jerome Groopman, the Harvard Medical School oncologist who became my informal patient advocate (which every patient needs and few get) and later my indispensable friend, told me that he wished he had a nickel for every patient he knew who was told he had an "incurable" disease and is still doing just fine. Groopman's new best seller, *How Doctors Think*, explains the self-protective psychology behind the pessimism of so many doctors, who don't like to view the death of a patient as a comment on their abilities. So they resort to saying it's a "bad disease" or "incurable." What doctors should say—and often do—is that a particularly challenging cancer might be incurable now, but if we can keep you alive a while longer, a cure might come, as it did for Lance Armstrong's testicular cancer. Patients need to do their part by enrolling more readily in clinical trials, which most avoid. And they should stop pressing their doctors for an exactitude that doesn't exist.

The climax of my treatment was a bone-marrow transplant in August of 2004. There are two kinds: an allogenic transplant—the only true cure—involves a donor. But I had no sibling match, and using an unrelated donor carries a one-third morbidity rate. Because the earlier rounds of chemo had achieved remission, I was eligible for a less danger-ous autologous transplant. I was hooked up to a machine that extracted (or "harvested") millions of my stem cells, which were then frozen. Once admitted to Sloan-Kettering for a 23-day stay, I was hit with high-dose chemotherapy, the most toxic in the chemo family. The point was to knock my white blood cell count down to zero, a process that confined me to my room for two weeks. Had I, with no immune system, wandered into the hall and caught something, I would have died. After my stem cells were defrosted and transplanted back into me, along with several other blood transfusions, my blood counts slowly increased.

For me, the experience was not as bad as advertised. Before I felt the brunt of it, I even managed to bang out a *Newsweek* column from the hospital. I avoided the horrible mouth sores and most of the other common side effects. Family and friends visited every day, as long as they washed their hands carefully and stayed on the other side of the room. Even when I was too weak to move or say much, I enjoyed their chatter. When I got home I could walk only a few steps. But within a few weeks I was walking a mile and by Election Night 2004 I was back on TV after eight months, balder if not wiser.

During my *annus horribilis*, *Newsweek* let me work at home and helped me navigate the insanity of the American health-care system. The claims forms are impenetrable and accompanied by pseudo-sympathetic bill collectors. How do other patients with life-threatening illnesses even begin to handle it? Cancer is seriously expensive, and no insurance company covers all of it. I met a lymphoma survivor whose wife left him after he sold the house to pay for his transplant. Now he's clinically depressed, too. But at least he's not uninsured or bankrupt. The majority of personal bankruptcies in the United States come from medical expenses, not sloth. In its hideous 2005 bankruptcy "reform," Congress sided with credit card companies and kicked cancer survivors when they were down.

Six weeks after my transplant—and again at six months—I received additional infusions of Rituxan, one of the new, less toxic and more targeted cancer therapies. In the two years since, my checkups have consisted of colonoscopies (I've had eight altogether) and CT scans. Recently I graduated from three-month scans to six-month scans. I grow anxious before each one, of course, terrified that I will be exiled once more to the penal colony of the sick.

In between, every little ache or pain sends a jolt of dread. But I run three miles a day to stay in shape, and I try to channel some of what my father has taught me about being a combat aviator in World War II, where he learned to balance fear and fatalism. At home, my children seem unaffected, insulated by the glorious narcissism of adolescence. I can even envision a time when a day finally passes without my thinking of cancer.

Serious illness has a way of crystallizing life, which is why so many people change jobs or spouses or views of the world when they fall ill. On some level, they weren't at peace with their old life and suddenly found the motivation to change it. I was happy with my old life, and all I wanted was to get it back, without having to become a professional cancer survivor or expert on coping.

In a taxi en route to lunch on that awful Super Tuesday, I experienced a powerful premonition: I have cancer, it's going to be bad, but I'll live until I'm 90. Probably not, but I turn 50 this year and, full of hope, recall that great line from *The Shawshank Redemption*: "You can get busy living, or get busy dying." For me, it's no contest.

Finding Grandma Cel

—— 2001 ——

SOMETIMES, a mere press junket can be a deeply personal experience. When I took a ferry across New York Harbor a couple of weeks ago to preview the new interactive installation at Ellis Island, I found more than just another new Web site and exhibit. I found my flesh and blood.

My Grandma Cel died a few years ago in her early 90s. She was the gentle and artistic matriarch of our family—the moral core of our universe.

Cel was a classic flapper in the 1920s; a wife and mother in the '30s and '40s; a world traveler in the '50s and '60s, visiting remote regions of dozens of Third World countries; and a figure of uncommon grace and wisdom in the final decades of the 20th century.

When prompted, Cel would recall her early childhood as a Jew in Czarist Russia, including dark memories of the day the Russian Cossacks terrorized her town. She told us about sailing for the United States not to escape these pogroms, but to attend her older brother's wedding in Chicago. The transit through Ellis Island, the decision to stay—all of this was vague. She was only a little girl at the time of her arrival.

So even after I heard about the new American Family Immigration History Center, which opened at Ellis Island on Tuesday with a ceremony including Lee Iacocca and Tom Brokaw, I didn't imagine I could actually find her. She was among 22 million immigrants who came over between 1892 and 1924. Talk about a needle in a haystack.

But at the urging of Edwin Schlossberg, whose New York design company produced the project, I decided to try. Ed explained that the

Mormon Church, which considers collecting names of the dead to be a blessing and duty, had spent hundreds of thousands of hours painstakingly deciphering the handwriting of the Ellis Island customs officials, then entered the passenger list information into a huge database on a new Web site.

I began my search by narrowing the possible dates of Cel's arrival to a 10-year period between 1905 and 1915. Then I typed in her maiden name, Celia Kagen. Nothing came up. I tried "Cel" and different spellings of "Kagen." Still nothing. Finally, at Ed's suggestion, I used just "C. Kagen."

This couldn't possibly work, I thought. Kagen was a common Jewish name.

Bingo. Suddenly, there she was: Cecelie Kagen, age 5, arriving on June 7, 1911, with her mother and older brother. Point of embarkation: "Grudno, Russ." The Web site even produced a photograph of her ship, the *Kaiser Wilhelm II*.

As soon as I got home I called my mother: "I found Grandma Cel at Ellis Island!" It may sound strange, but this was as exciting a moment as I've ever experienced on the Internet. Technology was reaching deep inside my heart, bridging expanses of time and memory, binding me to family and to history.

I'm usually fairly immune to the bells and whistles of newfangled Web sites. But this one helped me fix my beloved grandmother in the quintessential American experience. If only she was here to see it.

My Mother's Painful Quandary

—— MARCH 17, 2008 ——

*This column was one of those times when the personal
and political overlap.*

M Y MOTHER, NOW 80, should be in clover this political year. She met Hillary Clinton in the early 1990s, and the then First Lady championed a tutoring program that Mom cofounded in the Chicago housing projects. She met Barack Obama a few years later and was so taken with him that she and my father hosted a fund-raiser for his 2004 Senate campaign. But what should have been a bounty of political riches has instead become an "excruciatingly painful" choice, as I learned when I interviewed her recently. My mother, facing the other pains of age, often finds herself favoring Clinton in the daytime and Obama in the middle of the night (even at 3 AM!), then vice versa.

Joanne Alter's dilemma is bound up in her own history in the women's movement and in the brutal world of Chicago politics. But it's also representative of the conflicting feelings experienced by some of the older women who make up Hillary's most committed base. In that sense, she's a Democratic Everymom.

This year I've run into lots of people who say that Hillary Clinton reminds them of their mother, and they mean it as a compliment. The world is full of can-do women who ran their complicated households and also did the grunt work in every local civic organization, but got little, if any, credit for it. In the workplace, these pioneers faced patronizing and abusive behavior that today's young women wouldn't tolerate for a nanosecond. One of the big questions this year for Democrats is how much this legacy of sexism should shape their choice.

My mother appreciates Hillary's toughness because she's been there. After taking my grandmother's advice to avoid secretarial school ("You'll be stuck behind a typewriter for life"), she juggled raising a family with hyperactive nonprofit and political work. In 1972, she went to see the legendary Chicago Mayor Richard J. Daley and told him that it was the 20th century and he should finally allow women to run for office. Boss Daley thought Mom was a pushy critic, but he was a clever politician. So he put her on the Democratic ticket (primaries being a mere formality in Illinois in those days) for commissioner of the Sanitary District, responsible for sewage. She campaigned as an early environmentalist (we had private joke posters printed up saying: WHEN YOU FLUSH, THINK OF ME) and, despite running for a minor office, led the ticket that year with more than a million votes, becoming the first woman Democrat ever elected in Cook County.

I've always thought of my mother as the Jackie Robinson of Chicago's gender politics. For many of her 18 years in public office, other politicians often treated her the way many white players treated Robinson when he integrated Major League Baseball. Her cutthroat colleagues routinely ignored or insulted her, with another commissioner in the mid-1970s even calling her "one of those brainless, braless broads," though that was mild compared with what they said behind her back. "They couldn't deal with a 'girl from the kitchen' making big-budget decisions," she recalls, noting that pathbreaking women engineers and lawyers she knows faced similar derision. When she was praised by the Chicago newspapers for saving taxpayers tens of millions of dollars, the often-corrupt hacks tried, and failed, to stop her re-election. All the while, as one of the early women members of the Democratic National Committee, my mother was engrossed in advancing the cause of women in politics. When I was growing up, our dining room was mostly a meeting room for aspiring women politicians from Illinois and beyond.

So it's no surprise that my mother, like so many other older women I've met, wants to live long enough to see the first woman president. She greatly admires Hillary and thinks her campaign will yield long-term benefits. "Politicians like [House Speaker] Nancy Pelosi will be taken much more seriously because of her candidacy," she says, adding that the "boys' club" is weakening, though not fast enough for her taste. "Younger women," she says with a sigh, "don't understand, because they didn't have to fight the battles we did."

But when it came time to vote in the Illinois primary on Super Tuesday, my mother was in a quandary. She didn't like the sexist comments about Hillary ("Iron my shirts," chanted a couple of imbecilic hecklers in New Hampshire, thereby helping her win there). But she was also upset that Obama has been depicted as connected to Louis Farrakhan, unaccomplished in the Senate and full of empty rhetoric. These charges, she says, are "ridiculous." For years she watched him work with great skill to bridge barriers of race, class, religion, and party in Illinois. The choice was beginning to jangle her nerves.

When my two sisters became active Obama volunteers and her granddaughters as well as grandsons grew excited about politics for the first time, my mother began to think about the contest in a new way. The next president was for them, not her, she reasoned. Slowly, idealism edged identity. Her sense that Obama was a once-in-a-lifetime candidate took a fragile hold over the cause of women in politics to which she had devoted so much of her career. She voted for Obama, and knows she might not live to see the first woman president. Joanne Alter can live with that, even if she still often tosses and turns over it at three in the morning.

Boxers or Briefs?

L IKE ALMOST ALL stories about Hunter S. Thompson, who committed suicide last Sunday, this one involves drinking and politics and the gonzo performance art that Thompson perfected in his everyday interactions. What's different about my tale is that Thompson didn't find out how it ended. I never told him, though it took me a while to figure out why.

Back in 1992, I took a part-time gig with MTV, analyzing politics on camera and helping produce the network's town meetings with politicians. My job was to work with Tabitha Soren, the MTV anchor, devising some fresh questions. She was a natural and effective interviewer whose youth and rock-and-roll vibe let her slip in more curve balls than her stuffier counterparts on the broadcast networks. Our aim was to make every question from Tabitha and the kids in the audience count.

The first "Rock the Vote" town meeting with Governor Bill Clinton, assembled on a sound stage in Hollywood, was a ratings smash. Clinton was then running third in the polls behind President George H.W. Bush and Ross Perot, and the appearance helped jump-start his campaign, particularly with young voters. It was also endlessly dissected by the media as the fusion of entertainment and politics.

At the end of the program, we launched what we called the "rapid round." In the rehearsal beforehand, we requested that kids pose very short questions to Clinton. On the show, one asked whom he would appoint to the Supreme Court if elected. When Clinton answered "Mario Cuomo" (who later turned down the appointment), it made news. Bush also submitted to an interview with Tabitha, from the back of a train, but he was testy that day and he wouldn't answer questions from kids, which hurt his campaign.

Around this time, I went skiing in Aspen, Colorado, with my brother and a couple of his friends. I mentioned to Terry McDonnell (now managing editor of *Sports Illustrated*) where I was going and he asked a favor. Dr. Hunter S. Thompson owed his friend Terry a piece about Jack Nicholson, who also had a place in Aspen. Thompson was months late delivering the Nicholson story for Terry's magazine. Would I make contact with the good doctor and remind him that Terry wanted the article? Having missed the glory days of *Rolling Stone*, when Jann Wenner was famous for hunting down Hunter for copy, I happily obliged.

Like every other political writer of my generation, I adored "Fear and Loathing on the Campaign Trail," though I knew Thompson only slightly. When I was profiling Garry Trudeau for *Newsweek* in 1990, he had raged at me one night for two hours about how the cartoonist had ripped him off for his Uncle Duke character in *Doonesbury*. I argued it was homage; he called it theft.

This time, Thompson agreed to meet me at the Woody Creek Tavern, the place outside of Aspen that he made famous as his second home. My brother, his friends and I arrived around 7 PM, expecting to have dinner with the great man per our arrangement. He showed up, not surprisingly, around 11 PM, in precisely the manic state we had hoped for, retreating every half hour or so to the men's room for apparent self-medication before resuming his exhilarating rant, which, if I remember correctly through the tequila haze, had something to do with the decline of sports. The Nicholson piece was quickly brushed off and forgotten.

At a certain point, Thompson had had enough of us and retreated to the bar.

Suddenly, one of my brother's friends, a Chicago commodities trader and no stranger to debauchery himself, loudly re-approached.

"Hunter," he slurred. "I have one more question."

A look of considerable irritation flashed across the legend's face as we recalled his fondness for firearms.

"Boxers or briefs?"

Thompson refused to answer this novel query, but whispered something to the barkeeper, presumably about harassment by fans, and the next thing I knew we were staggering around in the snow, tossed out of a tavern by Hunter S. Thompson for being too rowdy.

I must admit, I had never before heard the "boxers or briefs?" conundrum and proceeded to dine out on the story for many months. I saw Thompson a couple more times—once, strangely, when we had breakfast in Little Rock, Arkansas, on the day after the 1992 election, and he asked if I'd mind if his beautiful female sidekick "took notes" by videotaping me. I didn't mention the Woody Creek incident to him, but among those with whom I shared it was Tabitha Soren, who found it amusing.

After the success of the town meeting during the campaign, Tabitha had more access to the new president than any other journalist. She interviewed him in the Oval Office and Clinton held a second MTV town meeting in 1993, then a third in 1994, which would prove, for obvious reasons, to be his last.

Tabitha always had an easy way with the young studio audience, and during rehearsals for that final forum she introduced the high school and college-age students to the concept of the "rapid round." She suggested they ask anything they wanted of the president, as long as the questions were short. Then, she jokingly threw out a few possibilities, from "What's your favorite album?" to—yup—"Boxers or briefs?"

A 17-year-old in the audience, Laetitia Thompson (no relation), popped the historic question and President Clinton, after expressing momentary surprise, answered: "Usually briefs."

Long before Monica Lewinsky, this was seized upon by commentators as symbolic of everything Clinton did to degrade and embarrass the American presidency. When George W. Bush was elected in 2000 by promising to "restore honor and dignity to the office of president of the United States," he was tapping into perceptions of Clinton that began with him discussing his underwear on national television.

Hunter Thompson ran hot and cold on Clinton, though he liked him far better than Nixon, Reagan or the Bushes. For all of his brilliant eviscerations of politicians (Hubert Humphrey was "a rat in heat"), the most enduring began with a question that even he would not answer.

For a writer, that's painful, and I never had the heart to tell him.

Press 1 to Go Crazy

—— 2002 ——

SOME HEALTH RISKS are more immediate than others: Saddam Hussein has weapons of mass destruction, an ice shaft bigger than Manhattan has plummeted into the sea near Antarctica, signaling global warming ... and *I'm still on hold*. It was only one night last week, but it felt like a year in Jalalabad. Remember the anti-smoking ad that said you lose a minute of life for every minute you smoke? That was a bargain. I figured I was losing a full year of life for every hour of grinding aggravation spent on the phone with that peculiar species known as the customer-service representative.

At 2:20 AM I finally gave up, unsuccessful in my three-hour effort to restore my Internet service, which had been cut off for unexplained reasons. (No, it wasn't a late bill payment.) The particular company I was having trouble with was Comcast, but its ratings, according to the University of Michigan's American Customer Satisfaction Index, are in the middle of the pack for the industry. It could have been practically any company turning a perfectly healthy and even-tempered person into a promising candidate for a coronary.

Clearly, if Franz Kafka were alive today he'd be writing about customer service. Just calling directory assistance can set your teeth on edge. In my case, the reps were never rude; they treated me indulgently, as if I were a mental patient who had neglected his medication. But the rules under which they operate are enough to make anyone rage against the machine.

I was lucky. At least I talked to actual human beings. The *Wall Street Journal's* Jane Spencer reported last week that companies are spending billions on automated systems designed to prevent customers from reaching operators. The paper found one man who had to call AT&T WorldNet 15 times and endure 600 minutes on hold just to talk to someone.

My own "Groundhog Day" routine involved sitting on hold—often for the length of a sitcom—for "the first available customer representative," who insisted on hearing the details of my situation (which I had already explained several times before), then passed me through two higher levels of supervisor, who said the problem would be taken up by a "provisioning team" at some unspecified future date.

Around this time, I heard those fateful taped words ("If you wish to make a call ...") indicating I had once again been disconnected. Because the reps were not allowed to give me their extensions (for reasons of "efficiency," says a Comcast spokesman), I had to start the whole thing again. As the night wore on and I began tossing around the name of the company's CEO, "Reuben"—or maybe it was "Sue," "Marian" or "Robin"—informed me that my problem was being referred to "escalations." This is apparently their euphemism for: Customer may be armed and dangerous.

Of course, if I wanted to pay my tormentors a visit, I would have a hard time finding them. Customer-service reps are everywhere—and nowhere. They have become the disembodied household gods of the age, reminders of our helplessness in the face even of technologies we understand. They don't offend as much as exasperate, as if part of some cosmic conspiracy to see how much we will pay in high blood pressure for our amenities.

Customers bear a share of the blame because we've become addicted to speed. The modem that once seemed fast now feels interminable. But the real victims of technology are the companies themselves. Bad service in a "service economy" (80 percent of GDP) is a surefire strategy for losing money. Some consultants writing in the *Harvard Business Review* last year (no, not Suzy Wetlaufer) found that more than half of all efforts to improve customer relations fail, mostly because companies see it as an information-technology problem.

Wrong. As usual in corporate America, it's not the software but the soft thinking. How often have you heard the recording "We are experiencing a higher-than-usual volume of calls"? And how rarely, asks Charles Fishman in *Fast Company* magazine, have you felt you were "experiencing a higher-than-usual volume of staff"?

In a new book, *Once Upon a Town*, Bob Greene writes about a railroad station canteen in the tiny town of North Platte, Nebraska, where the locals fed 6 million GIs passing through during World War II. Greene argues that this was "the best America that ever was." Maybe so. Maybe we've lost some old-fashioned American humanity. But I'd argue that the problem is less the people than the roles they're asked to play by corporate America. Can't answer the calls too easily or it might encourage the customer to seek more such human contact. Can't fix the problem without authorization. Can't be accountable.

Actually, you could—if you'd just take me off hold.

America's Identity Crisis—And Mine

—— 2002 ——

AFTER THEY STOLE my identity, even I didn't recognize myself anymore. My dominant memory of that time is of acting like a maniac in the lobby of my bank. A few days before, the bank had called to ask my wife and me a couple of questions. Someone with a long and totally unfamiliar name was presenting checks made out to him from us, the most recent one for $9,000. That one didn't clear, but others totaling $1,700 already had. Now we had our money back and had begun the paperwork to get a new bank-account number, but I was seething. Here was the evidence before me—forgeries of our checks so perfect that you would need a magnifying glass to tell the difference from the real ones. Only the poor imitation of my wife's eccentric signature gave the scheme away. But the bank was telling me there would be no investigation and referral for prosecution.

"If someone put a gun to my head right here and took $1,700 from my wallet, you'd call the police," I said indignantly.

"Certainly," replied the bank officer. "But we don't in these cases."

I did. Right there. I dialed 911, and an NYPD officer came to the bank lobby, where I reported a theft of $1,700. The policeman smiled, while various bank officials acted as if I were Al Pacino in *Dog Day Afternoon*. My little gambit got their attention, but not their commitment to spend any time or money trying to crack my case.

Several weeks later an officer from a distant suburb called to say that local police had found a man with checks in his possession with our names printed on them. But the bank wasn't interested in pursuing it, and both the D.A. and the Feds took a pass. "The amount is just too small to prosecute," a harried detective told me. Apparently, crime does pay—if you steal small enough.

That was five years ago, and I now have more company among the victimized than I ever imagined possible. According to the Justice Department, 500,000 to 700,000 Americans a year have their identities stolen. When thieves succeed in extracting money, the average loss is $18,000, though banks and credit card companies usually reimburse anything over $50, then pass along the cost in higher interest rates and other fees. The average amount of time needed to straighten out the situation: a year and a half. The Federal Trade Commission says that identity theft is now its No. 1 consumer complaint, accounting for an astounding 42 percent of all reports of fraud.

Who's responsible? After worrying for years about hackers, many institutions are now focused more on inside jobs, like the one last week in New York. Federal authorities cracked what they call the largest identity-theft case in American history. More than 30,000 people were victimized when a former employee of a Long Island software company—one of those guys we trust on the "help desk"— sold personal information to a ring of Nigerians in the Bronx.

The real pressure to crack down didn't come until after 9/11. "People now understand that identity theft can be a gateway to other crimes, including terrorism," says Jonathan J. Rusch of the Justice Department. We can't stop terrorism until we know who is living here, and we can't know that until we know their real names.

Prevention is the key. It wasn't until this year that the Social Security Administration took Social Security numbers off the envelopes of recipients, where they could be easily stolen. Many businesses still ask for your number for transactions, and many consumers are foolish enough to provide it. Stephen Keating of the Privacy Foundation says the Social Security number has been a dangerous "skeleton key" ever since the late 1930s, when a secretary in a Lockport, New York, wallet manufacturer became the first known victim of identity theft. Her number was printed on a sample Social Security card inside the company's wallets, which were sold at Woolworth's and elsewhere. Thousands of retirees used her number as their own.

The experts have some advice for lessening identity theft, including reviewing financial statements closely, shredding credit card receipts and financial documents before throwing them out and obtaining your own credit reports at least once a year (start with freecreditreport.com). Many thieves use phony change-of-address cards, so lighter-than-normal mail often signals trouble.

But even if you prove you've been victimized, the chances of getting justice are still remote. That's because, as I found in my own case, the laws on the books just aren't being properly enforced, which means that while people like me get their money back, the thief is still out there to prey on someone else. At a minimum, financial institutions should be required to pursue identity-fraud cases, instead of writing them off as a cost of doing business. Then maybe the authorities could crack more cases like the one last week, and keep those like me from having to lose it in the lobby.

The Cubs: Curses, Foiled Again. And Again.

—— 2003 ——

THE T-SHIRT READS: ANY TEAM CAN HAVE A BAD CENTURY. I liked that sentiment until I realized that it might apply to *this* century, too. In the 1960s, I grew up a few blocks from Wrigley Field and got badly infected. In the 1975 World Series, I was in Fenway Park when Carlton Fisk hit his famous but ultimately futile homer in Game 6 for the Red Sox, my favorite American League club. Last week both teams choked with three-run leads and only five outs to go before bringing a pennant to their famished fans. Call me a two-time loser.

Actually, call me a combined 180-season loser still plumbing the depths of masochistic superstitional narcissicism.

On Wednesday, after witnessing the excruciating eight-run eighth, I asked 500 kids at Chicago's Francis W. Parker School how many blamed themselves in some way for the collapse. Had they worn something different that day? Eaten a new snack in front of the TV? Sat on the couch instead of the chair? Nearly three-quarters raised their hands. Of course, the Cub swoon wasn't their fault but mine, as always. This is the lot of all sports fans, especially in Godforsaken places like Chicago and Boston. We only destroy the ones we love.

The defining characteristic of fanaticism—in the Middle East or the Middle West—is that it turns reality on its head. We convince ourselves that we somehow influence how superstars put runs on the board. But when it comes to something in our own lives, we assume we're powerless to change the outcome. We can control Pedro Martinez's pitching but can't possibly prevent ourselves from reaching for another potato chip.

This is one reason "The Fan" in Chicago took so much abuse for the sixth-game fiasco that he may have to go into the Witness Protection

Program. Instead of blaming Alex Gonzalez for booting a grounder or Mark Prior for throwing a wild pitch or even the umpire for not calling interference, Chicagoans settled on 26-year-old "Steve Bartman." I don't believe that's his real name. It's too perfect a combination of Bart Simpson and Everyman.

My colleague Mark Starr suggests on his Newsweek.com sports blog that the Cubs were dead when they, too, bought into fan narcissism. "It was [Moises] Alou's finger-pointing [that] helped put the Cubs in the psychic crapper," he writes. "With their heads out of the ballgame and back in the stands contemplating the baseball cosmos," they were toast.

Whether jinxed by barring a billy goat from Wrigley Field in 1945 or selling Babe Ruth to the Yankees in 1920, losers need curses. "If there's a curse, the universe has deep meaning and order," says Bill Savage, who teaches English at Northwestern. "If it's just that the [team] is bad or unlucky, it's the abyss."

Then the abyss it is. It was the Marlins, not the Billy Goats, who beat the Cubs. It was Boston manager Grady Little, not the Bambino, who inexplicably kept starter Pedro Martinez in the game when any fourth grader knew it was time to pull him. The players I interviewed last week all went to pains to nix the hex, with a Cubs corporate den master saying officially, "We're out of the goat business."

And yet "the past isn't dead, it isn't even past," as William Faulkner wrote. Sammy Sosa's denial of any extra pressure was too vehement to be believable, and Dusty Baker admitted to me that—like all baseball men—he is plenty superstitious. He never steps on the foul line on trips to the mound.

When I went late Tuesday night to the scene of the crime and inspected Seat 116, Section 102, where Bartman had evidently consumed nachos and melted cheese (American, not goat) shortly before gooing the Cubs for good, I spotted a lonely man still in his seat in the empty ballpark. He was a supervisor of the cleanup crew, a 30-year veteran of Wrigley. His words were reassuring for the fateful Game 7. But the poor man looked as if his dog had just been run over by a beer truck on Waveland Avenue. I trusted the look.

What to tell the kids about the Yankees? That overdogs with power and money deserve to win? That War Admiral should have beaten Seabiscuit? Defeat is not ennobling, but it can be instructive. The late Chicago columnist Mike Royko loved the Cubs because they reminded him that most people fail most of the time and we all end up dead. The next year he was back for extra punishment. Me, too, unless they win more when I don't watch.

Jonathan, You Ignorant Slut!

—— 2004 ——

I have a perverse reaction to hostile mail. I like it.
And I enjoy responding. So I thought I'd share some of it with you.

"**A**LTER, I HAVE long restrained myself from exploding after reading the type of rotting, festering, pus-covered liberal dung that you have presented in this article. I often wonder which crack in the sewer of liberal America people like yourself have oozed out from. It bewilders me to try to understand where you cockroaches lose your way in life. I just wanted to mention a few of the maggot-infested piles of whipped cream on the liberal pie-of-life that I knew were near and dear to your pink heart. Your article felt like watching a horrific and brutal flesh tearing, sadistic automobile collision unfold before my eyes. Thank you for the inspiration."

Sincerely,
David Nyseth

(please excuse me while I read your article again and vomit-again)

David, I'm flattered that I help you pray to the porcelain god but I think you'd be in there on your knees even without my help ...

* * *

"You love playing with facts—such as that Bush "squandering $100,000 in taxpayer-funded training" when he stopped flying in the National Guard. That is an outright LIE."

Kevin Everett, MD,
Birmingham, MI

You're right, Kevin. I got that wrong. By some estimates it cost the government $1 million to train a pilot.

* * *

"You are a shameless deceiver and a rank hypocrite. If you had ANY honesty in you at ALL you would run to the radio and TV to attack Senator Kerry and ask him if he has "ever cheated on his wife." And then say how you don't think Americans should vote for Kerry because he is a liar and a cheater. You are a complete joke of a human being. And worse ... you are a coward."

CWB1@aol.com

I would like to reply to your attack on me as a "coward" but you were too brave to attach your name.

* * *

"Mr. Alter: You're so nailed. You're a left-wing phony. Drudge simply exposes you for who you are with your President Bush's 1992 affair research that never amounted to anything. You and your entire *Newsweek/Wash Post* outlet are a complete joke."

Will Kreidler

Ooh ... Ouch. It really hurts to be nailed. Except that I'm not. The hypocrisy Drudge alleges is simply factually inaccurate. I thought questions about sexual misconduct by politicians were relevant in 1992 and in 2004 and in all the years in between. This is the presidency we're talking about and it's an issue of character. But I also thought unsubstantiated rumors were sleazy then—and I do now. As it happens, Drudge also has the facts exactly backwards. In 1992, I didn't personally ask then-President Bush or his aides about the rumors and I did no research into them. I was not involved in that story, except to say that the issue was relevant. But last week in Wisconsin, I did ask Kerry aides about the rumors. In both cases, the rumors were denied. Short of any evidence, that's when I move on.

* * *

"Let me get this straight—Limbaugh, Fox News are biased?"

Mike Stleacio

That would be a yes, Mike.

* * *

"Mr. Alter, The day you ever wrote a decent column, the world will explode. Get over yourself. Do something great and tell America why

there are 50+ socialists in the Congress. Are you a Communist also?"
S. Shenk,
San Juan Capistrano, CA

No, I'm one of those birds that flies back to San Juan Capistrano.
* * *

"You are a fraud. I remember when you were busting George Bush's father's chops in 1992 about an affair he may have had. Now the shoe is on the other foot and just because your J. Kerry's punk you can't say anything about his bimbo. I have news for you son, she isn't Kerry's only bimbo. Your boy is going down no matter how much you try to cover for him."
Signed, The Fraud Detector

Dear Fraud Detector: You "remember" when I supposedly did something in 1992 that just happened to be on Drudge this week? Good detector work, Sherlock.
* * *

"As those of us who have done it know, every time you climb into a military aircraft you run the VERY REAL possibility of getting killed—try it sometime if you don't believe me. The aircraft doesn't care if you are Air National Guard or not—in fact those old birds are more likely to crash than active-duty jets."
Wm. Babbingon,
USMC-AV8-Harrier pilot

Good point. And that incoming fire from the Vietcong over the Oklahoma border back in '69 was something fierce, too.
* * *

"Enjoy your day, Jon, and weep come November as you see your diatribe result in a second term for W, and expanded majorities in the House and Senate. Will you then take a quiet moment and reassess your blind devotion to present-day liberalism?"
Clyde Middleton,
Sacramento, CA

Thanks for writing, Clyde. I'm honored and humbled that you think my "diatribe" could "result" in W. being re-elected. That makes me almost as powerful as Justice Scalia!

* * *

"A wonderful article. You put everything on the table and clearly stated the facts. Hopefully people will wake up to what a President should be and should do. We need more of this type of commentary to save our country."

Ethel Pepperman

Thanks, Ethel. But sarcasm has no place here.

* * *

"Please spare us your dribble. You are so duplicitous. You took an interest in an alleged Bush affair, and now you blast others for making the same inquiry of Kerry. Why don't you go drown yourself, you hypocritical rat."

John Koenig,
San Mateo, CA

John, please be a little more specific about how I might do that. Little weights attached to my tail and claws? It's not easy being a depressed rodent.

* * *

"Jonathan: You're still a complete jerk."

Regards,
Lenny, New Orleans

Well, Lenny, at least I'm consistent.

Index